S0-BYF-854

FOOD LOVERS'
GUIDE TO
SAN DIEGO

Help Us Keep This Guide Up to Date

We would love to hear from you concerning your experiences with this guide and how you feel it could be improved and kept up to date. Please send your comments and suggestions to:

editorial@GlobePequot.com

Thanks for your input, and happy travels!

FOOD LOVERS' SERIES

FOOD LOVERS'
GUIDE TO
SAN DIEGO

The Best Restaurants, Markets & Local Culinary Offerings

1st Edition

Maria Desiderata Montana

Guilford, Connecticut

To buy books in quantity for corporate use
or incentives, call **(800) 962-0973**
or e-mail **premiums@GlobePequot.com**.

Copyright © 2012 Morris Book Publishing, LLC

ALL RIGHTS RESERVED. No part of this book may be reproduced or transmitted in any form
by any means, electronic or mechanical, including photocopying and recording, or by any
information storage and retrieval system, except as may be expressly permitted in writing
from the publisher. Requests for permission should be addressed to Globe Pequot Press,
Attn: Rights and Permissions Department, PO Box 480, Guilford, CT 06437.

Editor: Amy Lyons
Project Editor: Meredith Dias
Layout Artist: Mary Ballachino
Text Design: Sheryl Kober
Illustrations by Jill Butler with additional art by Carleen Moira Powell and MaryAnn Dubé
Maps: Melissa Baker © Morris Book Publishing, LLC

ISBN 978-0-7627-8119-5

Printed in the United States of America
10 9 8 7 6 5 4 3 2 1

All the information in this guidebook is subject to change. We recommend that you call ahead
to obtain current information before traveling.

Contents

Recipes, 343

I dedicate this book first and foremost to God;
to my best friend and husband, John;
to my amazing children, Lucia and Frank;
and to my cat, Leo.
I cherish you all.

About the Author

Maria Desiderata Montana is the publisher of the award-winning food blog *San Diego Food Finds* at sandiegofoodfinds.com. She is also a published cookbook author, editor, and award-winning freelance food and wine journalist who learned how to cook and appreciate European cuisine from her parents, who were born and raised in the town of Cirella, near the capital city of Reggio Calabria in Italy. Maria's mother taught her how to cook at an early age using fresh, organic ingredients including fava beans, tomatoes, and an assortment of fruits and vegetables from her father's garden. She loves to cook and create new recipes and strongly believes that eating with family and friends is a celebration of life itself.

She is the author of *The Inn at Rancho Santa Fe Cookbook* and was a contributing editor of the award-winning cookbook *Flying Pans*. She has been a regular contributor to the *U-T San Diego* since 2005, where she has written a variety of food and entertainment stories, as well as her own monthly "Step by Step" recipe series. Maria has also been extensively published in a variety of magazines and newspapers.

She lives in San Diego with her husband, John, and their two kids, Lucia and Frank. She feels that her most important job in the world is being a mom.

Acknowledgments

Thank you to all my friends and family for all of your support and encouragement while writing this book. To my husband, John—thank you for staying up with me during all those late nights of writing, keeping the freezer stocked with my favorite chocolate-covered vanilla ice cream bars, and making me cappuccino every morning. You are my rock! To my kids, Lucia and Frank—thank you for taking time out of your busy schedules to eat out with me and for being the best kids in the world. I am proud to be your mom. To my Italian parents— thank you for teaching me about the health benefits of the Mediterranean diet, how to grow my own vegetables, and how to be my own chef in the kitchen. To my sister Terese—thank you for the much-needed lunches and shopping sprees every Friday, I love you dearly. To my three brothers—thank you for all the jokes and for making me laugh when I needed it most. To my mentor Jim—thank you for helping me learn to challenge myself and to believe that all things are possible. To my fur baby and cat Leo—thank you for never leaving my side and sitting comfortably on my keyboard for moral support. To my loyal audience—thank you for your dedicated readership of San Diego Food Finds and for all the compliments and kind words you send my way on a daily basis. To my editor, Amy Lyons, and Globe Pequot Press—thank you for acknowledging my journalistic capabilities and for recognizing me as a local authority of the food scene in San Diego. By offering me this wonderful opportunity, you paid me the highest compliment, and I am truly honored. To all the restaurateurs and chefs—thank you for having cultivated such a creative and extraordinary culinary landscape in San Diego. Many of you are true pioneers of the slow food movement, changing the way people eat and creating a healthy menu for all of us through your utilization of local farm-fresh produce and sustainable meats and seafood. To all of my dear friends and colleagues in the journalism and communications field—thank you for sharing your knowledge of great restaurants with me. Your hard work and dedication is a constant inspiration!

Introduction

Aptly named "America's Finest City," San Diego is famous for a moderate climate, friendly attitude, health-conscious lifestyle, and endless natural and man-made attractions. It is the eighth-largest city in the United States and second-largest city in California. With nearly 16 million overnight visitors a year (another 15 million visit for a day trip), it's no wonder that tourism is the third largest industry in San Diego County, joining defense/military, international trade, and research (high-tech, communications, and biotech) as the main employers. And it's not just a huge influx during the summer months, as statistics show only a moderate bump in tourism between June and September. People like to visit throughout the year, due to one of the mildest and predictable weather patterns in the country. It is one of the top five leisure vacation destinations in the US with nearly 90 percent of our visitors traveling for non-business reasons. The climate of San Diego is categorized as semi-arid or Mediterranean, with an average high temperatures ranging from the mid-60s to upper-70s year-round. Measurable precipitation is recorded only around 40 total days every year, which is half to a third of the national average.

A recent study found that 86 percent of national chefs pointed to three hot tendencies

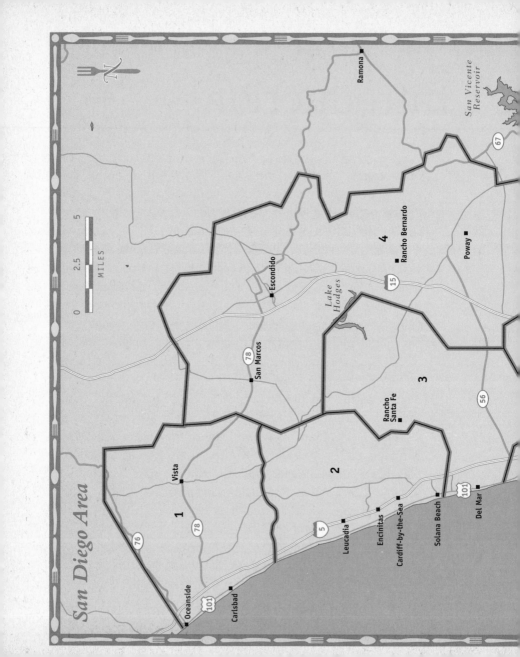

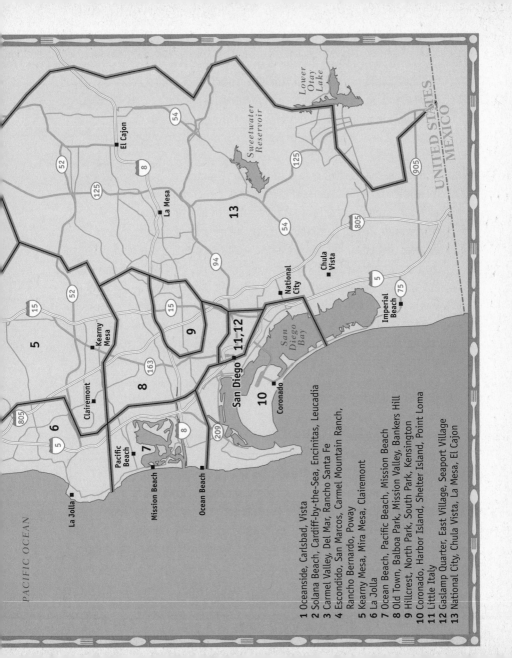

PACIFIC OCEAN

La Jolla

Mission Beach

Ocean Beach

Pacific Beach

Clairemont

Kearny Mesa

El Cajon

La Mesa

San Diego

Coronado

National City

Chula Vista

Imperial Beach

San Diego Bay

Sweetwater Reservoir

Lower Otay Lake

UNITED STATES
MEXICO

1 Oceanside, Carlsbad, Vista
2 Solana Beach, Cardiff-by-the-Sea, Encinitas, Leucadia
3 Carmel Valley, Del Mar, Rancho Santa Fe
4 Escondido, San Marcos, Carmel Mountain Ranch,
   Rancho Bernardo, Poway
5 Kearny Mesa, Mira Mesa, Clairemont
6 La Jolla
7 Ocean Beach, Pacific Beach, Mission Beach
8 Old Town, Balboa Park, Mission Valley, Bankers Hill
9 Hillcrest, North Park, South Park, Kensington
10 Coronado, Harbor Island, Shelter Island, Point Loma
11 Little Italy
12 Gaslamp Quarter, East Village, Seaport Village
13 National City, Chula Vista, La Mesa, El Cajon

in the culinary industry: locally sourced meats and seafood, locally grown produce, and sustainability. It is so true that diners want to know where their food is coming from and want to be sure it's nutritious for themselves and their families. San Diego's location makes it a perfect fit for this new direction, as fresh produce, seafood, and meats are easily sourced year-round. It is a true hot-bed for the slow food movement, a progressive mind-set for preserving traditional and regional cuisines by incorporating local ingredients in a fashion that preserves the ecosystem. Basically, it is the antithesis of the fast-food epidemic. In this book, you will often see me mention menus that are driven by farm-to-table attitudes. And it is so true! Many of the restaurants regularly use produce from local farmers, and even their own on-site gardens, to complete their recipes. No pesticides or preservatives here. The seafood? It's usually locally caught, or harvested using a sustainable practice to ensure the environmental impact is minimal. The meats? Many local chefs will only choose farm-raised animals that are typically grass-fed and free of hormones. Not only is the food better tasting, it is more nutritious, and leaves you with a sense of goodwill toward the planet and people.

Since the city is located on the coast of the Pacific Ocean and immediately adjacent to the Mexican border, the cuisine has serious Hispanic and Asian influences. You'll see this trend throughout the book. California modern cuisine is a trend taking hold throughout the region, fusing several different cuisines and styles to make great dishes even more extraordinary. Asian fusion is really the same concept, only focusing on the many individual flavors and cooking styles of the orient, and melding them together on one menu and even in one dish. Of course, French and Mediterranean styles and flavors are also widely used to perfection. You will also notice other, lesser seen cuisines becoming commonplace in almost every part of the city, including Indian, Latin American, African, and the Pacific Islands. Not to be outdone, there are plenty of traditional American restaurants, bakeries, dessertiers, and burger and pizza joints to satisfy any craving.

San Diego is an experience like no other. Obviously, it would be impossible to include *every* great restaurant within these pages, so the list has been narrowed to favorites. You are welcome to drop a note with your favorite destinations at sandiegofoodfinds.com. After all, food is meant for enjoyment and enrichment, and the choices are endless!

How to Use This Book

Altogether, San Diego contains more than 100 identified neighborhoods! In an effort to simplify your navigation, many of the adjacent neighborhoods are grouped into larger areas within the city. Be sure to use the area map located on page 2 as a high-level reference. Each of the 13 areas has a dedicated chapter with restaurants listed in alphabetical order, and represents a large portion of the book. There are also devoted separate chapters on industry-supportive subjects, including the Wine Scene (local wineries and wine bars), the Beer Scene (local brewers, bars, taverns, and brewpubs), Food Trucks, and Foodie Day Trips. The introductory chapter includes a summary of helpful tips for getting around the city, a helpful calendar of local culinary and food events, and a summary of the top favorite farmers' markets. And finally, there is a section featuring more than a dozen recipes from local chefs, highlighting some of their best dishes that you can re-create at home for a special occasion or that special someone in your life.

Foodie Faves

The restaurants that have made this section are the most noteworthy establishments that are worth a visit, from long-standing favorites to the latest on the scene. Bon appétit!

Landmarks

The listings in this section are the restaurants that have been San Diego's staples for a considerably long time and helped put San Diego on the food map, or ones housed in historic buildings or locations.

Specialty Stores, Markets & Producers

Some truly notable butcher shops, specialized groceries, and bakeries exist within this fascinatingly diverse city. Here we give you a list of must-visit specialty stores.

Recipes

At the back of the book (p. 343) we give new meaning to the phrase "continuing education" and help you re-create some of our favorite local dishes from some of the city's best chefs.

Price Code

The price range is covered in this book, immediately following the address listing, using the following guide.

$	**Cheap: you can have a full meal for $10 or less here.**
$$	**Economical: $10 to $25 per person**
$$$	**Moderate: $25 to $50 per person (a meal equivalent to an appetizer, entrée selection, and one alcoholic beverage)**
$$$$	**Expect to spend $50 to $75 for one appetizer, one entrée, and a glass or two of wine.**
$$$$$	**You will not walk out of this establishment having spent less than $75 to $100 per person; the sky's the limit.**

Getting Around

Walking

Depending on where you're at, this could be the most enjoyable option. Many of the areas in this book have central parts of town

COOKING SCHOOLS & CLASSES

Looking for an adventurous afternoon or evening where you can pair your love for food with a social but informative experience? San Diego is brimming with culinary educational options, ranging from short and simple to complex and elegant. Here is a sampling of the local offerings that will add a spark to your daily routine.

Carmel Valley Kitchen, 3955 Montefrio Ct., San Diego; (858) 382-2228; carmelvalleykitchen.com. Choose from a variety of lessons and learn how to make easy recipes using fresh and readily available ingredients.

Chef Jenn Felmley Cooks, (858) 212- 9054; chefjenncooks.com. Chef Jenn teaches large groups and hosts individual private classes and cooking parties. Classes range from cooking demonstrations on local farms to hands-on French cooking techniques.

Cooking 4 Life, 9145 Chesapeake Dr., San Diego; (858) 433-0085. Learn how to cook simple, healthy, and delicious meals that will keep you fit for life.

Cups Culinary, 7857 Girard Ave., La Jolla; (858) 459-2877; cupslj .com. Take part in hands-on cooking classes where, afterwards, you get to sit down, eat a full meal, and enjoy a Q&A with the chef.

Do It With Icing, 7240 Clairemont Mesa Blvd., San Diego; (858) 268-1234; doitwithicing.com. Have fun in the kitchen learning how to model chocolate to create roses and even small animal creatures, or learn how to make your own marshmallow fondant.

The Floating Chef Cooking School, Kona Kai Marina Shelter Island, 1561 Shelter Island Dr., San Diego; (858) 829-9021; thefloatingchefschool.com. Nothing beats learning how to cook while on a private yacht overlooking Mission Bay.

Great News Cooking School, 1788 Garnet Ave., Pacific Beach; (858) 270-1582, ext. 3; great-news.com. Helping students enhance their cooking knowledge since 1977, these professionally-driven classes are available nearly every day of the week.

Harvard Cookin' Girl, 7441 Girard Ave., La Jolla; (858) 888-3509; harvardcookingirl.com. This ex-Harvard MBA executive has turned to helping kids learn good habits and easy cooking techniques to enrich their lives and teach them how to eat healthy.

La Cocina Que Canta, Rancho La Puerta, Tecate, Baja California, Mexico; (800) 443-7565 or (858) 764-5500; rancholapuerta.com. Located on a sprawling 3,000-acre ranch near Tecate, Mexico, this world-famous spa offers weekly stays that include a variety of cooking classes and demonstrations for guests.

LaJollaCooks4u, La Jolla; (858) 752-4980; lajollacooks4u.com. Specializing in California cuisine and utilizing a private organic vegetable and herb garden, this is a great choice for hand-on experience at creating a farm-to-table meal.

Macy's Home Store, 1550 Camino de La Reina, San Diego; (619) 299-9811; macys.com. Experience professional cooking demonstrations from award-winning local chefs and celebrities in this polished kitchen environment, located in the Mission Valley Macy's.

Ro Z's Sweet Art Studio, 277 S. Rancho Santa Fe Rd., San Marcos; (760) 744-0447; rozsweetartstudio.com. Located within the School of Confectionary Arts, these classes focus on all things sugar, including cake/cookie baking and decorating, pulled sugar and fondant, candy making, and more.

Sur La Table, 1915 Calle Barcelona, Carlsbad; (760) 635-1319; surlatable.com. Professionally managed cooking classes with diverse offerings including Martha Stewart's American Favorites and Anthony Bourdain's Kitchen Basics.

with plenty of culinary options surrounded by shops, galleries, studios, cultural centers, or some of the most beautiful natural scenery around. San Diego is known for the best weather in the nation, and it is predictable every month of the year. Why not spend your time strolling on the sidewalks, enjoying the incredible views, or staying cool under tree-lined walkways? Most of the beach areas have well-maintained boardwalks that follow the ocean for long distances, and renting a beach cruiser is a very popular option. Besides, the exercise will give you a great excuse to sample more foods without the guilt!

By Car

Renting a car during your visit is a very smart decision, unless you plan to remain in one area. It's best to plan far ahead, making sure you understand the city layout, and consider traffic patterns. One of the best resources of information is AAA (aaa.com). Fortunately, the roadways in this area are well-designed to keep traffic flowing throughout the county. However, rush-hour traffic is as regular as the weather, so you should account for this added congestion between 7:30 to 9 a.m. and 4 to 6 p.m. Carpools are given a break on the main highways, and only require 2 or more passengers in the car. There is ample parking available in pay lots, along the streets (bring change for the meters between 8 a.m. and 5 p.m.), and in centrally-located parking garages.

The main freeways in San Diego County are I-5 (runs north/south along the coast from the US–Mexico border through

Oceanside), I-805 (runs north/south parallel to I-5, stretching inland from south of Del Mar to Downtown), I-15 (runs north/south through the inland area, from South County through Escondido and into Temecula), and I-8 (runs east/west from the East County to Ocean Beach). There are dozens of other smaller highways and thoroughfares throughout the county, including the famous 101, running from La Jolla to Oceanside, with stunning views of the coastline, and plenty of stoplights along the way.

By Taxi

San Diego is certainly not similar to the taxi havens of Los Angeles, New York, or Chicago. For the most part, you'll find the highest concentration in the downtown area, especially late at night when the bar hoppers are looking for a safe ride between parties or home. A number of websites can help you locate a good taxi service and also provide an estimated fare, including taxifarefinder.com or taxiwiz.com. If you're not in the downtown area, it's best to call ahead to be sure that your ride is available at the time you desire. For a more pampered experience, consider private town car or limo. There are plenty of options available online, and it is a booming business for the affluent in southern California.

By Bus, Trolley, and Train

The San Diego Metro and North County Transit systems (sdcommute.com) maintain one of the best options for travelers that want to see various areas without the hassle of a car rental. This includes an extensive light rail/trolley system that services 53 stations, nearly 90 fixed bus routes, and 2 commuter rail lines. The trolley covers a lot of ground, from the US–Mexican border, throughout downtown, up to Little Italy and the popular Old Town, and east through La Mesa, El Cajon, and Santee. Stops along the way include Petco Park (home of the San Diego Padres) and Qualcomm Stadium (home of the San Diego Chargers and other large sporting events). The Coaster is a commuter train that runs along the coast from Oceanside to downtown and teams up with its sister, the Sprinter, which runs inland from Oceanside to Escondido. The services also link into the Amtrak Pacific Surfliner and Orange County Metrolink. Fares vary depending on the length of your trip, but it's a scenic and convenient way to cover a lot of ground during your visit.

By Ferry

No visit to America's Finest City would be complete without taking a ride on the ferry across the scenic San Diego Bay. Enjoy the city skyline, views of the naval base and majestic ships, and of course the famous Coronado Bridge, stretching over 2 miles and 200 feet high over the Bay between downtown and Coronado Island. The Coronado Commuter Ferry (sdhe.com/san-diego-commuter-ferry.html) takes morning and afternoon commuters across San Diego Bay from the San Diego Broadway Pier, to the Naval Air Station North Island, and the Coronado Ferry Landing. San Diego Harbor Excursion (sdhe.com/san-diego-bay-ferry.html) operates ferry shuttles directly to and from the San Diego Broadway Pier, the Coronado Ferry Landing, and the Fifth Avenue Landing. Prices start at $4.25 each way. You also have many choices of day and dinner cruises throughout the year, where you can enjoy the skyline and water activities while sipping champagne or dancing the night away.

Food Festivals & Events

It's well known that San Diego has the best year-round weather in the continental states. That makes every month a good time to visit and stroll outside, enjoying the many cultural celebrations and food events. Although most of the events listed here are free, an admission cost will likely also include food and other perks. Parking can be a challenge, so plan ahead and consider utilizing public transport to ease congestion.

January

SD Restaurant Week, sandiegorestaurantweek.com. Sponsored by the San Diego Chapter of the California Restaurant Association, this semiannual event allows diners to experience everything San Diego has to offer at more than 180 of the county's best venues. Discounted, prix-fixe menus are available during the entire week. Since this is a great excuse for everyone to sample the best foods in San Diego, reservations are highly suggested. Also held in September.

February

Chinese New Year, sdcny.weebly.com. Now in its 30th year, head downtown for the San Diego Chinese New Year Food and Cultural Fair, where street vendors, entertainers, and artists light up the streets for this traditional celebration.

Mardi Gras, brazilcarnival.com. San Diegans are always looking for an excuse to celebrate, and Mardi Gras is no exception. Two long-standing, adult events occur on Fat Tuesday every year, so don your beads and get ready for some fun!

Vietnamese Tet Festival, sdtet.com. The lunar-solar calendar New Year is one of Vietnam's most celebrated holidays. Located in Balboa Park near downtown, this event features cultural festivities, entertainers, and food vendors.

March

Family Winemakers of California Tastings, familywinemakers.org. Hundreds of family-owned wineries converge in San Diego for a 2-day event including wine tasting and nibbling on small bites. Here's your chance to talk with the owners and vintners, gaining an understanding of the best vintages and varietals to pursue for a phenomenal wine.

St. Patrick's Day, stpatsparade.org. Although you can celebrate this occasion at nearly every local pub and tavern in the area, nothing is more attended than the St. Patrick's Day Parade and Irish Festival in Balboa Park, where you can celebrate everything green.

April

Adams Avenue Roots Festival, adamsaveonline.com. Situated in the uptown district, this weekend festival includes food, music, and other entertainment featuring folk, traditional roots music, Appalachian folk songs, bluegrass, Americana, cowboy, Cajun, and rockabilly.

Fallbrook Avocado Festival, fallbrookchamber ofcommerce.org. Located just a short drive north of San Diego, this festival celebrates the local agricultural heritage with arts and crafts, a farmers' market, food court, live entertainment, and even a guacamole contest!

Lakeside Rodeo, lakesiderodeo.com. Put on those boots, and don your best cowboy hat for this weekend rodeo, including traditional events and lots of barbecue-laden foods to enjoy.

May

Carlsbad Village Street Faire, carlsbad.org. Considered one of the largest one-day street fairs in the nation, over 100,000 people will stroll past 900 vendor booths, enjoying arts and crafts as well as an assortment of international cuisines.

Fiesta Cinco de Mayo, fiestacincodemayo.com. Due to San Diego's proximity to the Mexican border, it's no surprise that this festival is one of the most popular for locals and visitors alike. The festival is located in historic Old Town, considered the birthplace of California, and one of the most popular tourist attractions in the area, visited by nearly 250,000 annually.

Gator by the Bay, gatorbythebay.com. Located in Spanish Landing Park, this weekend festival celebrates everything that makes Louisiana exciting. Listen to zydeco, blues, and Cajun music as you dive into the 8,000 pounds of cooked crawfish and other regional fare.

Portuguese Festa, upses.com. This festival is the oldest ethnic religious celebration in San Diego, dating back to the time when the first families settled here in 1884. Including a parade and full weekend of activities, this is a must-see cultural event.

June

Greek Festival, sdgreekfestival.com. This weekend festival celebrates the heritage, culture, music, traditions, customs, and culinary skills of the Greek community, and serves the finest homemade Greek foods and pastries in all of California.

San Diego County Fair, sdfair.com. First opened as an agricultural fair in 1880, this premier summer event was relocated to the Del Mar Fairgrounds in 1936. Over one million people visit every year, making it one of the largest county fairs in Southern California. Featuring all of the expected animal exhibits and shows, you can also visit the many commercial and cultural exhibits, as well as the multitude of entertainers and carnival attractions, all ending with a spectacular Fourth-of-July fireworks show.

September

Festival of Beer, sdbeerfest.org. Considered a mecca for local craft beer, San Diego toasts this traditional brew. Admission to this 1-day celebration includes tastings from over 40 breweries, food vendors, and live music.

Julian Apple Days, julianca.com/events/#September. Just a short drive into the mountains east of San Diego, this harvest celebration spans nearly a full month of everything related to apples. No visit is complete until you fight your way through the long lines to savor freshly baked pies and other pastries.

SD Restaurant Week, sandiegorestaurantweek.com. Sponsored by the San Diego chapter of the California Restaurant Association, this semiannual event allows diners to experience everything San

FARMERS' MARKETS

San Diego is a hotbed for farm-fresh produce and products. It's no wonder that so many local chefs are visiting these treasure troves of the freshest produce nature has to offer. There's no doubt that you'll hear them haggling and joking with local farmers as they peruse ingredients for their next menu creation. In addition, many of these markets specialize in organically grown products. It's no wonder that a "farm to fork" philosophy has become one of the most widely used descriptions on restaurant menus.

One of the best resources available at your fingertips is the **Farm Bureau of San Diego** (sdfarmbureau.org). This website is updated regularly, providing the most comprehensive information on local farmers' markets, including maps and other relevant information. Most markets accept cash only, but many are beginning to accept EBT, credit, and debit cards for payment. All markets listed below are open year-round.

Here are some favorites:

Carlsbad Village Farmers' Market and Food Fair, Roosevelt Street, Carlsbad; (760) 687-6453; shopcarlsbadvillage.org. Open Wednesday and Saturday from 1 to 5 p.m.

Cedros Avenue Farmer's Market, 410 S. Cedros Ave., Solana Beach; (858) 755-0444; cedrosavenue.com. Open Sundays from 1 to 5 p.m.

Del Mar Farmers' Market and Food Court, 1050 Camino Del Mar, Del Mar; (760) 586-0373; delmarfarmersmarket.org. Open Saturdays from 1 to 4 p.m.

Escondido Certified Farmers' Market, E. Grand & Juniper, Escondido; (760) 745-8877; downtownescondido.com. Open Tuesdays from 2:30 to 6 p.m.

Hillcrest Certified Farmers' Market and Open Air Bazaar, 3960 Normal St. at Lincoln (adjacent to the DMV), San Diego; Hillcrest farmersmarket.com. Open Sundays from 9 a.m. to 2 p.m.

La Jolla Open Aire Market, corner of Girard Avenue and Genter Street, La Jolla; (858) 454-1699; lajollamarket.com. Open Sundays from 9 a.m. to 1 p.m.

Little Italy Mercato, Date & India Streets, Little Italy, San Diego, (619) 233-3769; littleitalymercato.com. Open Saturdays from 9 a.m. to 1:30 p.m.

The Mission Hills Farmers Market, West Washington & Falcon Streets, San Diego; (619) 795-3363; ourmissionhills.com. Open Wednesdays from 3 to 7 p.m.

North Park Farmers' Market, Herman Street between University and North Park Way, San Diego; (619) 233-3901; northparkfarmersmarket.com. Open Thursdays from 3 to 7 p.m.

Ocean Beach Certified Farmers' Market, 4900 block of Newport Ave. between Cable and Bacon Sts. in Ocean Beach; (619) 279-0032; oceanbeachsandiego.com. Open Wednesdays from 4 to 8 p.m.

Oceanside Certified Farmers' Market & Faire, Pier View Way & Coast Hwy 101, Oceanside; (619) 440-5027; msoceanside.com. Open Thursdays from 5 to 9 p.m.

Old Poway Farmers' Market and Faire, 14134 Midland Rd., Poway; poway.org. Open Saturdays from 8 to 11:30 a.m.

Pacific Beach Tuesday Certified Farmers Market, 901 Garnet Ave., San Diego; (619) 233-3901; pacificbeachmarket.com. Open Tuesdays from 2 to 6:30 p.m.

Rancho Santa Fe Del Rayo Village Farmers' Market, 16079 San Dieguito Rd., Rancho Santa Fe; (858) 922-5135; ranchosantafe farmersmarket.com. Open Sundays from 9 a.m. to 1:30 p.m.

Diego has to offer at more than 180 of the county's best venues. Discounted, prix-fixe menus are available during the entire week. Since this is a great excuse for everyone to sample the best foods in San Diego, reservations are highly suggested. Also held in January.

October

Little Italy Festa, littleitalysd.com/events/little-italy-festa. One of the largest Italian-American festivals on the west coast, enjoy Italian food served alfresco throughout the neighborhood, as well as cooking demonstrations, a stickball exhibition game, and bocce ball tournament. This is also the venue for one of the finest sidewalk chalk art demonstrations in the city.

Oktoberfest. Celebrated in many communities in and around San Diego, this is your chance to enjoy good beer, German food and festivities, just as they have for over 200 years. The largest parties are located in **La Mesa** (lmvma.com/SeasonalEvents/Oktoberfest .aspx), **El Cajon** (germanclubsandiego.org/events/Oktoberfest), and **Carlsbad** (rotaryoktoberfest.org).

November

San Diego Beer Week, sdbw.org. This 10-day festival focuses on the burgeoning craft beer culture in San Diego by offering events throughout the region at local breweries, restaurants, and more.

SD Bay Wine & Food Festival, worldofwineevents.com. Where classic cuisine, legendary wine, spirits and craft beer, and culinary all-stars come together for a weeklong event that culminates in a Chef or the Fest Competition that rivals any such event on the west coast.

Oceanside, Carlsbad & Vista

This coastal tri-city area is on the far north edge of San Diego County and just south of Camp Pendleton, one of the busiest Marine Corp bases in the US. There is a very strong military presence and community support for the local troops, as seen in many of the local businesses. The expansive coastline is always busy with tourists and locals taking walks or just enjoying beach-style activities. Inland areas are dotted with commercial and residential communities in one of the larger sections of North County.

Oceanside is home to one of the longest wooden piers in the western US. First built in 1888, this pier is central to the beach area and offers a 1,942-foot stroll of scenic beauty above the roaring Pacific. Perched at the end of the pier is **Ruby's Diner** (p. 33), which is open every day and offers great American drive-in food, but without the cars! The nearby amphitheater is host to many musical and cultural events throughout the year. Approximately

1 mile north of the pier is Oceanside Marina, where you can join charter fishing and whale watching tours anytime of the year.

Just south of Oceanside is the city of Carlsbad, which also boasts long stretches of beaches along the coastline, and is a favorite of local surfers and sunbathers. Since the terrain includes high bluffs over the ocean, many dining establishments are located along Carlsbad Boulevard, part of Highway 101. Carlsbad Village is a well-designed downtown area with tree-lined streets and plenty of boutiques, antiques shops, gift stores, restaurants, and art galleries. From March through May, nearly 50 acres of Giant Tecolote Ranunculus flowers color the landscape at Carlsbad Ranch, a popular spot for locals and tourists. Three lagoons cover more than 1,000 acres with nature preserves, hiking trails, and water recreation areas, and include Buena Vista, Agua Hedionda, and Batiquitos Lagoons. Bordering the Batiquitos Lagoon is the famous strawberry fields; 80 acres of this luscious fruit have been farmed in this location for 3 generations. Between January and July, the fields are open to the public. Carlsbad is also home to LEGOLAND California, only one of three in the world, and an oasis of activities for adults and children.

The inland part of the tri-city area is home to Vista, a city that operates 15 community parks—6 times the national average—that includes theaters, museums, recreation centers, picnic grounds, and athletic fields. Considered the "avocado capital of the world" in the 1940s and '50s, agriculture is still a strong component of this area.

This area also has a strong business focus, with over 800 companies calling Vista home. Be sure to visit the Antique Gas & Steam Engine Museum, with a collection focused on the period from 1849–1950. Unique from many museums, the equipment is maintained in operating condition and used for demonstrations.

Foodie Faves

BlueFire Grill, 2100 Costa Del Mar Rd., Carlsbad, CA 92009; (760) 929-6306; lacosta.com; California Modern; $$$$. Located inside the plaza of the La Costa Resort and Spa, BlueFire Grill makes for a fun and lively date night out complete with blue decor, mood lighting, and a beautiful outdoor patio with a large fountain and a fire pit. Although children are welcome, this is mainly an adult venue with live entertainment nightly. Executive Chef Hans Wiegand and Chef de Cuisine Greg Frey Jr. work side by side to bring you seasonal farm-to-table delights from organic gardens on-site, as well as the Carlsbad area markets. Spotlights from the menu are "From the Fields," an ayurvedic-inspired dish of the best local produce and grains; "From the Butchers Block," chops to chuck, the best the butcher has to offer; and "From the Sea," whole bone in-California striped bass. Vegetarian and vegan options are available.

Casa de Bandini, 1901 Calle Barcelona, Carlsbad, CA 92009; (760) 634-3443; casadebandini.com; Mexican; $$$. Located in the Forum Shopping Center in Carlsbad, this beautiful restaurant owned by Diane Powers features a wide array of authentic and regional Mexican entrees. The atmosphere is as festive as it gets with colorful Mexican decorations and strolling mariachis stopping by your table. An outdoor patio decked out with colorful lights and umbrellas is a hip gathering place in the evenings, so grab a seat when you can. Watch a señorita make tortillas by hand, while your server brings you a giant margarita from the cantina featuring over 50 of the most popular tequilas. My favorite is the Three Amigos Margarita, made with three generations tequila and Grand Marnier. Great food choices are the citrus marinated shrimp ceviche, the burrito de bandini filled with juicy seasoned shredded beef, or the pork carnitas served with warm tortillas, guacamole, salsa, and frijoles. Healthy dining options include fresh salads, vegetarian items, and a variety of gluten-free choices. Other restaurants by Diane Powers include **Casa de Pico** (p. 272) in La Mesa and Casa Guadalajara in Old Town.

Don's Country Kitchen, 2885 Roosevelt St., Carlsbad, CA 92008; (760) 729-2274; donscountrykitchen.com; American; $$. Reminiscent of a country inn with floral tablecloths and lacy ivory valences bordering the windows, this cute little eatery offers a ton of made-from-scratch specialties for breakfast and lunch. There are about six tables inside, as well as a long counter with barstools, and a small outdoor patio. Breakfast is a filling feast, with hearty helpings of fresh chorizo and beans with corn or flour tortillas, buttermilk biscuits with country sausage gravy, or luscious banana nut pancakes. For lunch, warm your soul with one of their hearty soups, especially the meatball or chicken tortilla. Other influential dishes include the warm and mildly spicy meat loaf sandwich with mashed potatoes and gravy, Don's country chili, and the deep-fried cod fillet fish burger. With reasonable prices and fast and friendly service, you can't go wrong here. In addition, they have a new location in Oceanside.

Elevation Burger, 2641 Gateway Rd., Carlsbad, CA 92009; (760) 683-5101; elevationburger.com; Burgers; $. "Ingredients matter" is Elevation Burger's slogan, where the proof is in a patty made with 100 percent USDA–certified organic and grass-fed, free-range beef that's ground right on the premises. With 30 percent less fat than similar burgers at competing chains, eating a burger doesn't have to expand your waistline. You can also opt for not just one but two organic veggie burger choices. You'll love the fresh-cut fries cooked in heart-healthy 100 percent olive oil as well as the hand-scooped milk shakes. Elevation Burger is also committed to environmentally friendly practices, including recycling waste—some of which becomes biodiesel fuel— and using sustainable materials and energy-efficient equipment in their restaurants.

Fish House Vera Cruz, 417 Carlsbad Village Dr., Carlsbad, CA 92008; (760) 434-6777; fishhouseveracruz.com; Seafood; $$.

Deriving its name from the commercial fishing boat the *Vera Cruz* built in 1965 in Costa Mesa, The Fish House Vera Cruz was born in the historic Old California Restaurant Row in San Marcos in December 1979. As the demand for seasonal and daily-delivered fresh fish selections continued to grow, two new locations were opened in Carlsbad and Temecula. Due to weather, fishing conditions, market availability, and local popularity, fish is subject to availability but can include anything from Atlantic salmon and yellowtail to wahoo, dorado, or ling cod. In addition to their standard menu, Fish House Vera Cruz features about 15 to 20 different fish daily. Recommended: a big bowl of the Boston-style clam chowder, Pacific oysters from the cold waters of the Northern Pacific, or the rainbow trout from the cool mountain streams of Idaho. All seafood is grilled over a mesquite charcoal grill.

The Fish Joint, 524 S. Coast Hwy., Oceanside, CA 92054; (760) 450-0646; Seafood; $$. From elaborate sushi and sashimi creations to imaginative salads and entrees, this laid-back beach-style bungalow is a fish joint you don't want to miss. Exceptionally prepared food and seafood variations, including eel and octopus, have brought this eatery a very loyal clientele. If you were a fan of the TV show *Gilligan's Island*, you will feel right at home. There are menu items named after the show's characters, including the Mary Anne Roll with crab, avocado, tempura shrimp, spicy tuna, masago, and teriyaki sauce and the Gilligan Roll with cucumber, sprouts, avocado, tomato, and spicy citrus. By far, the best-selling and most popular item on the menu is the flash-fried Chronic Roll of spicy tuna, crab, and avocado. Vegetarians can choose from rolls made with cucumber, carrot, tomato, or avocado, to name a few.

Flying Pig Pub & Kitchen, 626 S. Tremont St., Oceanside, CA 92054; (760) 453-2940; flyingpigpubkitchen.com; American; $$$. Located on a rather quiet residential street just 1 block west from the South Coast Highway, this small gastropub is a hidden gem. Husband-and-wife team Rodney and Aaron Browning have deep experience in the local culinary community, working with some of the most respected chefs in Southern California. Partnering with Chef Mario Moser, this new eatery is dedicated to the slow-food movement, a farm-to-table philosophy utilizing locally sourced and fresh ingredients. Rustic American cuisine is featured throughout the menu, with a touch of Southern-style comfort. One of the signature dishes is the Durac Pork Belly served with collards, caramelized apple, and polenta spoon bread. Favorite menu items include the chicken and dumplings or the shrimp and grits. And if you leave without having the bacon-studded mac 'n' cheese or the salt-and-vinegar fries, then you've really missed out. For dessert, nothing beats their vanilla ice-cream sundae topped with candied pork belly and chocolate chips. They offer a collection of craft beers on tap and in bottles, as well as a great selection of wines by the bottle or glass. Local artists are featured on a dedicated wall and available for purchase. Reservations are recommended on the weekend, as this cozy hangout is popular with the locals for its high-quality offerings.

Gregorio's, 300 Carlsbad Village Dr., Carlsbad, CA 92008; (760) 720-1134; gregoriosrestaurant.com; Italian; $$$. Reminiscent of a big Italian kitchen, the service at Gregorio's is friendly, the atmosphere is warm and welcoming, and the food is reasonably priced. Order a specialty pizza while catching a game on the TV indoors or on the enclosed heated patio, which has a partially enclosed awning and two more TVs. Bring the family because there is a little something on the menu for everyone, including appetizers and salads as well as specialty sandwiches, pizza, pasta, chicken, steak, and seafood. Try the USDA certified premium grain-fed beef New York steak prepared "Sicilian style," breaded in fresh bread crumbs, Italian herbs and spices, and cooked in a special steak oven. Some like it hot, and the shrimp and linguini in a spicy marinara fits the bill. Don't despair: you can cool off your tongue with a velvety rich spumoni-flavored gelato afterward!

Harney Sushi, 3964 Harney St., San Diego, CA 92054; (619) 295-3272; harneysushi.com; Asian Fusion; $$$. A second restaurant to the original location in Old Town, Harney Sushi, located near the Oceanside pier, is sexy-chic and sophistication all rolled into one. Accented with the color red, this roomy restaurant can seat up to 150 people inside. Grab a seat in one of the black booths, or at the environmentally friendly sushi and sake bars made of concrete and recycled glass. Of course, there is always room on the spacious outdoor patio if you prefer. No matter where you are in this restaurant, you'll be tapping your chopsticks to the beat of DJ music while indulging on elaborate seafood concoctions that melt in your mouth. My favorite rolls are the Bomb James Bomb, Hawaii 5-0, and the Flaming Lip. On a mission to protect the health of our oceans and bodies, sushi creations from a sustainable seafood menu are constantly reinvented here, keeping guests wondering what flavor combination will come next. Now your basic spicy salmon roll features Mt. Cook Alpine Salmon, which is eco-sustainably farmed in pristine waters high in the Alps in the South Island of New Zealand. As for happy hour, don't miss the sake oyster shooter—you'll be begging for more!

John's Neighborhood Bar & Grill, 1280 E. Vista Wy., Vista, CA 92081; (760) 724-7242; johnsneighborhood.com; American; $$$. One of the better family-friendly restaurants in North County, this place lends a nice, down-home feeling. With approximately 70 items on the menu, including a broad appetizer list, homemade soups, salads, sandwiches, pizza, steaks, and seafood, it's a guarantee that everyone in your party will walk away happy and full. Nothing beats the clam chowder, except for maybe the prime rib. Not many restaurants include soup or salad and a starch with your dinner, but this place does. The buffalo wings and calamari are great starters, and you can't go wrong with a juicy New York strip steak or filet mignon. Seafood options include scampi, halibut, salmon, sea scallops, swordfish, and my favorite, macadamia nut–crusted mahimahi. Whether you can carry a tune or not, join in on the karaoke fun on Wednesday, Friday, and Saturday.

KoKo Beach Restaurant, 2858 Carlsbad Blvd., Carlsbad, CA 92008; (760) 434-6868; kokobeach.com; American; $$$. Specialty of the house prime rib, hand-cut steaks, and fresh seafood have kept the locals coming for years to this cozy, old-fashioned hideaway with a dark atmosphere and red-leather booths. Enjoy breakfast or lunch, and don't worry about dinner, because they are open daily until midnight. The beef is aged, USDA Choice or higher, and entree prices are reasonable and include a choice of soup or dinner salad, steak fries, baked potato, house rice, or fresh vegetables. Try the 1-full-pound sweet red Alaskan king crab legs served with drawn butter and lemon or the slow-cooked barbecue baby back ribs finished on the char broiler. A cozy bar and lounge with a fireplace is the perfect setting for an after-dinner nightcap.

The Longboarder Cafe, 228 N. Coast Hwy., Oceanside, CA 92054; (760) 721-6776; American; $$. From a juicy pot roast sandwich topped with rich brown gravy to a bulky chicken chimichanga, a four-letter word called "food" is the reason there's a huge local following at this beach-style eatery for breakfast, lunch, and dinner. After experiencing the big portions, you might want to take a long walk on the Oceanside beach just steps away. I'm a fan of the popular medley of morning fare, including chicken-fried steak, almond french toast, the Hawaiian scramble, and huevos rancheros smothered with ranchero sauce. Lighter afternoon and evening options include a super tasty homemade garden burger and the turkey and avocado sandwich all melted with jack and cheddar cheeses on grilled sourdough.

Nozomi, 3050 Pio Pico Dr., Carlsbad, CA 92008; (760) 729-7877; nozomicarlsbad.com; Asian Fusion; $$$. Choose from three different Japanese dining venues all in one building. A favorite is the Tokyo room upstairs, where the sound of raindrops from a massive waterfall design evokes a sense of tranquility. Trained by a Master sushi chef of San Diego's **Sushi Ota** (p. 164), Executive Chef Ken Lee offers a notable selection of nigiri sushi, hand rolls, and sashimi as well as soups and salads, specialty tapas from land and sea, and larger entrees. Sip on a rare seasonal sake or a cold Japanese beer while savoring baby yellowtail tiradito drizzled with a citrus soy and white truffle oil or sirloin beef sukiyaki with glass noodles in a delicate broth. Whether it's lunch in a bento box, an elaborate dinner, or a luscious dessert paired with a handpicked tea imported from Japan, Nozomi will exceed your greatest expectations.

Pacific 333, 333 N. Pacific St., Oceanside, CA 92054; (760) 433-3333; 333pacific.com; California Modern; $$$. Located near the historic Oceanside pier, this gorgeous restaurant features indoor and outdoor dining areas, lively music, a big-screen TV, and an electrifying bar and lounge. The inside dining room offers a very nice ocean view, but the large outdoor patio gives you a closer view of the Pacific. If you are a vodka connoisseur, this is the place  for you. Choose from 100-plus vodkas from around the world while indulging in California-centric seafood, sushi, signature steaks, and chops. Chef Brian Hyre has a knack for using simple cooking techniques. The steaks are prepared in an 1,800°F broiler, ensuring a tender and juicy center with a perfectly charred outer crust. Don't want a steak? Venture out and try the tuna poke tacos, bleu cheese-crusted Australian Kobe beef meat loaf, or the shrimp and grits.

Ruby's Diner, 5630 Paseo Del Norte, Carlsbad, CA 92008; (760) 931-7829; rubys.com; American; $$. Open since 1982, this 1940s-style diner is famous for its great food and spectacular service in a sparkling-clean restaurant. It's a nice walk along the Oceanside Pier, and Ruby's is located at the very end. Inside there are two levels, all with beautiful views of the Pacific. The view is as good as you would find in a higher end restaurant, but without the high prices. Imagine waterside dining and a grilled-to-perfection Ruby's Signature Burger with melted double Swiss cheese and fresh sliced avocado on a grilled Parmesan sourdough *and* a side of chili fries—could it get any better than that? Oh yes—Ruby's all-natural USDA Choice beef comes only from hormone- and antibiotic-free cattle, raised naturally and fed on pasture grass, natural grains, legumes, and corn, and then allowed to mature slowly for optimal flavor and tenderness. Look for additional Ruby's locations throughout San Diego.

Twenty/20 Grill and Wine Bar, 5480 Grand Pacific Dr., Carlsbad, CA 92008; (760) 827-2500; twenty20grill.com; California Modern; $$$. In a magnificent airy space at the Sheraton Carlsbad Resort & Spa, you will find this warm and inviting restaurant complete with an outdoor patio offering views of the Pacific Ocean and the ever-blooming Carlsbad Flower Fields. And since the hotel is adjacent to LEGOLAND, you might see worn-out parents hunched over the bar unwinding over a much-needed martini. A diverse and globally inspired menu leans on playful flavor combinations from locally grown fresh ingredients for breakfast, lunch, and dinner. Executive Chef Robert Carr offers alluring starters in mason jars filled with anything from chipotle hummus to Sonoma goat cheese, and even a PB&J. Create your own hearth-baked pizza or go for the gusto with the sautéed duck breast or the Chardonnay-braised pork shank. Choose from a nice selection of affordable wines, draught beers, and specialty cocktails.

Vivace, 7100 Aviara Resort Dr., Carlsbad, CA 92011; (760) 448-1234; vivace-restaurant.com; Italian; $$$$. Italian for "alive," Vivace at Park Hyatt Aviara provides an elegant yet sophisticated ambiance with an irresistible contemporary Italian menu. Chef de Cuisine Jesse A. Paul likes to "let the ingredients speak," honing in on a market-driven cuisine that's always a perennial hit with locals and tourists looking for a seasonal and scintillating Italian dining experience. The pastas are made in-house daily, using only organic ingredients. Exquisite pasta options include a mouth-watering carnaroli risotto with lobster and gnocchi con agnello brasato with braised lamb and fava beans. Meatier favorites include wagyu flat iron steak, Berkshire pork tenderloin, and roasted Jidori chicken. Pick a great wine from Italy off the wine list, and your dinner is complete.

West Steak and Seafood, 4980 Avenida Encinas, Carlsbad, CA 92008; (760) 930-9100; weststeakandseafood.com; Steak House; $$$$. Located within walking distance of the Carlsbad beach, this sophisticated steak house with vaulted ceilings and stained-glass windows aims to please with prime beef, chops, and seafood. Born and raised in Venice, Italy, Executive Chef Eugenio Martignago is so passionate about the "farm to table" experience that he personally visits West's own 1-acre farm daily, picking the most seasonal vegetables for each and every entree. From an assortment of beets and lettuce, to strawberries and eggplant from the greenhouse, you'll get the gourmet organic "chef's touch" with every bite. Tantalize your taste buds with the crispy goat cheese and roasted beets before digging into a Durham Farms bison filet, or choose a USDA Prime cowboy bone-in rib eye steak and a side of zucchini-blossom tempura.

Tip Top Meats, 6118 Paseo Del Norte, Carlsbad, CA 92011; (760) 438-2620; tiptopmeats.com; Grocery/Market; $$. Customers return time and time again to this butcher shop, European market, and restaurant all rolled into one. You can't miss with the house-made sausages, the USDA Prime and Choice beef, lamb, veal, and fresh chickens. Plus, they always welcome special-order requests. Specialty meats include Diestel brand turkeys, boneless stuffed tur-duc-hens, fruit-stuffed pork roasts, barons of beef, suckling pigs, ducks, and geese. Their European market features specialty food items, cheeses, wine, and more. As for dinner in the restaurant, you get quality food at a bargain price; this truly is a bang for your buck! Opt for a massive portion of prime rib served with mashed potatoes and gravy. Other favorites are the liver and onions, the European sausage plate, or beef stroganoff.

Solana Beach, Cardiff-by-the-Sea, Encinitas & Leucadia

Located between Carlsbad to the north and Del Mar to the south, these oceanfront communities are stunningly scenic yet extremely laid-back. Dotted with vintage bungalows and quaint eateries, this is a local hot spot for the surfer and foodie alike. Nothing says vintage California more than this quaint area of San Diego. Although mostly centered on the historic Highway 101, these areas also stretch inland, where newer communities have developed.

Solana Beach is the southernmost community, where every residence and business is only a short distance to the ocean. Eden Gardens is one of the oldest residential areas of Solana Beach, formed in the 1920s by Mexican farmers. Some of the finest Mexican restaurants in San Diego are still operating here. One block east of Highway 101 is the Cedros District, which has grown into an upscale design district that attracts many artisans, decorators, and antiques dealers. Just a little farther north is Cardiff-by-the-Sea, formed in 1911 and named after the founders' birthplace of Cardiff, Wales. Many of the major streets in this community also bear familiar names from the UK. The town is very small, so most residents have views of the ocean and can easily walk between the ocean, community parks, and business areas. A must-see is the number of restaurants located directly on the beach in an area dubbed "Restaurant Row." Cardiff also includes the 900-acre San Elijo Lagoon Ecological Reserve, which is the largest coastal wetland in San Diego County and home to nearly 300 different bird species throughout the year.

Still farther north is Encinitas. The downtown area along Highway 101 is a 100-year-old coastal shopping district with examples of historic architecture, quaint shops, sidewalk cafes, and restaurants highlighted by beautiful flower baskets lining the street. Many residents consider Encinitas the Flower Growing Capital, and the city has been strategically developed around the preexisting flower growers. Be sure to visit the San Diego Botanic Gardens, which includes 4 miles of garden trails, flowering trees, majestic palms, and the nation's largest bamboo collection. Located directly on a clifftop off Highway 101 is the Self Realization Center. Founded in 1920 as a focal point for yoga and well-being, it is situated overlooking the ocean in a serene garden-like setting, and is open to the public. Also included in Encinitas is one of the most famous surfing locations on the Pacific, Swami's Beach, which is located at the far south end of town.

Last but not least is Leucadia, a small area just north of Encinitas, right along Highway 101. Many residents consider it a sub-town of Encinitas. Beaches here are difficult to find and not frequented by tourists, as the only access from the sheer cliffs are a few well-designed stairways leading to the rocky shore. These are very popular with the local surfing community.

Foodie Faves

A Little Moore Coffee Shop, 1030 N. Highway 101, Leucadia, CA 92024; (760) 753-8228; American; $$. Start your morning off right with a full-size breakfast at this vintage roadside diner, complete with French Country white windows, old-style tables, and a shiny countertop bar where you can sit and observe your eggs sizzling on an open griddle. Unlike the many chain coffee shops in town, this cute little cafe will take you back to the simpler life of the 1950s. That's when this little gem was first established in the quieter area of Highway 101 north of Encinitas. The locals know they can count on friendly, fast service and affordable prices while they get their fill of omelets, pancakes, and french toast. Do you like steak and eggs? They have it, along with Polish sausage or teriyaki chicken and eggs. Other substantial good-morning eats include a chili cheese omelet and eggs Benedict. And of course, you have to try their coffee! Also open for lunch.

Bangkok Bay, 731 S. Hwy. 101, 1B1, Solana Beach, CA 92075; (858) 792-2427; bangkok-bay.com; Thai; $$$. You'll fall in love with the dimly lit ambiance and the Thai decor and foliage. This hidden gem nestled in the Mercado del Sol complex reflects a rich variety of northeastern Thai drinks, crepes, soups, salads, noodles, curries, and desserts. Go with a bunch of friends and share a variety of entrees around the table. Try the half honey roasted duck on top of a bed of steamed young spinach, broccoli, and carrots topped with a honey sauce; kua rice noodles stir-fried with egg, brown sauce, and bean sprouts, then sprinkled with scallions and crushed peanuts; and of course, the fried bananas with coconut ice cream for dessert.

Beach Grass Cafe, 159 S. Hwy. 101, Solana Beach, CA 92075; (858) 509-0632; beachgrasscafe.com; Organic/Health Food; $$. You can dress up or come in flip-flops to this novel cafe with its white tablecloths in an informal setting. Guests who walk through these doors can expect a fabulous meal with friendly and personal service for breakfast, lunch, and dinner. There are plenty of vegetarian options. Since this is one of the few places that dishes up pasta for breakfast, it's a regular pit stop. The fried linguini scrambled with egg, tomatoes, feta cheese, and fresh basil is sublime. Another great breakfast item that's on the sweeter side and very popular with the locals are the luscious pineapple upside-down pancakes paired with a dark roast coffee. For lunch, don't miss the Kailua pork machaca tacos, and for dinner, opt for the spicy crusted pork chop or risotto with wild mushrooms.

Blue Ribbon Artisan Pizzeria, 897 S. Coast Hwy. 101, #102, Encinitas, CA 92024; (760) 634-7671; blueribbonpizzeria.com; Pizza; $$. Even with the long waits for dinner, this charming neighborhood pizza joint does pizza the organic, sustainable, and local way. The pizza dough undergoes a three-day fermentation process, mozzarella cheese is stretched by hand daily, and the fennel sausage is made from sustainable Berkshire pork on-site. Delicious pizzas are topped with unique ingredient combinations and cooked in a wood-burning oven. Favorites include truffled four-cheese pizza with mozzarella, bleu cheese, Parmigiana Reggiano, ricotta, and chives or the pizzaiolo topped with the chef's seasonal selections. As for drink options, Diet Coke isn't an option at this *au naturel* establishment. You will, however, find plenty of local craft beers on tap as well as organic, sustainable, and biodynamic wines.

Cafe la Bocca, 124 Lomas Santa Fe Dr., Suite 102, Solana Beach, CA 92075; (858) 792-2622; Italian; $. Born and raised in Rome, Owner Angela Sagnotti brought her love for gelato to the states, and be glad she did. She imports the ingredients from Italy and makes the gelato on-site at her cute little sidewalk cafe. Right across the street from the Solana Beach train station, the interior is suggestive of an Italian villa. Several comfy chairs are available inside, and there is also an outside patio shared with other businesses. She offers approximately 25 flavors of authentic gelato including sugar-free raspberry, rum raisin, bubblegum, peach, and mango. If you're not in the mood for gelato, Cafe la Bocca offers Illy Caffe coffee imported from Italy as well as genuine Italian pastries, sandwiches, salads, and pizza. A Napoleon of puff pastry layered with raspberry and cream filling is a decadent treat sold all over Italy. Now you can find them here!

Chief's Burgers and Brew, 124 Lomas Santa Fe Dr., Suite 108, Solana Beach, CA 92075; (858) 755-2599; chiefsburgersandbrew .com; Burgers; $$. Sports fans pack local sports bars on weekends to watch their favorite games, and this place is no exception. But beware: The owners and regulars are die-hard Denver Bronco fans, so the bar on NFL Sundays is filled with orange jerseys and screaming fans. It's all in good fun and competition, so feel free to wear your favorite team with pride and join the party. With great burgers, 23 TVs, lots of windows, and an outdoor patio, you will be cheering with new friends in no time. All burgers are prepared with ½-pound Angus beef except for the massive Super Chief One Pound Burger consisting of two patties with double cheese, lettuce, tomato, onion, and Thousand Island dressing. From fried dill pickle sticks to jalapeño poppers, and a heading on the menu called "Everything but the Kitchen Sink," everyone in your party will find something they like to eat!

Cicciotti's Trattoria Italiana & Seafood, 1933 San Elijo Ave., Cardiff-by-the-Sea, CA 92007; (760) 634-2335; cicciottiscardiff .com; Italian; $$$. Chef, restaurateur, and author Gaetano Cicciotti likes to cook his classic northern and southern Italian family recipes at this eatery just a step from the Cardiff beach. There is plenty of seating at the windows looking out over the Pacific, and also a spacious bar area. Lunch is a good time to visit if you like it less crowded. Choose the spaghetti and homemade meatballs or the in-house ravioli stuffed with fresh ricotta cheese and spinach, sautéed in a fresh tomato sauce and served with house salad or soup. Friday and Saturday are busy with live entertainment and a fun Italian waitstaff. You'll have no problem finding a great label from the wine list while you wait for the stuffed pizza with mozzarella, gorgonzola cheese, and walnuts—there's nothing like it!

Claire's on Cedros, 246 N. Cedros Ave., Solana Beach, CA 92075; (858) 259-8597; clairesoncedros.com; Organic/Health Food; $$. With a sustainable building and menu, this is the first LEED (Leadership in Energy and Environmental Design) Platinum–certified restaurant in San Diego. The menu is seasonal, but you will always find the award-winning original cinnamon or multigrain Clairecakes. Your morning sugar fix comes from utterly decadent stuffed spiced pear brioche french toast packed with fresh ricotta cheese, topped with toasted pecans, and served with spiced pear compote and homemade cinnamon butter. Egg lovers will savor a variety of hearty and healthful omelets and specialty items including Tuscan Benedict with homemade hollandaise and a delicious Caprese Frittata. Decorated like a country cottage, choose to sit in the warm and inviting dining room, or on the outdoor patio next to a bubbling fountain.

Crush, 437 S. Hwy. 101, #112, Solana Beach, CA 92075; (858) 481-CRUSH (2787); solanabeachcrush.com; Italian; $$$. This neighborhood Italian newbie is quickly becoming a favorite among the locals for its modish design, authentic Italian cuisine, and late-night happy hour scene. Longtime friends Executive Chef Jason Colabove and Head Chef Mike Lina trained together in culinary school and partnered to showcase a classically modern Italian menu featuring local and organic ingredients paired with over 160 bottles of hand-selected International wines. Live music is offered throughout the week, and there's plenty of seating on comfortable couches or outside next to the tabletop fire pit. Happy hour is especially busy. The restaurant is an extension of its sister restaurant of the same name, which has been delighting diners in Chico, California, for several years. This beautiful coastal destination offers lunch and dinner—with standout dishes including Old School Six Hour Ragu Bolognese Tagliatelle, Mom's Meatballs, and Roasted Chicken Rigatoni. Now that's my kind of Italian!

East Coast Pizza, 2015 San Elijo Ave., Cardiff-by-the-Sea, CA 92007; (760) 944-1599; eastcoastpizzaonline.com; Pizza; $. No doughy, soggy pizza crust here. East Coast serves the closest thing to the Big Apple in these parts. Pizzas are cooked in a brick oven with a good variety of traditional selections (meat lovers with meatballs, sausage, and pepperoni) and more contemporary options like the artichoke special, spicy chicken, homemade pesto, and Hawaiian barbecue with chicken and pineapple. There's a sister establishment located in San Marcos called Massachusetts Mike's (massmikes.com).

El Q'ero, 564 S. Coast Hwy. 101, Encinitas, CA 92024; (760) 753-9050; qerorestaurant.com; Latin American; $$$. Every neighborhood needs a Latin American restaurant like this one. Peruvian and South American specialties influenced by ancient times and cultures are offered in a romantic and enchanting candlelit setting decorated with Peruvian-style artwork and tablecloths. Since this small and exclusive eatery is often booked for lunch and dinner, reservations are highly recommended. There are two seatings offered for dinner, and there is rarely an open table for walk-in customers, unless a cancellation has occurred. The signature *Costillas en Jora* is fork-tender, prime grade beef short ribs braised in sacred *Chicha de Jora* corn beer and served over fluffy mashed potatoes with sautéed

Swiss chard. Quinoa, an ancient grain once considered the gold of the Incas, makes for a beautiful salad when combined with seasonal apples, winter squash, and lacinato kale. Only Peruvian and Brazilian beer and South American wine are served.

Ki's Restaurant, 2591 S. Coast Hwy. 101, Cardiff-by-the-Sea, CA 92007; (760) 436-5236; kisrestaurant.com; Organic/Health Food; $$$. This is one of Cardiff's best-kept secrets. Located just across the street from the Cardiff State Beach, Ki's offers a full spectrum of natural and organically raised foods without additives and preservatives. Choose from a fine selection of organic juices, smoothies, omelets, pancakes, salads, wraps, seafood, and meats. For breakfast try the tofu scramble in tamari spices and olive oil, and for lunch it's the thick millet veggie burger baked golden brown with cheese. If you visit for dinner, try the butternut squash soft rolled tacos. Gluten-free and vegan options are also available.

Lotus Cafe & Juice Bar, 765 S. Coast Hwy. 101, Encinitas, CA 92024; (760) 479-1977; lotuscafeandjuicebar.com; Organic/Health Food; $$. The Lumberyard in Encinitas is home to many trendy restaurants, and this is one of them. With indoor and outdoor seating for about 100 people, this healthy cafe is dedicated to serving fresh, locally sourced natural food at affordable prices. A comprehensive menu comprises many vegan, vegetarian, strict vegetarian, and gluten-free options. Choose from savory and homemade organic soups, salads sandwiches, pasta, vegetarian entrees, fish and chicken entrees, kiddies' meals, fresh juices, smoothies, shakes, and desserts, even homemade vegan cupcakes. Such items as the Pipe's Whole Wheat Pita with falafel balls, hummus, and tahini-ginger sauce, and the Swami's Carrot shake with organic carrot juice, vanilla ice cream, cinnamon, and nutmeg make this place unusual. Additional location in Hillcrest.

Naked Cafe, 106 S. Sierra Ave., Solana Beach, CA 92075; (858) 259-7866; thenakedcafe.com; Organic/Health Food; $$. Want a "Plate of Prosperity" with organic quinoa for breakfast? Or how about a Goddess Wrap with sautéed sesame ginger tofu wrapped in a spinach tortilla for lunch? You'll find it here where wholesome foods are turned into healthy delights that the whole family can enjoy. The concept of this eatery is that eating foods "naked" in their simple, clean, and natural state will not only please your palate but also nurture your body and mind. Start the day with an organic espresso or an Asian coffee, and a Buff Breakfast Burrito with egg whites and grilled chicken. Other great choices include the Fuzzy Monkey Pancakes with roasted grains and fresh bananas or, for lunch, the ginger rice and black beans. Additional locations in Encinitas, Carlsbad, and Point Loma.

101 Diner, 52 S. Coast Hwy. 101, Encinitas, CA 92024; (760) 753-2123; 101diner.com; American; $$. This roadside hole-in-the-wall/meets greasy spoon/meets diner is packed with locals who wouldn't dream of going anywhere else for breakfast and lunch. When you walk in, the friendly waitstaff will greet you with a smile and treat you like you've been coming in for years. In fact, they'll most likely remember you by name. Have a seat in one of the vintage booths and you'll be transported into a vintage beach-town hangout. If you've never had fresh-cut pork chops and eggs for breakfast, try it here, including your choice of potato and bread. The spicy beef Louisiana sausage or corned beef hash will knock your socks off. Warm and like nothing else you've ever tasted, don't miss the fluffy pineapple or banana nut pancakes. You'll love this place!

Pamplemousse Grille, 514 Via de la Valle, Ste. 100, Solana Beach, CA 92075; (858) 792-9090; pgrille.com; French; $$$$. Since 1996, this comfortable, yet elegant restaurant located across from the Del Mar Race Track has been surprising guests with eclectic inspirations from Chef-Owner Jeffrey Strauss. Drawing from his childhood visits to his grandparents' New Jersey farm, as well as his many travels to Europe, Strauss offers guests a modish and upscale mix of French continental cuisine featuring grilled fish and meats. I recommend the crispy half duck with sautéed gnocchi and cherry balsamic reduction or the lamb stew with braised potato, green lentils, and a mélange of in-season baby vegetables. Don't miss spaghetti and meatballs every Sunday evening. As for the vino, educate yourself while making your selection from a 65-page book of local and international wines. Pamplemousse Grille has received many local and national awards including "Best Restaurant, People's Choice," *San Diego Home & Gardens;* "Best New Restaurant," "Best Caterer," and "San Diego's Best Chef," *San Diego Magazine*; and Zagat Rated #1 Restaurant in San Diego for three consecutive years.

Panera Bread, 667 San Rodolfo Dr., Solana Beach, CA 92075; (858) 481-0050; panerabread.com; Bakery; $$. "A loaf of bread in every arm" is Panera's motto. They truly believe that a great slice of bread is key to any meal. Yes, this is a chain, but it always provides a fresh, delicious lunch that will leave you satisfied throughout the day. Walking in through the big arched front entryway, you see a large counter in front of you filled with baskets of bread and pastries. As you stand in line, they almost always have a sample of their warm bread for you to nibble on while deciding what to order. Their Asiago Roast Beef sandwich includes tender shredded roast beef, lettuce, tomatoes, onions, cheddar cheese, horseradish sauce, and their crusty Asiago bread. All meals are served with a pickle slice and a choice of either their Panera brand chips, a piece of their French baguette bread, or an apple. Other talked-about items are their soups and salads, which value the finest ingredients within each season. Consider stopping by to grab a large sourdough loaf to serve with a meal you prepare at home.

Parioli, 647 S. Hwy. 101, Solana Beach, CA 92075; (858) 755-2525; parioliitalianbistro.com; Italian; $$$. This wonderful Italian treasure is located in a simple little one-story beach house along Highway 101. This is the perfect place to enjoy upscale Mediterranean fare without the formality of a fine dining establishment. You'll be welcomed by a sunny front porch, prominent bar area, and stylish interior. The restaurant is co-owned and operated by two native Italian brothers whose food will draw you into another world. Chef Antonio admits there are many similarities between San Diego and southern Italy, and he utilizes seasonally fresh produce and ingredients in all his fabulous dishes. I fell in love with his Caprese salad, made with locally grown heirloom tomatoes, fresh mozzarella, and just the right touch of fresh basil, olive oil, and balsamic vinegar. For dinner, be sure to sample from the daily fish selections or one of the many traditional pasta dishes. Loyal patrons favor the homemade pappardelle or ravioli, prepared with the best available ingredients. The wine list is impressive, and there is also a large, interior courtyard area perfect for enjoying alfresco dining or reserving for a private party.

Red Tracton's, 550 Via De La Valle, Solana Beach, CA 92075; (858) 755-6600; redtractonssteakhouse.com; Steak House; $$$$. Beef, it's what's for dinner at this classical restaurant that planted its roots in San Diego more than 20 years ago, although it was first established in 1948. If you're looking for one of the finest steak houses in town, this is the place. Begin your meal with their famous Green Goddess Salad, followed by a gigantic 24-ounce eastern prime rib and a colossal baked potato. Although the menu features a wide selection of meats and fish, there are also daily favorites, like home-style meat loaf and roasted turkey. A more "mature" crowd of regulars likes to frequent this restaurant, featuring live entertainment from the piano bar. The young people like the bar.

Rimel's, 2005 San Elijo Ave., Cardiff-by-the-Sea, CA 92007; (760) 633-2202; rimelsrestaurants.com; California Modern; $$$. The locals know to come here for the grilled mahimahi tacos and the free-range antibiotic- and hormone-free meats. Offering up an Asian- and Mexican-inspired menu, this is a family-style restaurant adorned with simple wood tables that lend a log-cabin-type feel. Everything is done from scratch, including the delicious soups made daily from the freshest ingredients with no added butter or dairy. Specials include an 8-ounce fresh locally caught fish slow-cooked over a wood fire. A favorite is the grain fed California chicken cooked rotisserie style to a nice golden brown over Texan mesquite wood. Believe me, you can't go wrong with the slow-roasted, wood-fired half rack baby back ribs with Rimel's special dry rub and house barbecue sauce. Additional locations in La Jolla and Carmel Valley.

Sake House Yu Me Ya, 1246 N. Coast Hwy. 101, Encinitas, CA 92024; (760) 633-4288; sakehouseyumeya.com; Japanese; $$$. Open since 2006, Sake House Yu Me Ya (meaning House of Dreams) is a family-owned and -operated Izakaya restaurant that is only open for dinner. Chef-Owner Kiyohiro Nakai and wife, Hiroko, with daughters Yuka and Fumika, offer authentic Japanese specialties and sake in a 25-seat space with an intimate bar and bamboo decor. Signature dishes include Chef Nakai's homemade undo noodle, for which he is known for in Japan, and the barbecue beef salad with house dressing. Hiroko shares the love with her spicy tuna carpaccio creation of two fried wontons, avocado, and soy sauce, topped with spicy tuna and placed on homemade Japanese mayo. Other popular favorites include the broiled black cod with kyoto miso flavor and the baked bay scallop and shimeji mushrooms. Sake House only carries the pure rice sake known as Junmai. The Sake House Yumeya in Hillcrest opened in 2011, and has more of a lounge-type setting. Savor Fumika's secret spicy ramen noodle recipe at the Hillcrest location only.

Samurai, 979 Lomas Santa Fe Dr., Solana Beach, CA 92075; (858) 481-0032; samurai japaneserestaurant.com; Japanese; $$$. For 33 years, Samurai has been a mecca for Japanese food. From the cocktail bar to the multiple dining sections, including a sushi bar and large teppan grill, this place is fun for everyone. This is a more expensive restaurant that focuses on the quality of the food and drinks. The locals like to come in and dine on Monday and Tuesday evenings, which are slower nights. Weekends are louder, and there is more of a drinking crowd. The signature dish is definitely the chef's special specialty roll. I like sashimi, especially the tuna belly (toro) and the in-season live shrimp (amaebi). As for anti-sushi dishes, I highly recommend the chicken teriyaki and the assorted tempuras. If you decide you want red meat, invite your friends and dine around the teppan grill, which cooks the beef teriyaki or New York steak to a tender and juicy perfection.

Solace and the Moonlight Lounge, 25 E. E St., Encinitas, CA 92024; (760) 753-2433; eatatsolace.com; American; $$$. Located in Pacific Station in the heart of downtown Encinitas, this is the sister restaurant to the popular Urban Solace in North Park. Guests may need to aggressively hustle for a table as the natives do at this modern-day two-story newbie in Encinitas, but it's well worth it. The lounge and raw bar upstairs is a great place to sip on a specialty cocktail and slurp oysters on the half shell. Using only local, seasonal, and natural ingredients in his classic and modern American cuisine, Chef-Owner Matt Gordon dishes up warm cheddar and chive biscuits just out of the oven, warm house-made ricotta dip, and grass-fed steak tartare. He also offers Boylan Bottling Company's all-natural soda on tap as well as organic or biodynamic West Coast–produced wines. Gluten-free and vegetarian offerings are available.

Tony's Jacal, 621 Valley Ave., Solana Beach, CA 92075; (858) 755-2274; tonysjacal.com; Mexican; $$. Opened in 1946 and tucked away in Solana Beach, Tony's Jacal is a casual joint that serves some of the most traditional Mexican food you will find in San Diego. Originally serving customers on weekends and only accommodating

SUNDAY BRUNCH

Ever since I started a family, I've made Sunday a traditional time with the kids. We'll wake up in the morning, get dressed for church, and then celebrate the day with a Sunday brunch at one of the endless offerings in San Diego. It hearkens back to my simple childhood growing up in a small Northwest town, where Sundays were reserved for family, friends, and great conversation.

Whether you're interested in a simple menu-driven brunch or an extravagant room lined with every food imaginable, there's something for everyone in America's Finest City. If you search for "San Diego Brunches" online, you'll be bombarded with hundreds of options and plenty of advice on how to find the best choice to meet your taste and budget.

Below I have listed my favorites, with representation from around the county. Here you will find opportunities to visit high-end hotels, enjoy breakfast with waves of the Pacific lapping against the window, feast in lush gardens filled with tropical foliage, an urban neighborhood, and even a yacht. No matter what location you choose,

26 guests at a time, this restaurant has really grown into the place to be for delicious authentic food. Because it is family owned, you really get a sense of home when eating here. The atmosphere is rustic, and when the mariachi band begins to play, you really get the full dining experience. Start your meal off with their spicy and flavorful salsa served with fresh tortilla chips, and order the classic

be sure to bring your loved ones and friends, because Sunday brunch is meant to be enjoyed with great conversation and laughter. Isn't that the most important thing in life?

Crown Room at the Hotel del Coronado (Coronado), hoteldel.com

El Bizcocho at the Rancho Bernardo Inn (Rancho Bernardo), p. 105

Harbor Excursions (Downtown), sdhe.com

Hash House A Go Go (Uptown), p. 195

Humphrey's (Shelter Island), p. 215

Local Habit (Uptown), p. 196

Marine Room (La Jolla), p. 141

The Mediterranean Room at La Valencia (La Jolla), lavalencia .com

Ocean House (Carlsbad), oceanhousecarlsbad.com

South Bay Fish & Grill (Chula Vista), p. 277

Urban Solace (Uptown), p. 203

Vivace at the Park Hyatt Aviara (Carlsbad), p. 34

The Westgate Room (Downtown), p. 263

margarita, which is served in a large glass—you'll be able to drink throughout the whole meal. Favorites include the chiles rellenos, carne asada tacos, and their classic tamales. Make sure to try the huevos rancheros, two eggs covered in tangy mild yellow and green chilies and topped with onions and tomatoes. Finish that off with the decedent Mexican hot chocolate and you are set for the day!

Union Kitchen and Tap, 1108 S. Coast Hwy. 101, Encinitas, CA 92024; (760) 230-2337; localunion101.com; American; $$$. Grab a barstool when you can, because this Solana Beach hangout has become the talk of the town. Three separate dining areas allow you to view the latest sporting events on flat-screen TVs scattered throughout the restaurant. Local craft beers and Southern-style girl drinks served in mason jar glasses keep the locals happy. My favorite cocktail is the Strawberry Fields. Holding two culinary degrees, Executive Chef Jason Gethin offers an upgraded menu that follows his own love for local ingredients and Southern-style "lighter" fare cooked from scratch. Outrageous food surprises include the flatbread pizza topped with farm fresh eggs and greens, sage sausage-stuffed quail, and venison meatballs. The star of the show is the shrimp with grits, a dish that takes 8 days to make and uses grits imported directly from the South. See Chef Gethin's recipe for Union & Tap's **Strawberry Fields Cocktail** on p. 352.

Vigilucci's, 505 S. Coast Hwy. 101, Encinitas, CA 92024; (760) 434-2500; vigiluccis.com; Italian; $$$. Robby Vigilucci opened his first restaurant in Encinitas in 1994, and with a total of 7 Vigilucci's Italian Restaurants in San Diego County, he must have done something right. Born and raised in Milan, he learned the art of cooking by spending time in the family kitchen surrounded by relatives. With its largely Italian staff, diverse menu, and great wine list, it's no wonder this Encinitas eatery has become a favorite among regulars and Italians across the county who liken the fare to that served in Italy. One of their best appetizers is the non-fried, Luciana version of calamari, sautéed with garlic and white wine in a spicy marinara sauce. Come here for the large variety of fresh homemade pastas, especially the fettuccine with chicken in a classic Alfredo sauce. They also offer a full-scale catering service with custom menus designed to meet the needs of small or very large occasions.

Landmarks

Fidel's Little Mexico, 607 Valley Ave., Solana Beach, CA 92075; (858) 755-5292; fidelslittlemexico.com; Mexican; $$. Imagine walking into a neighborhood barbershop in the 1960s and having Owner Fidel Montanez cut your hair and offer you a taco for lunch. Seems the tacos became even more popular than the haircuts, so Montanez turned the place into a neighborhood cantina for the locals to hang out in. When the locals spread the word about the authentic food, the place boomed with business, and Montanez converted his two-story residence into three different levels and named the place Fidel's. This festive place is always packed. Favorite food choices include the meatball soup, a massive shredded beef burrito, and chile relleno filled with Monterey Jack cheese.

The Fish Market, 640 Via De La Valle, Solana Beach, CA 92075; (858) 755-2277; thefishmarket.com; Seafood; $$$. For over 30 years, this busy restaurant has been a Del Mar/Solana Beach favorite. Gather with friends at the popular oyster/cocktail bar and lounge. This is one of the few restaurants in town that serves a Crab Louie salad with traditional Thousand Island dressing. They also have delicious clam chowders available in traditional, New England, or Manhattan styles. A long list of fresh catches is available daily, cooked over mesquite wood broilers, and served with a choice of two side dishes. One of the most popular items on the menu is the hearty Dungeness Crab Cioppino, served with prawns, finfish, scallops, calamari, clams, mussels, cockles, and pasta with a house-made marinara sauce. Delicious! A retail fish market located at the front allows you to take home fresh, high-quality seafood selections, including the freshest fish, shellfish fish, smoked fish, and other menu items. Additional location at 750 N. Harbor Dr., San Diego; (619) 232-3474.

Specialty Stores, Markets & Producers

Chuao Chocolatier, 937 S. Coast Hwy. 101, Ste. 109-C, Encinitas, CA 92024; (760) 635-1444; chuaochocolatier.com; Desserts; $$. If you aren't a chocolate lover now, you might become one after a visit to this one-of-a-kind artisan chocolate shop. Named after a legendary cacao-producing region of central Venezuela, Chuao was founded in Encinitas in 2002 by Venezuelan-born brothers Michael and Richard Antonorsi. You will be *chew-wowed* with a sensual and spicy experience from these handcrafted world-class chocolates made with all natural ingredients. Crazy and crafty flavor combinations include a dark chocolate caramel fudge "Firecracker" with chipotle chile, salt, and popping candy, the "Chevere" with goat cheese, Pear Williams, and crushed black pepper butter cream, and the Cinco de Mayo with lemon tequila dark chocolate ganache topped with a preserved lemon chip. Additional location in La Jolla.

Jer's Chocolates, 437 S. Hwy. 101, Ste. 105, Solana Beach, CA 92075; (858) 792-2287; jers.com; Desserts; $$. It's all about the peanut butter at this gourmet chocolate shop. In fact, this place has rocked my chocolate world—in a good way of course! We all agree that these luscious confections made of all-natural peanut butter, gourmet milk, and dark chocolate— along with blends of toffee, caramel, rice crispy crunch, and pretzel—are everything a decadent chocolate should be and then some. We are not alone in our thinking: Jer's

Corporate Gift Chocolate Boxes and Peanut Butter Chocolate Gift Boxes have been featured on Food Network and the *Rachael Ray Show*. Chocolates are available for individual package purchases or as assorted gift boxes for any occasion.

Seaside Market, 2087 San Elijo Ave., Cardiff-by-the-Sea, CA 92007; (760) 753-5445; seasidemarket.com; Grocery/Market; $$. When you want fresh fruits and vegetables, head off to this seaside market. You'll have your pick of in-season produce, including some organic, from local growers, and even exotic fruits from faraway lands. If you're a sucker for shellfish, you can buy fresh seafood here and cook it for dinner the same day; it's almost as if you'd caught it yourself. A remarkable butcher shop ensures satisfaction with certified Black Angus Choice, organic Smart Chicken, and handmade gourmet sausages, veal, lamb, and fresh turkeys year-round. If you like your food prepared for you, you'll have your pick of sushi, imported cheeses, salads, sides, sandwiches, and homemade soups as well as pastries, cakes, pies, cookies, and more. They offer amazing wines and imported cheeses from around the world. You will also have your pick of wine and spirits galore.

St. Tropez Bakery & Bistro, 47 S. Coast Hwy. 101, No. 103-D, Encinitas, CA 92024; (760) 633-0084; sttropezbistro.com; Bakery; $$. Get your share of French bistro fare without the expensive plane ticket to France. Dine indoors or take a seat outside in the large outdoor patio, which resembles a sidewalk cafe—perfect for people watching with enough room for man's best friend. Walk by the large glass case inside, and take a long look at the traditional pastries. They also have a wide selection of filled cupcakes, cookies, patisseries, tarts, and cakes. If you're looking for a homemade treat on a special occasion, this is the place! I'm in love with the almond raspberry bars. Although my favorite time to visit is early in the morning for coffee and a light breakfast, the lunches and dinners are also excellent. Choose from soups, salads, hot and cold sandwiches, and plenty of delicious entrees. They also have a strong catering business throughout the local area. There are five locations throughout San Diego.

2GOOD2B Bakery & Cafe, 204 N El Camino Real, Ste. H, Encinitas, CA 92024; (760) 942-GOOD (4663); 2good2b.com; Organic/Health Food; $$. Out-of-this-world flavor and healthy ingredients collide at this trendy bakery where delectable gluten-free baked goodies include homemade artisan loaves, muffins, cupcakes, and cakes that taste so flavorful, no one will ever know they don't have gluten. Say goodbye to tasteless, gluten-free confections and say hello to flavorful, fresh meals, hot off the griddle, including breakfasts and sandwiches, all made with 100 percent gluten-, corn-, and soy-free ingredients. And 2GOOD2B doesn't stop there. Enjoy their Neapolitan-style personal pizzas, delicious quiche, and healthy gourmet salads. Comfort food items include gourmet chicken potpie, baked mac 'n' cheese, and homemade soups. The organic coffees, teas, and fresh squeezed orange juice hit the spot. Upon request, the chef will whip up vegan- and casein-free dishes.

VG's Donuts and Bakery, 106 Aberdeen Dr., Cardiff-by-the-Sea, CA 92007; (760) 753-2400; vgbakery.com; Bakery; $. There's really only one thing to say about this place, *doughnuts*! Made from scratch every day with no preservatives, these doughnuts are made with an old-fashioned style of baking that clearly tastes better. Open since 1969, they have been a favorite for generations of local residents as well as the surfing community who frequent the nearby beaches. Just stop by any morning and step in line. Although it can sometimes be quite long, it usually moves very quickly. Fortunately, doughnuts are baked twice daily, so there are always fresh selections available. Nearby businesses use them frequently for delivery to the hungry masses. They also carry a long list of special occasion and wedding cakes, cupcakes, pastries, muffins, cookies, breads, and bagels. During the holidays they also feature a number of traditional and festive baked goods. But really, it's all about the maple or chocolate old-fashioned doughnut.

Waters Fine Foods & Catering, 125 S. Hwy. 101, Solana Beach, CA 92075; (858) 509-9400; waterscatering.com; Grocery/Market; $$. Established in 1990, Waters Fine Foods & Catering offers full-service catering that allows guests to entertain with ease for their special event. Owner Mary Kay Waters is passionate about sustainability and meats from sound animal husbandry with no antibiotics or growth hormones. Waters believes in handcrafted, organic, artisan, and farmstead ingredients. Guests can also experience great food to go or on the premises at one of two Waters Fine Foods gourmet shops or at Fibonacci's Bistro in the newly redesigned and LEED certified Campus Pointe complex in La Jolla's UTC area. Choose from house-made soups, artisan sandwiches, and paninis as well as a variety of entrees, side dishes, and decadent desserts. Some favorites are Mary's all-natural farm chicken salad and the lemon crumble bars.

Carmel Valley, Del Mar & Rancho Santa Fe

New meets old in this area of San Diego, where historical and newly built residences share the land, sprawling from the Pacific Ocean to lushly landscaped communities spread inland for several miles. No visit to San Diego would be complete without visiting this haven for culinary excellence.

Carmel Valley is one of the newest areas in San Diego, a sprawling, master-planned community that replaced acres of tomato fields over the past 2 decades. The restaurants in this area will be located in many of the town centers that dot the landscape to add convenience and a sense of community for the residents. Although the homes can be densely packed into distinct neighborhoods, Carmel Valley also retains open spaces, including the westernmost end of the San Dieguito River Park, a series of trails from the Pacific

Ocean to the small town of Julian in the mountains. The nearby land is also used frequently by local hot air balloon companies as a take-off and landing area, especially in the summer, where you can often see colorful silhouettes in the afternoon sky, quietly floating over the vast valley with a stellar view of the Pacific.

The well-known city of Del Mar is located right on the coast and boasts some of the most expensive property near the Pacific. It also has a large concentration of the finest restaurants in the area, with nationally recognized chefs at the helm. If you're looking for a fine food experience, you'll never have to leave this small town. Summer is the most popular time to visit, as Del Mar is home to one of the largest fairs in North America based on attendance. June and July are filled with animal exhibits, contests, concerts, carnival attractions, and plenty of food. In August and September, you can join the flocks of spectators who try their luck at the Del Mar Racetrack, where Bing Crosby's crooning of "Where the Turf Meets the Surf" can still be heard before the first race every day.

Rancho Santa Fe is home to some of the most affluent residents in the continental US. The median property value is greater than $2.5 million. A small but centralized town center is dotted with high-end boutiques, galleries, and eateries. If you're looking to brush shoulders with the rich and famous, this is the place, at least in the few public areas. Most of the land is devoted to residential and agricultural use, with privacy getting a high priority. A strong equestrian presence is evident throughout the area at many exclusive horse parks and country clubs.

Americana, 1454 Camino Del Mar, Del Mar, CA 92014; (858) 794-6838; americanarestaurant.com; American; $$. **Chef-Owner** Randy Gruber has achieved the American dream with his successful restaurant nestled on a street corner in old Del Mar. Although they are open for breakfast, lunch, and dinner, it seems that folks like to gravitate here mostly for the morning fare, where you'll see people chatting and drinking cappuccinos while devouring buttermilk pancakes and eggs Benedict. Dine inside, or grab a chair at one of the cute tables along the front or to the side of the restaurant. While dining outside, passersby who can't help but get a glimpse of your food choice may want to join you. From green eggs and ham scrambled with spinach, pesto, and mozzarella to a homemade Belgian waffle, it's always busy for a reason. The locals know good food when they see it.

Board & Brew, 1212 Camino Del Mar, Del Mar, CA 92014; (858) 481-1021; boardnbrewdelmar.com; American; $. **Established in** 1979, this local legend is within walking distance of the Del Mar beach. Teenagers and surfer dudes of all ages like to hang out and eat some of the finest sandwiches in southern California. If you visit during lunch hours, expect a long, snaking line outside. Fortunately, the owners are well prepared for the onslaught, so everything moves quickly. Much of the available seating is on an outdoor patio, although many of the patrons are in grab-and-go mode. The most popular item is the Board Master, a roast beef and turkey breast combo with cheddar cheese and sweet-and-sour dressing served on a warm baguette. Also a local favorite is the Turkado, with thick layers of turkey, Jack cheese, avocado, onion, tomato, and lettuce on sourdough bread. With generous portions and inexpensive prices to boot, this place is hard to beat! Additional locations in Carlsbad and San Clemente.

Burlap, 12995 El Camino Real, Ste. 21, Del Mar, CA 92130; (858) 369-5700; burlapeats.com; Asian Fusion; $$$. From the food to the service and upbeat music, this is social dining at its best! Entertainment for your eyes is not too shabby either with an array of indoor and outdoor seating amidst pan-Pacific decor, two bars, a massive hanging dragon, Turkish lamps, longhorn cattle skulls, lion dance headpieces, koi ponds, and fire pits. A protein-driven menu focuses on local meats, seafood caught fresh daily, and hearty sides. I recommend ordering a little bit of everything on the menu and sharing. This Italian girl loves the venison carpaccio with truffle soy aioli and the miso-glazed black cod. However, my top choice is the whole angry snapper with a generous drizzle of fiery sauces—a phenomenal presentation and taste sensation. Pair your dinner with a handcrafted cocktail, an exclusive wine, or a local craft beer.

Cafe Secret, 1140 Camino Del Mar, Del Mar, CA 92014; (858) 792-0821; cafesecret.com; Latin American/Peruvian; $$$. It wouldn't be fair to keep this place a secret any longer. Dim the lights, turn on the Peruvian music, and let dinner begin at this capricious cafe, reminiscent of an old vintage Mediterranean cottage. Reminiscent of the street-side eateries in Europe, tables are placed close together in partially enclosed and heated covered areas. Enjoy made-from-scratch cuisine, including a vegan soup of the day, crostinis, and vegan vinaigrettes. Get your dinner off to a good start with the house-made sangria, moving on to the savory chowder with shrimp, red snapper fillet, prawn, and quail egg. I don't think I've had scalloped potatoes since I was a kid, but the Peruvian scallops au gratin with Parmesan cheese and lime juice is much better than Mom used to make . . . sorry, Mom. The highlight here is the ceviche bar where you can experience yellow whipped potatoes topped with avocado and charred shrimp. Specialty desserts are delectably divine and include key lime pie with Italian lime meringue, bread pudding, and tres leches. Open for breakfast, lunch, and dinner. Reservations are highly recommended for Friday and Saturday nights.

Caliente Mexican Food, 11815 Sorrento Valley Rd., San Diego, CA 92121; (858) 259-9579; Mexican; $. Popular among the locals, Caliente's is a great place to stop by for a quick bite. A menu of numerous dishes includes burritos, tacos, and combo plates at low prices. Whether you're a high school student from nearby West View

High or Canyon Crest Academy, or just a businessman on his lunch break, Caliente's is a must try. Large portions are satisfying and I guarantee you won't leave hungry. The most popular item on the menu is the very large order of carne asada fries topped with carne asada steak, guacamole, sour cream, cheese, and salsa. Caliente's is also well-known for its signature Caliente Burrito. This oversize burrito is perfectly compacted with a mixture of spices, salsa, shrimp, peas, and their house hot sauce, which is given on the side of every meal.

Cinepolis, 12905 El Camino Real, San Diego, CA 92130; (858) 794-4045; cinepolisusa.com; American; $$. Cinepolis is a new luxury theater in Del Mar that creates a one-of-a-kind "dinner and a movie" option! Walking in, it almost looks like a hotel, with the greeters dressed in all-black attire and a full bar to your left. There are tables and chairs as well as sofas all throughout the waiting area, and the menu includes paninis, sushi, and Angus beef sliders. I love the gourmet caramel or cheddar cheese popcorn. Movie tickets are sold as single seats and you actually get to pick exactly what chair you would like to be in. On top of that, each week a select theater is designated for only guests 21 and up where alcohol is allowed inside. Now, what makes this a great experience is the fact that inside your movie, the seats are actual leather recliners set into pairs with your own coffee table next to you on each side. During your movie you can push a little button on your chair and a waiter will quietly greet you and take any food orders you may have, then bring your order straight to you without your having to leave your reclined seat. I would consider this the trendiest, intimate, and upscale movie theater you will see in San Diego; it is definitely a place to check out.

Corner House Cafe & Pizzeria, 11815 Sorrento Valley Rd., San Diego, CA 92121; (858) 755-3183; cornerhousecafe.com; American; $. This popular sandwich joint on the corner of Sorrento Valley Road has become famously known for its hot and cold sandwiches, which are served with a signature sweet and sour sauce. The most popular items are the Baja chicken and the Ironman sandwich. The Baja chicken is a hot sandwich, which is made up of grilled chicken breast, jack cheese, grilled onions, jalapeños, tomato, lettuce, and mayonnaise, all served on a French baguette. The Ironman consists of grilled chicken breast, avocado, Swiss cheese, honey mustard, tomato, and sprouts, all inside two soft sourdough slices. Corner House doesn't just stop at sandwiches though; they also serve a mouthwatering specialty burger, fish-and-chips, a great gyro plate, and more. Corner House is located outdoors, which provides beautiful, quaint, tiled tables located on the side patio for customers to enjoy their meal in the quiet scene viewing Sorrento Valley. There aren't many places such as Corner House that serve such a wide menu. The options are just about limitless!

Delicias, 6106 Paseo Delicias, Rancho Santa Fe, CA 92091; (858) 756-8000; deliciasrestaurant.com; California Modern; $$$$. Consistently recognized as one of San Diego's best, Chef Paul McCabe is an expert at preparing world-class cuisine. As executive chef-partner at this long-standing restaurant in "The Ranch," McCabe focuses on offering a cache of seasonal selections at this affluent destination where the rich and famous like to dine. Utilizing only the finest local, organic, and sustainable ingredients, he makes it a priority to update his menus often. From Crows Pass Tahitian Squash Soup with local apples to wood-roasted poussin and natural bison New York steak, the culinary options at this haven are immeasurable. Delicias is known for its outstanding wine selection; diners select their wines on an iPad using the i-Somm interactive wine application.

Del Mar Rendezvous, 1555 Camino Del Mar, Del Mar, CA 92014; (858) 755-2669; delmarrendezvous.com; Chinese; $$$. Share unexpected pleasures at this trendy restaurant that just completed a quarter-million-dollar renovation. The sophisticated atmosphere looks sharp, yet still offers a romantic and upscale ambiance complete with a high-end wine cellar and a beautiful outdoor patio. The most striking part of the decor is the ancient Chinese artwork consisting of traditional pieces and sculptures from China, some dating back 200 years. A new open kitchen lends an opportunity to sneak a peek at what options you want cooked up for you from the large 100-plus-item menu. I like to gather with friends and share a variety of spruced-up and exhilarating entrees, such as walnut shrimp, Mongolian rack of lamb, and the wild and crazy banana cheesecake Xango for dessert. In addition, there over 40 gluten-free and vegetarian options available. Choose from over 20 local, import, and craft beers, as well as organic, free trade, and sustainably produced teas and coffees, in French presses.

Eda-Mami, 2282 Carmel Valley Rd., Del Mar, CA 92014; (858) 755-4777; edamami.com; Asian Fusion; $$$. This place has a modern and comfortable feel, especially on the second floor where there are unobstructed views of the Torrey Pines State Reserve and Los Penasquitos Lagoon. This is one restaurant where the prices are very reasonable given the outstanding view. Diners craving more action can take a seat at the sushi bar with TVs airing nonstop sporting events, or enjoy the San Diego weather on a beautiful outdoor patio. A full menu includes inventive sushi rolls, sashimi, teriyaki entrees, Udon noodles, skewers, salads, and more. Open for lunch or dinner, and the happy hour specials are extremely popular with the local business crowd. A second location is in Tierrasanta.

Flavor Del Mar, 1555 Camino Del Mar, 3rd floor, Del Mar, CA 92014; (858) 755-3663; flavordelmar.com; California Modern; $$$$. This is Restaurateur Jeff Hunter's first San Diego venture, and it's proving to be the new Del Mar hotspot located atop the Del Mar Plaza. Executive Chef Brian Redzikowski re-invents the wheel with unexpected food pleasures that keep you guessing as to whether you're going to feel fantastically French, articulately Asian, or idyllically Italiano. External pleasures include a close proximity to the ocean and a fashionable bar vibe that's anything but low key. My close encounter with the butternut squash soup with marshmallow and brown butter was of the creamy and silky kind. The big eye tuna tataki, dolled up with tomato-ginger dressing, is a powerhouse of flavor, and I will never tire of the ricotta agnolotti with Berkshire prosciutto and broccolini.

Jake's Del Mar, 1660 Coast Blvd., Del Mar, CA 92014; (858) 755-2002; jakesdelmar.com; California Modern; $$$$. Jakes on the water's edge in Del Mar is where you'll want to spend a romantic day or evening with your special someone. The place embodies the coastal living and lifestyle that is envied by anyone outside of Southern California. Where else can you enjoy a meal in the dead of winter and gaze at a multitude of beach activities in the warm sunshine? Take pleasure in upscale beachside eats for lunch, or relax and savor dinner and a dazzling sunset view from the floor-to-ceiling windows. This is clearly one of the more romantic dining venues in the entire city (and the rest of the country, for that matter). Jakes takes full advantage of the ocean's bounty, offering great seafood selections including macadamia nut-crusted salmon, wok char spiced mahi, sesame wasabi ahi, and grilled shrimp scampi. No visit would be complete without tasting their signature Hula Pie dessert, a frozen treat that is a feast for the eyes and large enough to share with the whole table. Don't miss Jakes' happy hour, where you can eat and drink at extremely affordable prices; but grab a seat early, as it fills up fast every day of the week!

Kitchen 1540, 1540 Camino Del Mar, Del Mar, CA 92117; (858) 793-6460; laubergedelmar.com; California Modern; $$$$. Overlooking the Pacific Ocean, L'Auberge Del Mar is a 120-room hotel located in the coastal village of Del Mar. Located just inside is Kitchen 1540. Whether you're lucky enough to dine at a table for two in front of the indoor fireplace, outdoor fire pit, or private wine room, you'll get a special pampering from Executive Chef Scott Thomas Dolbee and an attentive waitstaff. Described by Dolbee as "playful, whimsical, and modern," the menu offers plentiful portions that incorporate fresh local produce, seafood, and meats. The open kitchen is a great place to watch him cooking and plating beautiful food. Dining here is always an epicurean adventure that electrifies the taste buds with flavors rarely experienced. From roasted veal sweetbreads with smoked black trumpets to barbecued pig tails with warm potato salad, the surprises keep coming. See Chef Dolbee's recipe for **Seared Rare Ahi Tuna Tower** on p. 360.

MARKET Restaurant + Bar, 3702 Via de la Valle, Del Mar, CA 92014; (858) 523-0007; marketdelmar.com; California Modern; $$$$$. The cuisine at this restaurant is so product-driven, it seems to carry a type of pedigree that sets it apart from other restaurants in the area. Chef Carl Schroeder continues to hone his craft, while customers keep the place packed on any given night.

The atmosphere is modern, yet casual, with brown and orange decor. Sushi is available in the bar and lounge. Order off the menu and dine in the fully enclosed red room with red curtains or the temperature-controlled patio area. Schroeder has the menu set up as three courses (although you don't have to eat three courses if you don't want to). His specialty is the Cabernet-braised short ribs. The menu changes daily depending on what's in season or what he feels like making. The place is always packed. Reservations are highly recommended.

Pacifica Del Mar, 1555 Camino Del Mar, Del Mar, CA 92014; (858) 792-0476; pacificadelmar.com; Seafood; $$$$. One of the first modern restaurants to open in the Del Mar Plaza, this local favorite has won awards yearly for its impeccable California cuisine, contemporary style, and stunning views of the Pacific Ocean. Perched on the hill in one of Del Mar's most sought-after locations, Pacifica is one of the most consistent and high-quality seafood restaurants in San Diego. The Ocean Bar is always busy and lively, boasting a selection of at least 150 of the world's finest vodkas, daily specials, and a beautiful aquarium teeming with tropical fish. But it's their creative dishes that take center stage, tugging on all of your senses with colorful arrangements and wonderful aromas and tastes. One of those dishes that has pleased patrons for years is the sugar-spiced salmon, paired with Chinese beans, garlic mashed potatoes, and a subtle mustard sauce that coaxes every bit of flavor out of every ingredient. Nights and weekends are always packed with local and visiting patrons alike, so be sure to make reservations early for the best seating.

Pannikin Coffee and Tea, 2670 Via De La Valle, Del Mar, CA 92014; (858) 481-8007; pannikincoffeeandtea.com; Coffee/Tea; $. With delicious, freshly roasted coffee beans made daily as well as the wide selection of teas, this is a great place to work on your computer or see live acoustic bands on occasional Friday evenings. With three locations (Encinitas, La Jolla, and Del Mar), it makes it easy to stop for some tea or gelato after walking around some of the best areas in San Diego. Specifically at the Del Mar spot, resting upstairs above the restaurants below, there is plenty of seating and a wide variety of pastries to choose from. Many comfortable couches and tables make it easy to spend hours here. My favorites include their decadent Mexican hot chocolate as well as the "Jimi Hendrix," a great pick-me-up that includes 4 shots of espresso, hazelnut syrup, Mexican mocha mix, and steamed milk. Add whipped cream to that for a very fulfilling drink!

Paradise Grille & Bar, 2690 Via De La Valle, Del Mar, CA 92014; (858) 350-0808; paradisegrille.com; California Modern; $$$. Tucked away in the Flower Hill Mall near I-5 and less than a mile from the Del Mar Fairgrounds, Paradise Grille has become favored among locals for serving California cuisine with island flair. Three unique dining areas are available, including a more intimate dining room on the top floor facing an open kitchen, a downstairs lounge and bar, and an outdoor patio set in a courtyard with palms and fire pit welcoming you to relax. The latter location is the most popular spot in the evenings, especially during happy hour when the conversation and laughter reach a crescendo. Some of the more popular and creative food items include firecracker shrimp, bleu cheese burger sliders, and ahi poke crisps.

Poseidon on the Beach, 1670 Coast Blvd., Del Mar, CA 92014; (858) 755-9345; poseidonrestaurant.com; Seafood; $$$$. Think of this place as an island getaway, somewhere to go when you want to relax by the ocean in an up-close and personal way. Large retractable windows create a nice open-air feeling, and an indoor fire pit and lively bar are big draws. Although there is a view from every seat in the house inside the dining room and bar, we prefer to sit on the heated outdoor patio because it feels as though we are basically sitting on the beach itself. This place is great for breakfast, lunch, or dinner. The menu offers a variety of unique salads and sandwiches, as well as grilled meats and seafood. We like to sip on fancy cocktails and munch on tempura-style soft-shell crabs while waiting for the sun to set. A creamy bowl of New England style clam chowder always keeps us nice and warm.

Rubio's, 3545 Del Mar Heights Rd., San Diego, CA 92130; (858) 481-8002; rubios.com; Mexican; $$. No book about San Diego cuisine would be complete without including one of the more famous local culinary success stories. While still a college student, Ralph Rubio frequently visited the local border communities in Mexico for great surfing, entertainment, and snacking at the seaside *taquerias*. It was there that he first tasted the fish taco, a simple mix of beer-battered local fish, combined with shredded cabbage, salsa, and creamy sauce, all wrapped in a flour tortilla. Inspired (and somewhat obsessed) with his newfound love, he was committed to bringing this taste sensation north of the border. In 1983 Rubio opened his first taco stand in San Diego, centered on this unique combination of ingredients that has now become a national staple for fresh California cuisine available in 5 states spanning the southwest. Now having served over 150 million fish tacos, Rubio's has become synonymous with local cuisine. A trip to one of the many local establishments is a casual experience, with a simple menu of traditional small plates and a self-serve salsa bar featuring a variety of different tastes ranging from mild to extra hot. Next time you're in town, visit this local landmark and enjoy the cuisine that sparked a cultural shift in Southwest American cuisine.

Ruth's Chris Steakhouse, 11582 El Camino Real, San Diego, CA 92130; (858) 755-1454; ruthschris.com; Steak House; $$$$. On the way to celebrating 5 decades, this modern and well-designed 2-story chophouse, boasting posh white linens and candlelight, continues to please steak worshippers from around the globe. You may think you're a grill master at home, but once you sink your teeth into a Ruth's Chris cut of beef, you may never want to eat a steak anywhere else. Signature, high-quality steaks are seared at 1,800°F, topped with fresh butter, and brought sizzling to your table. Non-steak lovers can opt for the extra-thick lamb chops, cold water lobster tail with blackening spice, or the oven-roasted free-range double chicken breast stuffed with garlic herb cheese. A deluxe dessert of bread pudding with whiskey sauce is nothing short of exquisite. Additional location in San Diego at 1355 North Harbor Dr., as well as locations in other states.

Sbicca, 215 15th St., Del Mar, CA 92014; (858) 481-1001; sbiccabistro.com; American; $$$$. Loyal customers have been savoring clever modern American cuisine at this lighthearted and friendly neighborhood eatery for many years. Experience a fine dining experience indoors, relax on the casual patio out front, or walk up a little flight of stairs to the covered and heated ocean-view terrace to enjoy a big bowl of lobster bisque. A great happy hour with girl drinks and a bar menu offers anything from Stone Pale Ale mac and cheese to sautéed shrimp with basil, or a jumbo crab cake with chipotle kimchi. Half-priced bottles of wine are offered on Tuesday and Thursday with zero corkage fees on Sunday and Monday. The grilled beef filet brandt with gorgonzola mashed potatoes and the roasted pork prime rib with bourbon demi-glace are a big hit, along with the scallops. Splurge on the giant peanut butter cup, which is enough for two to share. Susan Sbicca's deliciously creamy Millie's Gelato is a wonderful vegan dessert option.

Smashburger, 1555 Camino Del Mar, Del Mar, CA 92014; (858) 461-4105; smashburger.com; Burgers; $$. Feel as though you are on vacation at this Del Mar location resting just steps from the ocean. Walking into Smashburger, you can't help but notice the retro red and white atmosphere that has a definite old-fashioned diner feel. Order your food at the counter up front before grabbing a seat at a booth or table. Choose from the pre-made burger selections or build your own burger from an array of optional toppings and sauces. My favorite is the San Diego burger, which includes their 100 percent fresh Angus beef patty, avocado, cilantro, onions, pepper jack cheese, lettuce, tomato, sour cream, and spicy chipotle mayo. Don't care for a burger? Try a freshly made black bean veggie burger or a crunchy salad. The Sunset salad is my favorite and includes balsamic tomatoes, raisins, dried cranberries, sunflower and pumpkin seeds, as well as blue cheese. If anything, feel the breeze as you sit on the patio right outside the shops and enjoy an icy cold root beer poured over a mountain of vanilla ice cream with a side of sweet potato fries. Additional locations throughout San Diego.

Trattoria Ponte Vecchio, 2334 Carmel Valley Rd., #A, Del Mar, CA 92014; (858) 259-9063; pontevecchiodelmar.com; Italian; $$$. This exceptional dining destination will remind you of a cozy New York–style Italian restaurant without the hassle of crowded sidewalks, honking taxis, and parking nightmares. Besides, what could be more romantic than a view of the peaceful Torrey Pines Lagoon? There is something wonderful about nestling into a little corner table for two, sharing a bottle of red wine, and rolling pasta from large bowls. Owner Daniel Nobili is always present to greet you in Italian. Old world recipes from his homeland in Milano, Italy, are brought to new life with creative presentations. A specialty of the house is the Spaghetti alla Puttanesca with olives, capers, and anchovies in red sauce; or try the Linguine Ai Frutti Di Mare with mussels, clams, calamari, and shrimp in marinara sauce. Come here and find a little table for two. Call it "Pasta Therapy" for you and a companion!

Urban Plates, 12857 El Camino Real, San Diego, CA 92130; (858) 509-1800; urbanplates.com; American; $$. Fresh off the farm delights in this open kitchen at the brand-new Urban Plates in the Del Mar Highlands Town Center. Dine in for lunch or dinner, or take your food home. All the ingredients are conveniently displayed in front of you. Basically, pick out which foods you like best, and your meal is prepared immediately. The menu is divided into a variety of sections. Try the "Carve Up" with barbecue-glazed turkey meat loaf, "Pile Up" with a marinated and grilled wild ono sandwich, or "Load Up" with grilled free-range, cruelty-free chicken. Don't miss Urban

Pizzettes made with hand-stretched organic dough as well as the made-from-scratch cream pies, layer cakes, and brownies.

Landmarks

Addison at The Grand Del Mar, 5300 Grand Del Mar Ct., San Diego, CA 92130; (858) 314-2000; thegranddelmar.com; French; $$$$$. Timeless and classic, Addison within The Grand Del Mar is the single most important destination for dining in San Diego. In Southern California's only Five-Star/Five Diamond restaurant, you will relish in Relais & Chateaux Grand Chef William Bradley's artisanal approach to cooking, as well as enhance your culinary IQ. Contemporary French cuisine with an emphasis on seasonal California ingredients make for masterfully presented entrees with intense flavor characteristics. This is a destination to enjoy the true "dining experience," savored for hours over several courses, each a masterpiece in flavor and presentation. Watch as the formally clad attendants whisk your next course to the table, hesitating until everyone receives a covered dish, and then simultaneously lifting the lids to reveal the culinary art. Every aspect of the evening will leave an impression. One of the few Master Sommeliers in Southern California, Jesse Rodriguez will help you pair your meal with the perfect vino from Addison's world-class wine room. Menu highlights include avocado and golden caviar, parmesan and arugula spring lamb, or the persillé with toasted pistachio purée, dates, and sauce chèvre. I would strongly suggest you choose one of the multicourse dinners, highlighting some of the best dishes in Bradley's repertoire, sequenced from savory to sweet, delighting your palate with every taste. See Executive Chef William Bradley's recipe for **Grilled Prawns with Fines Herbes Vinaigrette** on p. 347.

Bully's, 1404 Camino Del Mar, Del Mar, CA 92014; (858) 755-1660; bullysdelmar.com; Steak House; $$$. Where's the beef? It's been right here in old Del Mar since 1967. This iconic restaurant, reminiscent of a dark old-world homestead, has never wavered from offering *beef* as its answer to all woes. And not just any beef, but hormone- and antibiotic-free all-natural Montana-raised 100 percent Angus corn-fed beef. Get your fill from a 22-ounce prime rib or choose a steak, including porterhouse, filet mignon, New York, and USDA "Prime" top sirloin. Nothing fancy here, just a really good steak dinner, a glass of beer or wine, and good conversation from the dedicated staff willing to cater to your every whim. Non-beef lovers may choose from other menu options including fish, shellfish, seafood, and chicken. Additional location in Mission Valley, San Diego.

En Fuego Cantina & Grill, 1342 Camino Del Mar, Del Mar, CA 92014; (858) 792-6551; enfuegocantina.com; Mexican; $$$. You'll feel like you're south of the border at this boisterously decorated authentic Mexican eatery that is the longest standing restaurant in Del Mar. Back in the 30s, La Tienda was Del Mar's first hot spot restaurant at this very location. For the last 16 years, En Fuego has respected tradition by pleasing diners with Mexican cuisine, seafood, and tangy margaritas at this 2-story restaurant where you can dine alfresco in covered areas. My favorite part of the restaurant is the indoor La Tienda Wine Room that has been restored to retain the old style ambiance with old beams and the original 1930s fireplace. En Fuego (loosely translated to "on fire") offers bold flavors from the Mexican Riviera such as sautéed filet mignon smothered in a roasted tomatillo chipotle sauce, pan-seared Cajun-style tilapia topped with a spicy mango salsa, or the large black tiger shrimp skewers sautéed in a sweet and spicy red chile sauce.

Mille Fleurs, 6009 Paseo Delicias, Rancho Santa Fe, CA 92067; (858) 756-3085; millefleurs.com; French; $$$$$. Food lovers with an appetite for the lighter side of French know they can count on a true fine dining experience at this restaurant in the village of Rancho Santa Fe. Martin Woesle became chef de cuisine in 1985 and has been impressing customers ever since. The recipient of multiple awards, including *Food and Wine*'s top 25 restaurants in the nation, Mille Fleurs serves French California cuisine in an elegant yet comfortable setting. A daily changing menu for lunch and dinner ensures the freshest and finest ingredients. And since Woesle was born in South Germany, you will see touches from his roots, including the venison rib chop with dried blueberries and hazelnut spätzle or the "wiener schnitzel" of

Strauss Farm veal with wild arugula salad, caperberries, and lemon parsley butter.

The Restaurant at Rancho Valencia, 5921 Valencia Circle, Rancho Santa Fe, CA 92014; (858) 756-1123; ranchovalencia.com; California Modern; $$$$. The Restaurant at Rancho Valencia, located inside the Rancho Valencia Resort, embodies the unpretentious grace and sophistication of its Rancho Santa Fe location amidst a beautiful 40-acre landscape of rolling hills and 49 luxuriously appointed suites, each with a fireplace and private garden terrace. Stunning valley views from the dining room or outdoor dining terrace will make you feel as if you are somewhere in the Mediterranean. Springtime is a particularly special time to visit, as the citrus trees are in full bloom and fill the air with a distinctly fragrant aroma.  Executive Chef Eric Bauer presents his farm-to-table philosophy with artfully crafted dishes for breakfast, lunch, and dinner. You'll often find him roaming through the local farmers' markets in the morning, choosing special ingredients to inspire his menu. A great example is the cornucopia salad, with diced apple, grilled chicken, avocado, bleu cheese, mandarin oranges, and candied almonds. My favorite dinner entrees are the succulent veal picatta and savory pan-roasted Chilean sea bass.

Specialty Stores, Markets & Producers

Chino Farms, the Vegetable Stand, 6123 Calzada del Bosque, Rancho Santa Fe, CA 92067 (off Via de la Valle, S6); Recorded farmstand information: (858) 756-3184; Grocery/Market; $$. Situated on 50 acres in the lush backcountry of Rancho Santa Fe, you forget that this little vegetable stand is so close to some of the most expensive housing parcels in the nation. Alice Waters stated in her hugely successful book, *Chez Panisse Vegetables,* "The Chinos have made an art of farming. For two generations now, they have tended their land with an inexhaustible aesthetic curiosity, constantly searching out new and old varieties of dozens of fruits and vegetables from all over the world, and planting and harvesting year round." Their produce is trucked to some of the most famous Southern California restaurants on a weekly basis. On any given day, you could be bumping elbows with some of the most brilliant chefs in the local area, all looking for the finest ingredients to prepare unique dishes on their menu. Considered traditional Japanese, the family keeps the secret of successfully growing exotic and organic produce a secret. It may be the best-kept secret next to the Coca-Cola or Kentucky Fried Chicken recipes!

Dallman Fine Chocolates, 2670 Via De La Valle, Ste. A270, Del Mar, CA 92014; (858) 720-1933; dallmannconfections.com; Desserts; $$. Using only the finest and freshest ingredients, Guenther Dallmann opened his pastry shop in St. Gilgen, Austria,

WHOLE FOODS

Founded in 1980, this supermarket was designed to support the growing natural foods industry by offering the largest selection of natural and organic products, including foods, beverages, and household items. They are dedicated to buying from local producers as much as possible to support the communities and farms. You'll especially enjoy sampling the variety of delicious prepared foods in the immense deli section. There are four locations in the San Diego area:

Del Mar: 2720 Via De La Valle, Del Mar; (858) 481-2904

San Diego (Uptown): 711 University Ave, San Diego; (619) 294-2800

La Jolla: 8825 Villa La Jolla Drive, San Diego; (858) 642-6700

Encinitas: 687 South Coast Highway 101, Encinitas; (760) 274-1580

in 1954, offering only three types of pastries, which were baked fresh daily. Soon, the word spread and more pastries were in demand. Today Guenther's daughter, Sylvia, together with her husband, Franz, expanded Dallmann, gaining a worldwide reputation. In 2006, Franz and Sylvia's daughter, Isabella Valencia, brought the family business to El Cajon, with a second fine chocolate boutique retail store recently opened in the Flower Hill Promenade of Del Mar. This mini chocolate factory is where Valencia hand-makes exquisite artisan chocolates using the original family recipes. My favorite is the Fleur de Sel. Once you taste this buttery caramel with sea salt, sheathed in bittersweet chocolate and garnished with Fleur de Sel, you'll understand why it's Dallman's bestseller. Another popular favorite is The Mozart Kugel, a blend of hazelnut nougat with a pistachio marzipan center, named after the famous composer Wolfgang Amadeus Mozart.

Jimbo's Naturally, 12853 El Camino Real, San Diego, CA 92130; (858) 793-7755; jimbos.com; Grocery/Market; $$. Everyone who lives in Carmel Valley knows about this natural food store. Jimbo's is a great place to shop for fresh and organic ingredients. Aisles are easy to navigate and are stocked with all kinds of "good for you" foods. To start, there are a variety of organically grown fruits and vegetables in the produce section. Get fresh-squeezed carrot juice from the juice bar paired with a healthy pastry from the bakery case. Freshly made soups, sandwiches, and salads are always on hand in the refrigerated case. Meats include Vintage natural beef, Rocky and Shelton natural poultry, and a variety of wild and farm-raised seafood. Aisles are filled with bins holding dry ingredients, healthy chips, and cereals. I like the vitamin center, where you can ask questions about herbs and supplements.

Milton's, 2660 Via De La Valle, Del Mar, CA 92014; (858) 792-2225; miltonsdeli.com; American; $$. When you walk into Milton's, you will instantly be attracted to the bakery case boasting brownies, cookies, and loads of other goodies. An adjacent meat counter includes deli-style meats such as corned beef, pastrami, and salami. I come here often for the fresh baked bagels, cinnamon raisin, sourdough, and rye breads. The restaurant is casual with white freezer paper for tablecloths and nostalgic pictures on the brick walls. It's easy to imagine you're dining in an old-fashioned New York or Chicago deli. A large menu offers nearly everything you can imagine for breakfast, lunch, and dinner. Where else can you order eggs Florentine or an old-fashioned meat loaf dinner any time of day or night? They are most well-known for large homemade dishes, famous oversize sandwiches, and pub-style foods. A new Chicago-style deep-dish pizza for two has become quite a hit here. As for dessert, my once-a-year indulgence is the German chocolate cake for my birthday. You can buy whole cakes here, or get it by the slice. They also run a very successful catering operation.

Thyme in the Ranch, 16905 Avenida De Acacias, Rancho Santa Fe, CA 92091; (858) 759-0747; thymeintheranch.com; Bakery; $$. Nothing beats spending an afternoon driving up a gorgeous tree-lined winding Rancho Santa Fe road and ending up at a bakery's doorstep where the aroma of freshly baked apple pie lures you to come inside. This friendly eatery with small tables scattered about has a simple country charm. Stop in for breakfast and savor quiche by the slice or a warm muffin out of the oven. For lunch, it's a bowl of chili served with a Dutch crunch baguette or old-fashioned turkey meat loaf. Other made-from-scratch goodies include cookies, scones, pies, bread pudding, lemon bars, triple chocolate brownies, and specialty cakes topped with butter cream or whipped cream frosting.

Venissimo Cheese, 2710 Via De La Valle, #B138, Del Mar, CA 92014; (858) 847-9616; venissimo.com; Grocery/Market; $$. With multiple locations in San Diego, this cheesemonger hangout in the Flower Hill Mall just off I-5 offers the best cheese varieties from all over the world. You can taste before you buy, and with selections changing daily, you more than likely won't have the same cheese twice. Receipts complete with pronunciations, country of origin, and milk type will make it easier for you to know exactly what you are buying. Accouterments include artisanal breads and crackers, chocolate, olive oil, and more. The staff at Venissimo will also help you design the perfect gift basket or party tray for your next occasion.

Zumbar Coffee and Tea, 10920 Roselle St., San Diego, CA 92121; (858) 622-0000; zumbarcoffee.com; Coffee/Tea; $. Located in the busy tech center of Sorrento Valley, Zumbar is a diminutive shop with a huge reputation for serving some of the best coffee in the area. Taking a craftsman's approach to roasting, they have perfected the process using a vintage, cast-iron coffee roaster situated right behind the ordering counter, giving every patron a chance to see/hear the action. A small selection of pastries and breads are also available, delivered from **VG's Donuts** (p. 62) and **Opera Patisserie** (p. 123) every morning. Some regulars believe that the coffee actually advances science, and I have to agree, given the buzzing conversation during my last visit. They also sell fresh-roasted beans at the shop or online, so you're never too far away from a great cup of joe.

Escondido, San Marcos, Carmel Mountain Ranch, Rancho Bernardo & Poway

This expansive inland area north of San Diego is rich in history dating back to the early 1800s. Settled in a long valley between coastal mountains, Escondido is surrounded by citrus and avocado groves. Primarily a residential area, neighborhoods include Victorians next to Craftsman bungalows, as well as eclectic Art Deco and post–World War II residences. This city is home to the California Center for the Arts, a facility that attracts over a quarter million visitors from the surrounding area to enjoy musical and cultural events. Be sure to also take a walk on the wild side at the San Diego Zoo Safari Park. Located east in the San Pasqual Valley, it is one of the largest tourist attractions in the San Diego area. With over 1,800 acres of natural enclosures, showcasing more than 400 species of animals, it is visited by over 2 million people every year.

San Marcos is considered a centerpiece of higher education in San Diego, as it is home to Palomar College, California State University San Marcos (CSUSM), and several technical schools. For dining, you must visit Old California Restaurant Row. It is North County's largest dining and entertainment center, with 18 restaurants, an Edwards Cinema Complex, and many quaint village boutiques.

Just south of Escondido is the community of Rancho Bernardo, a well-established master-planned community situated along rolling hills and canyons. It is dotted with a number of exclusive country clubs and golf courses, as well as being home to the corporate headquarters for companies like Sony and Hewlett-Packard. The Bernardo Winery is one of the oldest operating wineries in Southern California, established in 1889 and family owned and operated since 1927.

Carmel Mountain Ranch is situated at the eastern end of the 56 freeway, a newly built feeder highway that directly links the coast and inland areas, from I-5 to I-15. Primarily residential and commercial in nature, it is home to several large shopping centers, easily accessible from the main roads. It is here that you will find a majority of the restaurants, primarily of the chain variety.

Traveling farther south will land you in Poway, nicknamed "The City in the Country." Originally used by the missions as a range for feeding livestock, this area eventually became a centerpiece of agriculture. Although it has become a draw for residential living, Poway is home to the Blue Sky Ecological Reserve, Lake Poway, and many minor hiking and horse riding trails throughout the many canyons. If you're looking for a great picnic spot, Poway offers many options.

Foodie Faves

Bamboo House, 320 N. Midway Dr., Escondido, CA 92027; (760) 480-9550; Chinese; $$. Since 1982, Owner Yee Leung has been impressing customers with affordable good-quality food and some very impressive dishes that have lived up to his restaurant's reputation. The dining room, adorned with bright pink tablecloths, is the ideal gathering place for family and friends. Leung, a cook for many years, works at his establishment daily and created the menu. A big seller is the deluxe beef, chicken, and shrimp chow mein. The Hong Kong pan-fried egg noodles are heartily paired with barbecue pork, chicken, shrimp, and vegetables. The fillet of sole in black bean sauce melts in your mouth, and the Szechwan pork is spicy good. A great vegetarian option is the braised eggplant and black mushrooms with oyster and soy.

The Brigantine, 421 W. Felicita Ave., Escondido, CA 92025; (760) 743-4718; brigantine.com; Seafood, $$$. Located near the California Center for the Arts, Escondido, this beautiful restaurant has large dining areas and three connecting patios complete with an ample number of heat lamps for alfresco dining. I personally like to sit inside, with brick walls holding plenty of sea-faring items, and high ceilings to accommodate a tall ship's mast, complete with a rolled-up sail. Guests flock here for the oyster bar featuring several varieties on the half-shell, shooters served in a shot glass with horseradish, and Rockefeller style with spinach, bacon, and parmesan aioli. If you aren't a fan of oysters, you might want to try the fresh diver scallops Rockefeller. You will get more flavors than you bargained for when you try the lobster relleno poblano chile stuffed with lobster and jack cheese, served with jalapeño white sauce and mango relish. Although this location focuses mainly on seafood, there are a few meat dishes worth noting, such as the slow-roasted prime rib and chicken piccata. Open for lunch and dinner, the Brigantine has multiple locations throughout San Diego.

Cafe Luna, 11040 Rancho Carmel Dr., San Diego, CA 92128; (858) 673-0077; cafelunasd.com; Italian; $$$. Cafe Luna is definitely the go-to place for wining, dining, and splurging on pasta dishes galore. Hidden in a strip mall in Carmel Mountain Ranch, just off I-15, this small and comfortable Italian eatery features homemade pastas galore in a European-type setting. Tables are placed close together, making it an ideal romantic dining destination. The signature pasta is the Rosetta, a homemade pasta sheet rolled with ham and Swiss cheese that's sliced and baked with cream and Parmesan cheese. They make delicious spinach- and cheese-filled ravioli in a light cream sauce, topped with ground walnuts and the fettuccine Bolognese of prime ground filet mignon is as good as the Bolognese that comes out of my Italian kitchen.

Cavaillon, 14701 Via Bettona, Ste. 200, San Diego, CA 92127; (858) 433-0483; cavaillonrestaurant.com; French; $$$$. This Black Mountain Ranch neighborhood hideaway, tucked away in the 4S Ranch area of North County, makes for a beautiful dining adventure. Enjoy fine wines and alfresco dining on the lovely patio or at one of the cozy tables inside, where a softly lit and intimate setting will transport you to a cottage nestled in the hills of a French countryside. Swiss-born Chef de Cuisine Michael von Euw relies on modern technology to perk up traditional French recipes and desserts. Although they offer prix fixe, their main dinner menu, has a number of favorites, such as the cocoa and Sichuan pepper-crusted venison loin, beef bourguignon with roasted garlic, or pork loin with mustard glaze. The rotating risotto flavors are more than fabulous, and I have yet to find another restaurant that does risotto better. For dessert, you must have the warm chocolate molleux with citrus ginger sorbet and warm chocolate soup.

Centre City Cafe, 2680 S. Escondido Blvd., Escondido, CA 92025; (760) 489-6011; sandiegohomecooking.com; American; $$. Open since 1997 in Escondido, this was the first of now 5 locations for the San Diego Home Cooking group. The service is extremely friendly and very prompt, just like you would expect. Offering traditional American comfort food, they also specialize in homemade Hungarian dishes like goulash, cabbage rolls, and stuffed bell peppers. Savor freshly made dinner rolls, biscuits, secret recipe homemade dressings, hearty soups, gravies, house-ground hamburger patties, oven-roasted turkey breast, and a large selection of "mama's" homemade pies. Who could deny craving meals like beef stroganoff, meat loaf and mashed potatoes, or chicken and dumplings? They are open for breakfast, lunch, and dinner with a variety of choices spanning an extensive menu, offering affordable prices in a family-friendly setting.

Domenic's Italian Ristorante, 12719 County Hwy. S4, Poway, CA 92064; (858) 748-9563; domenicsristorante.com; Italian; $$$. With red and green decor, and festive white lights enhancing the atmosphere, dinner at Domenic's is like having a holiday celebration all year round. Open since 1991, it is a very popular spot for locals who count on getting their fill of pizza, pasta, salads, and sandwiches. Their homemade focaccia bread is baked fresh and delivered to your table warm and tasty. If you're in the mood for pasta, try the fettuccine Alfredo or homemade gnocchi (potato dumplings) covered in luscious gorgonzola cheese cream sauce. The regulars know they can count on a bang for their buck by choosing one of the house specialty entrees that includes a choice of minestrone soup or house salad, potatoes, fresh vegetables, and focaccia bread. How many restaurants still provide all of those extras for a reasonable price? My favorite has to be the baked eggplant parmesan. It's truly authentic. The place can get quite busy, so reservations are highly recommended.

Flippin' Pizza, 342 S. Twin Oaks Valley Rd., San Marcos, CA 92078; (760) 736-3180; flippinpizza.com; Pizza; $$. Flippin' Pizza in San Marcos is the first of the chain of restaurants to include a bar, a chopped salad station, and a spacious interior that's an ideal place for guests to gather. This tasty pizza pie recipe originated in Sicily over 30 years ago, and gained popularity in New York before the concept moved to its San Diego location The Triboro is a favorite, packed with red sauce, meatballs, sausage, and pepperoni. Other styles include plenty of white pie options, as well as calzones and salads. Beer, wine, and a full bar are also available. Additional Flippin' Pizza San Diego locations in Carlsbad, Encinitas, La Costa, and Vista, as well as locations in other states.

The Grand, 150 W. Grand Ave., Escondido, CA 92025; (760) 735-3333; thegrandongrand.com; California Modern; $$$. Reminiscent of a Chicago-style speakeasy with a Vegas-style ultra bar built right into it, experience fine dining at its best at this large and newly remodeled restaurant in Escondido. The inviting ambiance is complete with gorgeous warm colors, black table linens, decorative Persian rugs, and a plush lounge with big comfy chairs and leather barstools. Choose from a 30-drink handcrafted cocktail list made with fresh juices, limes, mint, and dill plucked fresh from the Escondido farmers' market every Tuesday. French-born Chef Vincent Altavilla keeps busy in the kitchen creating made-from-scratch soups and sauces, and you definitely don't want to miss his french onion soup. Other great choices include juicy steaks, tender lamb, and daily seafood specials. The locals like to come for the chicken picatta and the zesty gumbo with Andouille sausage. An extra benefit here is that entrees come with a choice of soup or salad and a side dish consisting of a veggie, couscous, or mashed potatoes. A 42-seat live music room opens up into a 62-seat open back patio. Live music is offered every Thursday, Friday, and Saturday night. Karaoke Wednesday is always a ton of fun!

The Grand Tea Room, 145 W. Grand Ave., Escondido, CA 92025; (760) 233-9500; thegrandtearoom.com; American/Tea; $$$. Here's a concept that you don't see very often, especially in our busy, electronic-focused world: a full-service tearoom offering traditional teas and snacks that will transport you to a simpler time. Get your friends together and enjoy the slow life. Although you can walk in any time and order from the a la carte menu, I strongly suggest you call ahead and reserve a traditional afternoon tea, including a table for 2 hours to enjoy 4 to 5 courses and freshly steeped tea.

Your meal includes soup, assorted tea sandwiches, seasonal fresh fruit, scones, and petite desserts. Casual business attire is the most common practice, but on many days you will also find some guests wearing tea dresses with hats and gloves. There are three times available Tuesday through Saturday, so be sure to call ahead.

Hacienda De Vega, 2608 S. Escondido Blvd., Escondido, CA 92025; (760) 738-9805; haciendadevega.com; Mexican; $$$. This 1.6-acre Hacienda, nestled in an original adobe home dating back to the 1930s, features alfresco dining at its best. Come here to eat genuine Mexican cuisine while relaxing among tropical flowers in a bountiful garden amidst striking ponds and waterfalls. Made exclusively at Hacienda de Vega, start your meal with a spicy margarita containing the Mexican fruit *tamarindo*. I recommend the Filete de Vega, an eye-catching choice filet mignon that is grilled and topped with pasilla chile sauce. Another entree with unique flavor characteristics is the Pacific snapper wrapped in banana leaves and cooked in roasted tomato sauce with olives and herbs. After dinner, savor the Mexican flan tipico dessert by the River Lounge, a haven featuring seven HD televisions, three fire pits, and four Mexican rain cape *palapas*.

Mama Kat's Restaurant & Pie Shop, 950 W. San Marcos Blvd., San Marcos, CA 92078; (760) 591-4558; mamakatsrestaurant.com; American; $$. Somewhat hidden in a strip mall along busy San Marcos Boulevard, this simple little eatery has become a haven for locals interested in a hearty breakfast or lunch. The great comfort food you crave is made from scratch here, and the roasted turkey, roast beef, and corned beef are all baked on-site. Reminiscent of an old-fashioned country kitchen, this is one of the best places for early risers to get a filling breakfast and a luscious homemade pie. Savor specialty omelets, Benedicts, pancakes, french toast, and waffles. They are well-known for the homemade cream sausage gravy and hollandaise sauce, which are phenomenal when paired with chicken-fried steak or the homemade biscuits. I love the caramel apple Belgian waffle topped with hot apple pie filling and whipped cream. Pies are baked fresh on the premises and include fruit pies, cream pies, and my favorite lemon meringue.

Nugent's Firegrille, 12015 Scripps Highlands Dr., Scripps Ranch, CA 92131; (858) 566-3474; fishgrille.com; Seafood; $$$. For over 30 years the Nugent family has been serving great food on both East and West Coasts. Choose from a wide variety of American seafood dishes emphasizing Northeastern classics at this bright, airy restaurant with lots of windows and outdoor seating. Appetizers are creative and enticing, especially the lump crab cake made with blue crab meat, and the littleneck clams simmered in wine butter garlic broth. My favorite pastime is to dunk warm sourdough bread into a big bowl of New England clam chowder, Manhattan seafood chowder, or shrimp bisque. For non-seafood lovers, there are plenty of fire-grilled steak, burger, and chicken choices. Another great option is what they like to refer to as a "clambake in a bucket" (Babo's Bucket). This feast of steamed clams, shrimp, and sausage with red potatoes and corn on the cob in a savory garlic butter broth is definitely enough for two people to share. The broth is so sumptuous, you'll want to continue dunking bread for every last bit. If you feel like being your own chef, check out the seafood market and take home some local white sea bass, ahi tuna, scallops, or clams.

Phil's BBQ, 579 Grand Ave., San Marcos, CA 92078; (760) 759-1400; philsbbq.net; Barbecue; $$$. The secret's in the sauce—the barbecue sauce, that is! Since opening its doors in San Diego in 1998, Phil's BBQ has served over 1 million pounds of barbecue sauce (enough to fill Shamu's whale tank at Sea World). The long lines waiting for huge portions of Phil's mesquite grilled baby back and beef ribs, chicken, burgers, and sandwiches are well worth it! Pull up a chair at this fun and energetic restaurant where all sides are made from scratch, including the hand-dipped colossal onion rings. By the end of your dining experience you will have something in common with your fellow diners—those paper towels on your table used to wipe the barbecue sauce off your messy hands and faces. Additional Phil's BBQ location in Point Loma.

Que Pasa, 9932 Mercy Rd., San Diego, CA 92129; (858) 578-7272; quepasamexicangrill.com; Mexican; $$$. Located in the Rancho Penasquitos area, the most difficult part of eating at this relaxed neighborhood spot is simply deciding what to choose off an imaginative menu boasting fresh ingredients. The handpicked staff from five-star restaurants and nightclubs will tend to your every need. Dine indoors or on an outdoor patio and sip on a specialty margarita, martini, or draft *cerveza*. You really can't go wrong with anything you order, whether you opt for the lobster chimichanga topped with creamy jalapeño sauce, chicken enchiladas in mild creamy tomatillo sauce with cream and cotija cheese, or chiles rellenos topped with Spanish sauce. Don't forget to save room for the flan or the deep-fried ice cream for dessert!

Vincent's, 113 W. Grand Ave., Escondido, CA 92025; (760) 745-3835; vincentsongrand.com; French; $$$$. It is through the inspiration of the seasons that makes me want to call the food here "French a la California style" at this historic downtown Escondido restaurant. Diners clamber to get a table here to taste the delicacies prepared by Chef Vincent Grimel. Dip your bread into the steamed local Carlsbad Aqua farm mussels in herbs, garlic, white wine, and cream, while you wait for Chef Grimel to prepare you half of a roasted Maple Leaf Farm duckling prepared in a candied-orange and crystallized-ginger sauce, served with potato gratin and a medley of seasonal vegetables. Having been honored with the "Award of Excellence" from the *Wine Spectator* many times over, there isn't a wine you won't discover and love from the massive on-site wine cellar.

Yummy Sushi, 11835 Carmel Mountain Rd., No. 1305, Carmel Mountain Ranch, CA 92128; (858) 673-2279; yummysushisd.com;

Japanese; $$$. Escape to Yummy Sushi in Carmel Mountain Ranch, where it's all about big flavors and bringing them all together at this Japanese eatery with a Korean twist. Grab your seat at the sushi bar or at a table by an eye-catching aquarium. As busy as this place gets, it still feels like a soothing Zen-like environment. Lift up the wok lid and kick-start your appetite with the thick and spicy Yum Yum Udon Pan-Fried Noodles with chicken or beef and vegetables. Off the sushi menu, I like the Tropical Fever, with a fruity addition of mango paired with tuna, avocado, masago, and asparagus. If it's lobster you crave, get the baked lobster beach roll with crab, cucumber, and avocado.

Landmarks

Cocina del Charro, 890 W. Valley Pwy., Escondido, CA 92025; (760) 745-1382; cocinadelcharro.com; Mexican; $$. Praise Baja! For over 30 years there's been Mexican magic in the air at this loud, boisterous, and colorful restaurant in Escondido. A feast for the eyes, as well as the palate, I highly recommend the *Cochinita Pibil*. A little pocket of flavor, it's Mayan-marinated pork cooked in the authentic Yucatan process with achiote and exotic spices, then wrapped in banana leaves and baked. Delving into the fiery Cancun burrito is high-risk behavior. Six large Mexican shrimp are garlic buttered, sautéed, and added to a tomato chipotle sour cream sauce with onions, bell peppers, squash, and rice and stuffed inside a huge flour tortilla, smothered in its own sauce and topped with cheese. Sister restaurant located in San Marcos.

El Bizcocho, 17550 Bernardo Oaks Dr., San Diego, CA 92128; (858) 675-8500; ranchobernardoinn.com; French; $$$$. When I walk into the dining room nestled inside the Rancho Bernardo Inn, I feel like I am being channeled to a different era when fine dining was ageless and classic. With white linens, candlelight, and plate after plate of absolute deliciousness coming out of the kitchen, this is definitely a destination for a romantic evening out. Raised on a working farm by his French father and American mother, Executive Chef Nicolas Bour learned firsthand about the farm-to-table concept from his parents. Today, he offers a simple and fresh ingredient-driven fine dining experience at El Biz that everyone will enjoy. If you really want to experience this chef's talents, I recommend his 4-course or 6-course tasting menu. You'll want to visit again and again!

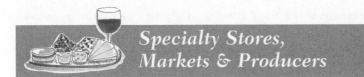

Specialty Stores, Markets & Producers

A Delight of France, 126 W. Grand Ave., Escondido, CA 92025; (760) 746-2644; adelightoffrance.com; Bakery; $$. This beautiful French bakery and bistro is located right in the center of Escondido on scenic Grand Avenue. Focusing on breakfast and lunch, it has become one of the more popular destinations for locals. Authentic recipes are used throughout the menu. In the morning, most patrons are enjoying one of the many fresh pastries with a cup of coffee, but don't overlook the larger breakfast items. The eggs Benedict is served on a wonderful baked brioche, and their strawberry crepes are the best I've tasted. For lunch, try one of the flavorful quiches, or splurge on my favorite, the vol Au vent: a puff pastry shell filled with chicken, mushrooms, and curry stew. Sandwiches, paninis, soups, and salads are also available. Not surprisingly, they offer an extensive assortment of freshly baked cakes and tarts for parties and other special occasions.

Edelweiss Bakery, 11639 Duenda Rd., San Diego, CA 92127; (858) 487-4338; edelweissbakerysandiego.com; Bakery; $$. I have two words for this place: "Apple Strudel," the best in town! Offering much more than strudel, Edelweiss has been pleasing guests with these old-world European-style desserts for over 2 decades. From wedding and birthday cakes filled with Bavarian cream and raspberry, to the best-selling German Apple Ring, there isn't a dessert here that I don't crave on a regular basis. Grab a seat and sip on a Kona Blend coffee in one hand and a bear claw in the other. Some other favorites are the English scones, almond raspberry croissants, custard-filled éclairs, and cheese Danish. Chocoholics come here for the chocolate cake with chocolate mousse. I have a soft spot for any Italian pastry, especially the cream-filled cannoli. Second location in Mira Mesa.

Vinz Italian Bistro, Pizza and Deli, 120 S. Kalmia, Escondido, CA 92025; (760) 745-8007; Grocery/Market; $$. One of the oldest operating businesses in Escondido, this old-fashioned deli specializes in Italian and German fare. With seating inside and out, this isn't a fancy place, but the down-home food at reasonable prices is worth the trip. A big refrigerated case is filled with Thumann's Meats, authentic German sausages and Italian meats and cheeses. The Reuben made with hot pastrami is a big seller and pairs great with one of the many homemade soups or the German potato salad served hot or cold with fresh dill and Black Forest ham. Other great selections include ready-made vegetarian lasagna, chicken parmesan, and an assortment of hot Italian subs. Don't miss the New York–style thin-crust pizza. The deli also offers a selection of bottled wines and imported candies.

Kearny Mesa, Mira Mesa & Clairemont

In the early 1900s this land was initially purchased as a ranch by newspaper tycoon Edward Scripps, who longed for an escape from the hectic East Coast but didn't want to settle in the downtown San Diego area. Most of the existing developments were built in the post-war boom of the 1950s as one of the primary residential areas for the military, since the Naval Air Station was nearby. Now called the Marine Corps Air Station Miramar, this military base became famous as the backdrop for *Top Gun*, an extremely popular movie starring Tom Cruise.

Highly industrialized, most of the main thoroughfares are lined with commercial property. This area was one of the first in San Diego to include fully designed suburban neighborhoods, with many city amenities included in the overall layout. Much of the land has been developed, except for San Clemente, Los Penasquitos, and Tecolote Canyon Parks. These are great areas to hike or bike along the natural canyons and imagine what most of San Diego looked like before modernization.

More so than any other area of the city, you will find large pockets of Asian cultures, including Chinese, Japanese, Korean, Thai, and Vietnamese. Convoy Street is a great example of this ethnic influence, with a large concentration of authentic restaurants and markets. Oftentimes, you'll know the cuisine is good because a majority of the patrons are local and speak the language most appropriate for the location. Many of the menus will also be written in both native language and English. In general, the prices are very reasonable, any time of day. The markets can be a fun experience, as you will find aisle upon aisle of exotic spices, packaged foods, and fresh items not found in a normal grocery store.

Foodie Faves

BUGA Korean B.B.Q., 5580 Clairemont Mesa Blvd., San Diego, CA 92117; (858) 560-1010; bugabbq.com; Korean; $$$. This Korean barbecue restaurant has a successful business based on quality ingredients and authentic recipes. Prices for dinner are higher than many comparable eateries in San Diego, but this is reflective of their choice to use Kobe and Neiman Ranch beef. There's always something special and delicious about natural meats that avoid hormones or antibiotics, and this is reflected in every dish. Two of my favorite barbecue dinners are the *Joomuluck* (boneless rib) and *Seng Deung Shim* (rib eye). For something truly authentic, choose one of the stews or hot pot casseroles. Reasonably priced lunch specials are available during the week. The spacious dining room can accommodate a good crowd, so finding a table is easier than many smaller restaurants in the area.

China Max, 4698 Convoy St., # 101, San Diego, CA 92111; (858) 650-3333; chinamaxsandiego.com; Chinese; $$. I like to call this "pish-posh white tablecloth" Cantonese seafood and New Hong Kong–style cuisine, which will have you so addicted, the staff may have to pry you out of your chair to get you to leave. It's a little pricey for a Chinese place, but when you walk in and smell the fresh spices wafting out of the kitchen, you'll spare no expense. Seriously good eats include the daily dim sum and the light and crispy fried baby squid with a touch of garlic salt. The sizzling beef with black bean sauce will warm your bones, and you can actually order live seafood from their tank, including Boston lobster, scorpion fish, sheepshead fish, and abalone. Don't miss the mango pudding for dessert. Beer, wine, and sake are always available.

Di-Chan Thai Restaurant, 5535 Clairemont Mesa Blvd., San Diego, CA 92117; (858) 569-0084; Thai; $$. Owner Sang Bonsynat has been offering delicious and authentic Thai dishes at Di-Chan Thai (translation: My Thai Restaurant) for over 20 years. The restaurant is a small hole-in-the-wall offering honest portions that are not only flavorful but healthy too! While vegetarians have their choice of vegetables and fish entrees, carnivores can opt for beef, chicken, and pork. All dishes are cooked to order, and you can order your food any way you like. Don't miss the Pad see-Iw, the spicy basil fried rice with shrimp, or the pad Thai.

Do Re Mi House, 8199 Clairemont Mesa Blvd., San Diego, CA 92111; (858) 565-2085; Korean; $$. There's a justified, quiet pride in the Korean offerings at this tiny hole-in-the-wall tucked away in the Kearny Plaza strip mall. With just a few tables and two TVs lurking in the background, the decor isn't fancy, but the food is fabulous. If you've never had Korean cuisine before, don't let the large 45-item menu intimidate you. Definitely consider one of the fabulous Korean stews (called *chigae*), including the popular *Yookgaejang*, a hot and spicy broth with shredded beef and vegetables. The mixtures of flavors are extraordinary. For your main dish, I suggest you try one of the specialties, including *galbi* (barbecue short ribs) or *bulgogi* (barbecue beef). If you want a nice dinner for 4 people, I suggest you try the bibim noodles, thin wheat somyeon noodles paired with small pieces of cabbage and zucchini. In addition, there are also plenty of fish and vegetarian choices, especially the raw crab, black cod, and delicious tofu soups. The complimentary cinnamon tea offered at the end of the meal is even better than dessert!

Jasmine Seafood Restaurant, 4609 Convoy St., #A, San Diego, CA 92111; (858) 268-0888; jasmineseafood.com; Chinese; $$. This is an extremely large and casual restaurant that resembles a dining hall where live seafood chosen from any of the 6 tanks in the restaurant is prepared Cantonese style. Live fish changes daily and includes lobster and crab. Choose from a large menu of authentic fare, including noodle and barbecue specialties, as well as duck, squab, pork, beef, and chicken dishes. The specialty of the house is the Cantonese-style roast duck, which serves 4 people. The big draw here is the Cantonese-style dim sum brunch, served daily. Choose from over 50 intricate mini-dishes presented on steamed carts and brought right up to your table. Try the barbecue pork bun, the stuffed crab claws, and the fried shrimp balls—or, if you're brave enough, the chicken feet! Weekends are very busy, so come early.

Khan's Cave, 9350 Clairemont Mesa Blvd., Suite F, San Diego, CA 92123; (858) 279-9799; khanscave.com; Asian/Fusion; $$. This hidden jewel in North County is located in a small strip mall with convenient parking nearby. The interior is quite spacious and can accommodate happy hour partiers as well as diners seeking a more intimate dining venue. A heated patio is also a nice option for guests wishing to dine outdoors. The focal point is a bar with over 20 local and international beers on tap, as well as plenty of wine choices. The diverse menu includes an impressive variety, including exotic Asian fusion tapas. The best strategy is to order a few items and share with your dining partners, as this guarantees you'll get to experience various flavor combinations. One of the house specialties is the Chilean sea bass with steamed vegetables and a choice of garlic ginger or black bean sauce. Also be sure to try the Mongolian lamb shank, super-tender meat that abounds nicely with a mildly sweet sauce and vegetables. One of my all-time favorites is the spicy eggplant in Kung Pao sauce, served over rice.

Kitchen 4140, 4140 Morena Blvd., San Diego, CA 92117; (858) 483-4140; kitchen4140.com; American; $$. Just off the beaten path, this organic bistro bejeweled with a crystal chandelier and a rustic, oversize picnic table offers fresh produce from local farmers as well as healthy greens from its impressive on-site herb garden. Executive Chef-Owner Kurt Metzger has definitely found his niche, continuing to astonish guests with his inimitable and twisted regional American cuisine. Dedicated to his ingredient-inspired and ingredient-driven menu, Metzger never wavers on his daily morning trips to the farmers' market. Break your morning fast in style with the Bistro Omelet with feta cheese, roasted bell peppers, heirloom tomatoes, garden vegetables, and home-fried potatoes. As seen on the cooking channel, a must-have for lunch is the beer-braised short rib sandwich with pickled onion, mango chutney, and Asian slaw on roasted pepper bread.

Mignon Pho + Grill, 3860 Convoy St., San Diego, CA 92111; (858) 278-0669; sandiegopho.com; Vietnamese; $$. Fabulous food and colorful dishes make for amazing memories at this modern, yet comfortable eatery in the Sunrise Plaza. Genuine Vietnamese family recipes, passed down from generations, are served in generous portions meant for sharing. The pho (beef broth noodle) is made from the bone marrows of large beef bones. Each bowl of pho comes with your choice of three ingredients and a side dish of vegetable. I like to order this big bowl of savory goodness with beef meatballs (*bo vien*), shrimp balls, and soft tofu. For guests who are sensitive to gluten, their brown rice noodles are 100 percent gluten free. Two other popular favorites include the fried chicken wings tossed in fish sauce and the refreshing julienne green papaya salad. The servers here will educate you on *soju*, a distilled beverage native to Korea. Drop *soju* into a pint of draft beer, or vice versa for some real fun!

Mr. Dumpling, 7250 Convoy Ct., San Diego, CA 92111; (858) 576-6888; Chinese; $$. A large variety of dumplings are sure to please at this comfortable eatery on Convoy Court. Enjoy 4 or 5 dumplings to an order, which can be steamed or pan-fried (turning it into a pot sticker). Popular favorites include the special seafood, vegetarian, and pork and dill dumplings. The centerpiece of the meal is the broth-based soup, better known as hot pots. Explosive with sweet, sour, salty, and bitter flavors, hot pots are customized and prepared by diners at their table. Flavor choices include a hot and spicy Szechuan, spicy cumin, or the Beijing and Dong Gui-style broth. As soon as the hot pot starts bubbling, diners add ingredients chosen from a varied list of meats, veggies, seafood, tofu, and noodles. Once the ingredients in the boiling pot are cooked, diners spoon out the ingredients and dig in!

The Original Sab-E-Lee, 2405 Ulric St., Linda Vista, CA 92111; (858) 650-6868; originalsab-e-lee.webs.com; Thai; $$. Opened since 2008, this tiny understated eatery in Linda Vista offers authentic Isaan (northeastern) style at reasonable prices. Choose from delicious appetizers, soups, salads, meat, and vegetable entrees, and noodle and rice dishes. I am a big fan of the curries, which can be made as spicy as you like. My favorite is the moist garlic and red chili based curry made with bamboo shoots and eggplant. All curries are served with a choice of beef, pork, chicken, vegetable, or tofu. Don't worry, if your mouth feels like it's on fire, cool it down with a Thai ice tea or the "Sweet Sticky Rice with Mango." You won't be disappointed. Additional location at 9159 Mission Gorge Rd., Santee.

Pho Ca Dao & Grill, 8373 Mira Mesa Blvd., San Diego, CA 92126; (858) 564-0917; Vietnamese; $. Pho Ca Dao is a spacious and colorful dining room that is packed for lunch and dinner. However, service is quite prompt, so tables turn over very quickly. The quality and price are really unbeatable, with many items less than $5. The seafood pho and the broken rice dishes are excellent. There are three other locations in San Diego.

Phuong Trang, 4170 Convoy St., San Diego, CA 92111; (858) 565-6750; phuongtrangrestaurant.com; Vietnamese; $$. You don't want to miss this authentic Vietnamese restaurant in Convoy Plaza. An extremely large menu boasts appetizers, soups, noodle dishes, and main courses including chicken, beef, pork, and seafood as well as vegetarian entrees. Your palate will remember the oodles of noodles in the broth-based vegetable Bun Nuoc, a warm vermicelli noodle soup served with shredded red cabbage, bean sprouts, jalapeño peppers, fresh mint, and lime. Two real highlights are the oven-roasted whole catfish served with vegetables, fish sauce, and rice paper or the Dungeness crab plucked live from the tank, then lightly battered and fried and tossed with garlic, salt, pepper, red bell peppers, and scallions. Okay, one more—the locals know to come here for the strawberry or Key lime ice-cream pie for dessert!

Robata Ya Oton, 5447 Kearny Villa Rd., Suite D, San Diego, CA 92123; (858) 277-3989; Japanese; $$. Just look for the crowd hanging out at the open bar watching the chefs in action, and you'll know you've arrived at one of the finest Japanese restaurants in town. This is prime territory to experience exotic Japanese cuisine in your own private booth, a cozy setting that's conducive to hand holding and kissing, as well as eating, of course. Take your shoes off before you step into your booth where you sit on mats placed on a bench close to the table. It's almost as if you are sitting on the floor, but you're not. The Shabu-Shabu allows you to cook your own food, at your own pace, and to your own liking, adding sliced beef, tofu, and assorted vegetables over a pot of boiling water, seasoned with kelp. If you want to leave the cooking to the master chefs, try the Kakuni, braised Kurobuta pork, or the Tara no Saikyo Yaki, grilled marinated black cod with miso flavor.

Sher E Punjab, 9254 Scranton Rd., Ste. #102, San Diego, CA 92121; (858) 458-2858; sprestaurant.com; Indian; $$. Located in a strip mall, this cozy Indian getaway offers a family-friendly atmosphere and a menu filled with Indian favorites. There are multiple platters of vegetarian, chicken, lamb, tandoori, and seafood specialties. With your meal it is suggested that you order the homemade naan, plain bread, which is absolutely delectable and melts in your mouth. I recommend the lassi, a popular mango yogurt smoothie, which goes well with just about any dish in the restaurant. Sher E Punjab offers an all-you-can-eat buffet on Friday and Saturday nights, allowing you to choose from all of the favorites. The buffet contains appetizers, salads, rice, a variety of delicious curries, and dessert.

Siam Nara, 8993 Mira Mesa Blvd., San Diego, CA 92126; (858) 566-13002; amarinthaisandiego.com; Thai; $$. Before you know it, you are pursuing the exotic cuisine at Siam Nara, a fine dining restaurant with a menu that spans a myriad of Thai cuisine specialties, including starters, soups, rice, noodles, and more. From the culture to the cooking, customers know this is as authentic as Thai food gets. Once the dishes start rolling, each one looks more like an edible work of art. I like the *goong num pla wan*. Eaten the during winter months, when the nem flowers (*dork sadao*) and river prawns become plentiful, beautiful prawns are grilled and served with tamarind sauce (*num pla wan*), roasted shallots, and Thai chili. Another off-the-grid standout is the crispy golden sole fillet topped with five signature sauces: pineapple puree, roasted garlic, and a trio of chili sauces. Dotted with kaffir lime leaves, it is a sweet and spicy Thai favorite.

Studio Diner, 4701 Ruffin Rd., San Diego, CA 92123; (858) 715-6400; studiodiner.com; American; $$. Featured on the Food Network's *Diners, Drive-ins, and Dives*, this eye-catching, neon-lighted diner continues to turn heads. It's nearly impossible to miss this place after the sun sets. Take a trip back to the 1940s where food was simple and the menu was easy to read. With a flashy, domed ceiling and movie-making equipment throughout the dining room, you'll feel reenergized at this 24-hour hot spot. No fluff, just good, down-home burgers and fries, hot dogs, sandwiches, fried clams, and maybe even a Bud Light with a warm Julian apple pie a la mode. One of my sinful indulgences for breakfast is the chicken-fried steak and eggs, with hash browns and toast. Or try their Grip Burger, a half-pound cheeseburger you might have a hard time finishing. Low-carb dieters will appreciate being able to order their burgers "protein style," substituting buns for leaves of lettuce.

Wa Dining Okan, 3860 Convoy St., #110, San Diego, CA 92111; (858) 279-0941; okanus.com; Japanese; $$. You can taste the history and the culture of the people through the food at Wa Dining Okan where, through their own independent channels, they import seasonal ingredients direct from various areas in Japan to prepare a true Japanese cuisine that will leave you completely fulfilled. From a variety of Japanese casseroles to rice cooked in a "Kama" Kettle, the ingredient-driven menu rivals the best at this small, all-occasion restaurant. If you're lucky enough to get a seat at this small restaurant, this is a great place to enjoy your tapas while mingling with the staff. Twelve different tapas rotate daily, and are served in the dining room as well, and include bean starch noodle salad, Japanese potato and macaroni salads, fried eggplant with spicy miso sauce, deep fried tofu with Japanese gravy, simmered pumpkin in broth, boiled asparagus mixed with miso and vinegar. Other worldly and daring dishes include roasted bonito sashimi, beef tongue steak and egg omelet with eel. Open for lunch and dinner. Reservations recommended.

The WineSellar & Brasserie, 9550 Waples St., Ste. 115, San Diego, CA 92121; (858) 450-9557; winesellar.com; French; $$$. In a modest location on a corner in Sorrento Mesa, there is a wine cellar and a brasserie under the same roof. The WineSeller, located on the ground floor, offers domestic and international wines from around the world. They hand-select wines that possess special character and quality. Find a great wine at a reasonable price, or go for the gusto with an expensive collector's wine. Located up a short flight of stairs, the Brasserie offers impeccable service matched with artful plates of innovative California French cooking based on homemade, seasonal, and locally grown ingredients. You won't find the French classic beef bourguignon here, because it has been given an American makeover. You will, however, find a salty and smoky scallop and pork belly bourguignon that's become an extremely popular signature dish. Not your ordinary BLT, the lobster tartine BLT, richly tastes of avocado butter paired with applewood-smoked bacon, melted leeks, roasted tomatoes, and garlic aioli. For dessert, this Italian girl loves the profiteroles; luscious cream puffs, stuffed with homemade chocolate, caramel, or vanilla ice cream.

Yokohama Yakitori Koubou, 3904 Convoy St., #108, San Diego, CA 92111; (858) 277-8822; yokohamayakitorikoubou.com; Japanese; $. Tucked away in an area of San Diego filled with Asian choices, this unassuming Japanese restaurant is an excellent choice. The semicircular bar and small dining room decorated with dark woods is frequently occupied with locals enjoying authentic food and conversation. An open kitchen allows you to watch the chefs slicing and dicing various meats and vegetables for skewers grilled over traditional Japanese bincho charcoal. Plenty of other rice and noodle dishes are also available. A unique dish is the *nippon no nikomi*, a Japanese-style meat and vegetable stew cooked in a fish base. Be sure to also try their excellent selection of hot or cold sake and *soju*.

The Godfather, 7878 Clairemont Mesa Blvd., #G, San Diego, CA 92111; (858) 560-1747; godfatherrestaurant.com; Italian; $$$. From the moment you enter this dimly lit landmark, you know you're in for a special treat. Since its opening in 1974, The Godfather has been considered one of the finest authentic Italian restaurants in Southern California. Tucked away in a neighborhood widely known for its Asian influences, this deeply Sicilian eatery has defied the odds and remained true to Chef Isodoro Balistreri's vision when he arrived from Palermo to share his cuisine. Don't look for any fusion dishes or modern music and decor. Here you will find comfortable booths, cloth-laden tables, tuxedo-clad servers, and soft music from a live piano filling the air. Upon your arrival, fresh baked bread and lightly breaded zucchini slices are placed on your table. The wine list is impressive and chock-full of excellent Italian varietals. Equally stunning is the menu, a comprehensive tour of the finest Italian dishes and suggested wine pairings, making your decision all the more difficult. Must-haves are the linguine ai frutti di mare, a medley of the sea mounded over pasta, and the cannelloni medaglione, pasta shells filled with filet mignon, Sicilian marsalla wine, and fresh mushrooms. Be sure to save a little room for the house-made Tiramisu, one of the best in the city. A large banquet room is also available for private parties. Dinner reservations are highly recommended.

Specialty Stores, Markets & Producers

Big Joy Family Bakery & Cafe, 4176 Convoy St., San Diego, CA 92111; (858) 627-0888; bigjoyfamily.com; Bakery; $$. Located in the Convoy Plaza, this is your chance to splurge on some sinfully tasty treats at this small bakery and cafe with seating for up to 50 people. Get the full effect of the cafe atmosphere by sipping on good coffee and grabbing a seat on one of the many comfortable loveseats that border the interior. Choose from a nice selection of artisan breads, pastries, sandwiches, specialty cakes, desserts, strawberry shortcake, brownies, croissants, and more. Love macaroons? Get macaroons fresh out of the oven in flavors of chocolate, strawberry, blueberry, and pistachio, to name a few. I really like the smoothies, sandwiches, salads, and the mini Hungarian nut cakes. My all-time favorite is their special raisin nut bread that has no yeast and trans fats added. It is made by a special enzyme and has an especially rich aroma. It is also abundant in dietary fiber and vitamin E and digests easily.

99 Ranch Market, 7330 Clairemont Mesa Blvd., #112, San Diego, CA 92111; (858) 565-7799; 99ranch.com; Grocery/Market; $$. Walking into this market is like stepping into another dimension. One minute you're driving past chain restaurants and a Walmart, the next minute you're surrounded by aisles of products from nearly every Asian country. This Asian-American supermarket was established in 1984 and now boasts locations in 30 states. Well-known for its product diversity and quality, this is an essential store for many locals, Asian or otherwise. Stroll through the store and marvel at the multitude of spices, canned foods, packaged products, and practically endless items for an authentic meal. The fish counter is a kaleidoscope of colors, with the freshest catches available whole or prepared as steaks or fillets. A full-service deli and take-out counter is usually the busiest section of the store. But my attention is drawn to the bakery, where bread, pastries, and cakes are made fresh daily. You won't leave without a full cart!

Opera Patisserie, 9254 Scranton Rd., San Diego, CA 92121; (858) 458-9050; operapatisserie.com; Bakery; $$. Find a safe haven in this museum of French food specials written on a chalkboard, including salads, sandwiches, crepes, soups, and house specialties. The carefully made *croque monsier*, a French style grilled cheese sandwich with Gruyère cheese, béchamel sauce and Black Forest ham has a gratifying charred and chewy texture. Another popular favorite is the vegetarian quiche, a French-style custard pie filled with oven-roasted tomatoes, sautéed spinach, feta cheese, and fresh buffalo mozzarella. Ambitious desserts of raspberry mascarpone mousse, a luscious pastry made with pistachio strawberry pomegranate, and my favorite gluten-free chocolate lava cake.

Surati Farsan Mart, 9494 Black Mountain Rd., San Diego, CA 92126; (858) 549-7280; suratifarsan.com; Middle Eastern; $$. Serving San Diegans for over 26 years, this Indian food market and eatery is one of the most popular of its kind in Southern California. They don't serve the typical curry-smothered dishes normally found in most Indian restaurants, boasting instead a wide variety of vegetarian dishes, snacks, and sweets. Many patrons frequent this hot spot for their reasonably priced street food (often called tapas locally). Most of the items are sold by the pound or half-pound, and reasonably sized portions are less than $4 each. Walking through the front door is a feast for the senses, with exotic spices filling the air, and glass cases lined with colorful foods. Quality, consistency, and the freshest ingredients are top priority. The sweets are perfectly delightful. Choose a tray of assorted items to broaden your knowledge and satisfy your sweet tooth, like sugar-free date rolls and rose kaju badam rolls.

La Jolla

La Jolla is home to some of the most affluent residents in the area. And for good reason: It is culturally dense, packed with high-end, ocean-view restaurants, 4-star hotels, art galleries, boutiques, and lots of shopping. Although the geography stretches from beaches to rolling residential hillsides, it is the small area nearest the natural cove that garners the most interest from visitors. Considered one of the most beautiful (and photographed) beaches in Southern California, the La Jolla Cove includes a couple of small swimming beaches, a grassy picnic area, and high bluffs with the waves crashing into foam during high tide. The popular underwater park is a haven for swimmers, scuba divers, and snorkelers of all skill levels. The area is also frequented by packs of sea lions that lie on the beach and nearby rocks, and sea birds of all kinds, including gulls and pelicans. Prospect Street runs along the coast and is lined with various eateries and hotels that have some of the best views (and food) in San Diego.

La Jolla Shores is just a short walk north of the cove, and has a long stretch of beach lined with a boardwalk until it intersects with the Scripps Pier. Drive a few miles north up a steep hillside, and you'll find yourself at the entrance to the Torrey Pines Reserve, with extensive walking paths and nature trails. Farther east is UC San Diego and more shopping at University Towne Center and other nearby commercial centers.

Foodie Faves

Barbarella, 2171 Avenida De La Playa, La Jolla, CA 92037; (858) 454-7373; barbarellarestaurant.com; Italian; $$$. This simple and stylish mainstay in La Jolla is the perfect dining venue for guests wanting to feel as though they have stepped into a charming, modern, California-style bistro with a Mediterranean-inspired menu. Offering indoor and outdoor seating, Owner Barbara Beltaire thinks of this place as her home, where her staff takes an honest approach to organic and seasonal food by allowing the flavors to express themselves in simple and fresh ways. An engaging crowd of tourists and after-work locals know to come here for the french onion soup with melted Gruyere and the fresh organic salmon tartare. For diners craving Italian fare, Beltaire does Italian right with a variety of delicious pizzas and baked orecchiette pasta with gorgonzola, pecorino, parmesan, and pancetta in a light cream sauce. In addition, if you have a hungry pooch, a special Doggie Menu will do the trick!

Beaumont's, 5662 La Jolla Blvd., La Jolla, CA 92037; (858) 459-0474; beaumontseatery.com; California Modern; $$$. Located in the Bird Rock Community of La Jolla, this down-to-earth restaurant has customers lining up for progressive American cuisine paired with live music on select nights, as well as a "Blues Brunch." Whether you want to sample exclusive appetizers or take a voyage through some incredible meat, seafood, and pasta courses, Beaumont's proves ideal. From gutsy duck confit tacos and pork chile relleno to rustic prime short ribs bourguignon or roasted chicken pappardelle, Beaumont's expertly prepared cuisine is a mainstay for diners seeking unforeseen flavors. Signature martinis and hazelnut gelato bon bons for dessert further bolster the allure!

Brockton Villa, 1235 Coast Blvd., La Jolla, CA 92037; (858) 454-7393; brocktonvilla.com; American; $$$. Originally a historic La Jolla cottage built in 1894, Brockton Villa is now the locals' go-to for the view of the ocean, the barking seals on the seashore, and of course, the coastal-inspired fresh catch seafood cuisine. Both the dining room and open-air patio face the incredible shoreline and famous seaside cliffs where waves continuously crash against the rocks. Simple, flavorful, and seasonal, the menu includes a richly decadent clam chowder or lump blue crab cake sliders for lunch that never disappoint. There is no better location for a romantic dinner, watching the sun set over the

Pacific, and enjoying savory meals over a candlelit table. The hours linger nicely with oysters "Brockafeller," fiery dill shrimp butter leaf wraps, and almond-chili–crusted scallops. Not just for breakfast, top off your meal with their legendary Coast Toast served "a la mode" with cinnamon or vanilla gelato.

Burger Lounge, 1101 Wall St., La Jolla, CA 92037; (858) 456-0196; burgerlounge.com; Burgers; $$. A healthy and delicious burger does exist! Say goodbye to conventionally grown beef, and hello to hormone- and antibiotic-free beef that comes from one farm where the animals' diet consists of tall green grass from a Kansas prairie. You'll get a flavorsome burger sandwiched between a soft, organic whole-wheat bun made with a little unbleached white flour and blackstrap molasses, organic white cheddar or American cheese, fresh or grilled onion, tomato, and house-made Thousand Island sauce. Non-beef lovers can opt for a veggie burger made with quinoa, salmon, or all-natural turkey, or choose a green salad topped with grilled or crispy chicken breast. French fries and onion rings are cooked in 100 percent refined peanut oil. Splurge on the chocolate malt or the ginger beer float with vanilla ice cream. Draft beer and wine are available. There are several burger lounge locations throughout San Diego.

Cafe Japengo, 8960 University Center Ln., San Diego, CA 92122; (858) 450-3355; cafejapengo.com; Asian/Fusion; $$$$. Consistently

ranked among the best restaurants in San Diego for its urban flair and style, this dynamic and energetic restaurant ventures into exotic culinary territory and features fancy cocktails, wine, and sakes, a renowned sushi bar, and an audacious menu focusing on Asian and Pacific Rim cuisine with French and Mediterranean influences thrown in. Executive Sushi Chef Jerry Warner offers his signature Stuffed Tomato Tuna Sashimi and his own Yellowtail Ceviche creation, while Executive Chef Jay Payne offers curry-dusted calamari and duck pot stickers with cilantro-mint pesto and ponzu. From the wok the Vietnamese pork delicately entwined with glass noodles, jalapeño, portobello mushrooms, eggplant, asparagus, and hoisin sauce will definitely ignite your taste buds. Word to the wise: Happy hour in the full-service bar is a big draw here!

Chedi Thai, 737 Pearl St., #110, La Jolla, CA 92037; (858) 551-8424; chedithaibistro.com; Thai; $$$. Executive Chef, Restaurant Designer, and Owner Sutharin Pia Kampuntip cooks traditional Thai cuisine prepared in a more contemporary way at this enchanting and attractively decorated eatery on Prospect Street. Since each dish on the menu boasts its own unique twist, order multicourses to share. Great starters are the Thai crispy calamari cooked in sweet roasted chili sauce, crispy corn cakes served with cucumber relish, or the steamed vegetable dumplings generously stuffed with shiitake mushrooms, corn, tofu, and spinach. The pad Thai rice noodles mingle deliciously with shrimp, eggs, bean sprouts, tofu, and chopped peanuts in a tamarind sauce. Most impressive of all is the crispy and boneless red snapper with cherry tomatoes and bok choy in a three-flavor sauce. A daily happy hour is a great way to try many dishes at an affordable price.

The Cottage, 7702 Fay Ave., La Jolla, CA 92037; (858) 454-8409; cottagelajolla.com; American; $$. Surrounded by boutiques and galleries, this little cottage has it figured out for breakfast, as well as late lunches and dinner. The lines can be long in the mornings, but wait patiently for the fried egg sandwich. This sumptuous concoction of applewood bacon, Gruyere cheese, tomato, arugula, red onion, and lemon aioli all griddled on sourdough bread will make you really happy and full. On the sweeter side, the french toast stuffed with strawberry compote and mascarpone cheese is the perfect pairing with your morning cappuccino. For dinner it's none other than comfort food therapy with the turkey and Angus ground beef meat loaf with Yukon Gold potatoes and cabernet gravy, or the melt-in-your-mouth polenta cakes with tomatoes, mixed vegetables, goat cheese sauce, and arugula. So much fun food, so little time!

Crab Catcher, 1298 Prospect St., La Jolla, CA 92037; (858) 454-9587; crabcatcher.com; Seafood; $$$$. With spectacular ocean views throughout the dining room and outdoor patio, the Crab Catcher specializes in California and Pacific Rim–inspired seafood selections. Be sure to schedule your visit when you can enjoy the scenery and colorful sunsets, as the dark of night will limit your sight line. I am a sucker for a great Crab Louie, and in my opinion, they serve the best in town! With a blend of crabmeats, mixed field greens, tomatoes, cucumber, avocado, and special dressing, it's priceless. Other specialties include savory crab cakes, crab-stuffed mushrooms, king crab ceviche, and Maryland blue crab wontons. Of course, they serve plenty of other offerings from both land and sea, so be sure to bring your sunglasses and an appetite!

Eddie V's Prime Seafood, 1270 Prospect St., La Jolla, CA 92037; (858) 459-5500; eddiev.com; Seafood; $$$$. With its expanse of windows, a *très* chic lounge, and two decks overlooking the La Jolla Cove, this newbie is a strong contender for the city's best view. As for the California cuisine, it's a matter of splurging on top-notch steaks and fresh seafood with a few Asian twists thrown in. A *Wine Spectator* award-winning wine list doesn't hurt either. Premium hand-cut steaks include a 12-ounce filet mignon embellished with cracked black peppercorns and cognac sauce and an enormous 22–ounce USDA Prime bone-in rib eye that's enough for two to share. Experience the joined tang and texture in the broiled Pacific swordfish with Jonah crab and avocado, perked up with red chile vinaigrette, or the North Atlantic scallops sautéed with citrus fruits, almonds, and brown butter. The bananas Foster flambéed tableside is the only way to close! See Chef Patri Ponsaty's recipe for **Chocolate Godiva Cake** on p. 350.

George's California Modern at George's at the Cove, 1250 Prospect St., La Jolla, CA 92037; (858) 454-4244; georgesatthecove .com; California Modern; $$$$. Inundated by locals and visitors wearing everything from tailored suits to designer jeans, an exceptional, unsurpassed flawlessness exists at George's California Modern. An unobstructed ocean view, perfectly placed candles on white tablecloths, impeccable service, and a beautiful wine list are just the start. Named one of America's top 10 chefs by *Food & Wine*, Executive Chef Trey Foshee continues to unfurl a menu of exceptional seasonal California cuisine so transcendent, you'll petition for more. Earthy and robust dishes include the braised lamb shank with butternut squash risotto, roasted squab, and smoked Maine lobster. Foshee hits the mark with vegetarian offerings prepared at the peak of freshness, including rapini-ricotta ravioli or chanterelle stew. Another meatless wonder, the slow-roasted Chino Farms carrot takes on the texture and flavor of fall-off-the-bone braised beef when paired with curried apple puree, glazed turnips, maitaki mushrooms, and toasted buckwheat-brown butter vinaigrette.

Goldfish Point Cafe, 1255 Coast Blvd., La Jolla, CA 92037; (858) 459-7407; goldfishpointcafe.com; American; $$. This café is located uphill from the La Jolla Cove, and the locals like to congregate here for the ocean view and to relax in the classic, yet casual setting. Choose from a large range of specialty drinks including cappuccino, white mocha, hot cider, and Italian soda. A great selection of lighter fare is served for breakfast and lunch. Start your day out right with a veggie burrito or lox and bagel with cream cheese, red onions, capers, and tomatoes. For lunch, choose from a nice selection of salads, specialty sandwiches, and paninis. I like to order the Bird Rock Sandwich, triple-decked with layers of turkey, ham, bacon, and Swiss cheese. Locals come here for the Panini Milano with pepperoni, salami, melted provolone cheese, and tomatoes on grilled ciabatta bread.

Harry's Bar and American Grill, 4370 La Jolla Village Dr., #150, San Diego, CA 921221; (858) 373-1252; harrysbarandamericangrill .com; American; $$$$. Located across the street from the UTC Mall, this upscale bar and grill is a great place to meet a friend for lunch or to relax and unwind after a fun day of shopping. The atmosphere is light and bright with linen-covered tables and a large covered outdoor patio with a fireplace. From the Maine lobster burger patty with caper aioli and homemade potato chips to the seafood Cobb salad or Harry's Filet Mignon Steak Sandwich, the food is consistently delicious. Favorites include the grilled 14-ounce veal chop marinated with fresh herbs and the cannelloni filled with veal, spinach, and ricotta cheese. Live music on select nights.

The Melting Pot, 8980 University Center Ln., San Diego, CA 92112; (858) 638-1700; meltingpot.com; American; $$$. Never fear, fondue is here! After first noticing the romantic and quiet atmosphere, you are taken back to your booth delightfully colored in rich browns and burgundys. In the middle of your table there are burners for where your fondue pot will be placed. Choose from an array of menu items such as the "Traditional Swiss Cheese Fondue" starter, which is a blend of Gruyère and Emmenthaler Swiss cheeses and a splash of white wine as well as some spices for flavor, served with bottomless bread chunks and vegetables. A popular main course is the "Land and Sea," which includes filet mignon, chicken breast, and shrimp. Now, don't be alarmed when a plate of raw meat comes your way. The best part of this whole experience is being able to cook the food in your choice of fondue broth. Delicious sauces accompany the main course, and you will leave feeling satisfied. If you do happen to save room for dessert, make sure to try one of their famous chocolate fondues, which come in many different flavor profiles and are served with sweets including marshmallows, cheesecake bites, and even strawberries and bananas. It's a classy and romantic spot to go for a different, yet memorable dining experience.

Museum Cafe, 700 Prospect St., La Jolla, CA 92037; (858) 456-6427; mcasdcafe.com; California Modern; $$. Located inside the Museum of Contemporary Art San Diego, this cozy bistro is open daily for breakfast and lunch. Chef-Owner Giuseppe Ciuffa serves European-inspired cuisine with his own personal Italian touch. It's a perfect stopover before or after visiting the museum, but many of the patrons frequent the cafe for their superior cappuccinos and culinary delights. All of their offerings are made with only the finest ingredients, often organically grown and sourced locally, and the meats and poultry are free from hormones and antibiotics. Be sure to try the made-from-scratch blueberry pancakes and Sonoma chicken-apple sausage, or my favorite lunch item, the white albacore tuna salad sandwich. Chef Ciuffa also operates a fine catering business that is extremely popular with local companies and private parties (giuseppecatering.com).

Nine-Ten, 910 Prospect St., La Jolla, CA 92037; (858) 964-5400; nine-ten.com; California Modern; $$$$. Escape to Nine-Ten located inside The Grande Colonial Hotel for an unforgettable gastronomic experience! Executive Chef Jason Knibb passionately redefines California cuisine with eloquent presentations and spice-laden touches from his Jamaican background. By gathering veggies and herbs from a garden just outside the back door of the kitchen, Knibb honors his commitment to create innovative cuisine using only the freshest, local ingredients. Treasured dishes include Jamaican Jerk pork belly with spicy jellies and seared duck breast with an 18-year aged balsamic and duck jus. Allow the chef to utterly pamper you, and opt for his "Mercy of the Chef" special prix-fixe and wine-pairing menu. San Diego's most admired Pastry Chef Jack Fisher takes care of the sweeter side of things by offering a variety of handcrafted desserts using seasonal products from local farmers. Don't miss the warm hazelnut cake with mascarpone cream, figs, balsamic syrup, and Concord grape sorbet. Thank you, Jack!

Prospect Bar & Grill, 1025 Prospect St., #210, La Jolla, CA 92037; (858) 454-8092; prospectbar.com; American; $$$. Prospect Bar & Grill is a second-story restaurant-bar that gazes out over the Pacific Ocean, offering guests a simply put and easygoing, yet indulgent Californian-themed menu. Bottom line—this place is really fun, offering crafty cocktails and trendy appetizers, salads, sandwiches, burgers, pasta, and more. If you want to try the Waiver Wings, you must sign a form from the manager. If you eat all wings in under 11 minutes, you'll receive a complimentary Prospect T-shirt. Grilled soba noodles over buckwheat pasta, lobster ravioli and blue moon battered Atlantic cod and chips—it's all here! This is the only place in town where you'll find a fried strawberry swirl cheesecake, a traditional dessert that this restaurant has twisted into something much more unique than the creators of cheesecake intended. A crispy fried wonton shell substitutes for the outmoded crust, subtly dusted with sweet brown sugar and topped with fresh strawberry slivers. The contrasting texture of crunchy wonton, soft cheesecake filling, and fresh strawberry slices definitely keeps your palate satisfied!

Puesto Mexican Street Food, 1026 Wall St., La Jolla, CA 92037; (858) 455-1260; eatpuesto.com; Mexican; $$. Located in downtown La Jolla, this upscale fast-casual eatery features a walk-up counter where you can dine in or get your food to go. The menu offers a variety of authentic Mexican food ingredients including all-natural meats, sustainable seafood, local and seasonally organic vegetables, homemade all-natural stone-ground corn tortillas, and 6 homemade signature salsas made from scratch daily. Customize your *guisados* (grilled foods), which can be mixed and matched and are served as tacos that are layered with crispy hot cheese. Diners can choose from a variety of toppings such as fish, shrimp, chicken, carne asada, and gourmet Mexican vegetarian items like zucchini flower, corn truffle, and soy chorizo potatoes. For a healthy dessert or refreshing side, Puesto serves a Mexican street cup of sliced jicama, cucumber, carrots, mango, and dried mango sticks with lime, chili, and sea salt.

Roppongi Restaurant and Sushi Bar, 875 Prospect St., La Jolla, CA 92037; (858) 551-5252; roppongiusa.com; Asian Fusion; $$$$. This higher-end remarkable Asian restaurant and sushi bar offers a unique, contemporary, Asian-influenced menu ideally designed for sharing. With an atmosphere inspired by the flamboyant nightlife district in Tokyo, you'll take your seat in a lively sushi bar, loosen up in the lounge, or relax around the outdoor fire pit. Personally, I like to sip on international sake and dine with a view of the extraordinarily beautiful aquarium. Asian tapas are more than prominent, including Hamachi Taro Tacos with sweet mango and the Mongolian shredded duck quesadilla with spicy Asian guacamole. As for main entrees, don't be surprised at the envious stares when you order the barbecue mini lamb chops with pineapple egg fried rice or the grilled Szechuan peppercorn-crusted top sirloin with broccoli rabe and gorgonzola croquette. Are you hungry yet?

The Steakhouse at Azul, 1250 Prospect St., La Jolla, CA 92037; (858) 454-9616; brigantine.com; Steak House; $$$$. Azul is a fine dining steak house where you can count on a really good piece of prime cow cooked to perfection on a special high-temperature upside-down broiler. Guests may dine inside the building's main interior with a stunning view of the La Jolla Cove or opt for a seat on the ornate courtyard patio, complete with a modern fire pit. The menu offers USDA prime steaks and grain-fed wagyu beef. Other outstanding options range from tender rack of lamb to numerous seafood selections. Perhaps the star of Azul's show is the surf and turf. This sought-after entree features a tender petite filet accompanied by choice Maine lobster. For more private occasions, Azul's Wine Room is an intimate abode surrounded by glass walls that gaze northward upon the shoreline of the Pacific.

Sushi On The Rock, 1025 Prospect St., Ste. 205, La Jolla, CA 92037; (858) 459-3208; sushiontherock.com; Asian Fusion; $$$. Listen to Metro-style music at this high-energy restaurant near the La Jolla Cove. Creative and freewheeling sushi masters in the kitchen offer some wild and crazy sushi combinations that will tantalize your taste buds. Customers drive near and far for the salmon and crab stuffed yellow chilies (Dragon Eggs), cooked tempura style and drizzled with wasabi cream sauce. Two dishes that are worthy of prolonged discussion are the jumbo black tiger shrimp, cooked with a sweet and spicy barbecue sauce served over sweet mashed potatoes, and the peppered seared tuna with a sesame ginger ponzu, avocado slices, and red onion.

Tapenade, 7612 Fay Ave., La Jolla, CA 92037; (858) 551-7500; tapenaderestaurant.com; French; $$$$. While this isn't a "maison" located in France, it might as well be. Award-winning Chef Jean Michel Diot has done something right, because when you dine here, you'll feel like you're in a refined Parisian bistro. Since 1998, Diot has been a magician in the kitchen, combining traditional French techniques with natural aromatic ingredients to create simple, yet classic dishes. Eating authentic is easy with the burgundy escargots with fresh herbs and garlic butter. Wild game lovers, try the Scottish partridge with root vegetables or the venison loin with huckleberry and burgundy sauce. Having an affinity for those rich French sauces, I adore the pheasant breast with chestnut cream and port wine reduction. With so many French options, you will definitely need more than one visit!

Whisknladle, 1044 Wall St., La Jolla, CA 92039; (858) 551-7575; whisknladle.com; American; $$. In 2008, friends and partners Arturo Kassel and Chef Ryan Johnston established this little neighborhood eatery on the map in La Jolla. The concept was perfect for La Jolla: quaint, cute, modern, and comfortable—you name it! The food is simple, humble, and straightforward with some esoteric choices thrown in. This approach has won acclaim in a number of national and local publications, adding to their positive reputation throughout the culinary community. From flatbread to burgers to charred bone marrow or fried sweetbreads, this made-from-scratch food is fresh, local, and seasonal. One of my favorite starters is the Cutting Board, an assortment of house-cured meats, artisan cheeses, mustards, spreads, and pickles. Another very popular dinner item is the fork-tender braised beef cheek with balsamic cipollini onions, potato puree, and pecorino. Additional locations now include shorter-order items and take-out at the PrepKitchen in La Jolla, Del Mar, and Little Italy.

Landmarks

A.R. Valentien, 11480 N. Torrey Pines Rd., La Jolla, CA 92037; (858) 777-6635; arvalentien.com; French; $$$$. The Lodge at Torrey Pines is home to A.R. Valentien, one of San Diego's most notable and refined restaurants. You will certainly feel transported whiling away the hours in a charming dining room with a beautiful view of the Torrey Pines Golf Course and the Pacific Ocean just off the bluffs in the distance. Classically French-trained, with more than 30 years of experience, Executive Chef Jeff Jackson offers a temple of flavor in his market-driven cuisine from some of California's finest organic farms, orchards, and fishermen. The menu revolves around the seasons, assuring superb freshness and taste with every bite. The charcuterie section of the menu is one of my favorites, offering duck and pistachio pâté platter of three terrines, with house-made pickles and Dijon mustard. Artisanal and farmhouse cheeses are outstanding, and the meat and seafood options range anywhere from lobster and swordfish to duck, Niman Ranch pork loin, and dry aged rib eye steak. The spiced crepe with warm apples and cream is worth writing home about. In 2008, foodie website epicurious .com honored A.R. Valentien among the top 10 farm-to-table restaurants in the nation.

The Marine Room, 2000 Spindrift Dr., San Diego, CA 92037; (858) 459-7222; marineroom.com; French; $$$$. Opened in 1941, this iconic restaurant with its opulent dishes and million-dollar beachfront location continues to attract celebrities, world figures, residents, visitors, and nightly regulars who wouldn't dream of having dinner anywhere else. The seahorse symbol of The Marine Room has long stood for its dramatic on-the-surf location, where waves have been known to crash up against the windows, especially during their popular High Tide breakfast offered on select days during the winter months. Food is magic here, and Executive Chef Bernard Guillas and Chef de Cuisine Ron Oliver bring an international influence to their cuisine, so much so that they wrote a cookbook called *Flying Pans* in which they tell of their traveling tales from around the globe with recipes to match. From local seafood favorites to the seasonal and exotic, the menu is an elegant and everlasting tale of two chefs. Soothe your soul with a fennel escargot casserole dressed with white sage gnocchi, pomelo glazed organic tofu with spaghetti squash, or free-range veal osso bucco braised in plum wine. See Executive Chef Bernard Guillas's recipe for **Caramel Star Anise Pot de Crème** on p. 357.

The Shores, 8110 Camino Del Oro, La Jolla, CA 92037; (858) 456-0600; theshoresrestaurant.com; California Modern; $$$$. How many places can you step off the sand and immediately into a casual but stylish dining experience? Look no further than The Shores Restaurant, located within a Spanish-style hotel bearing the same name. With a wall of windows right on the beach, you can't find a bad seat in the dining room, lounge, or open-air patio. Serving breakfast, lunch, dinner, and Sunday brunch since they opened in 1970, it's a perfect choice for a family gathering or romantic evening. Each of the menus is extensive and sure to delight even the pickiest of diners. The prix-fixe menu changes regularly, and is offered at a reasonable price, especially when you allow the sommelier to pair your dishes from their extensive wine list. A kids' menu is also available.

The Sky Room, 1132 Prospect St., La Jolla, CA 92037; (858) 454-0771; lavalencia.com; California Modern; $$$$$. An elevator ride up to the 10th floor of the La Valencia Hotel and you have arrived at The Sky Room, where 180-degree views of the Pacific Ocean will leave you breathless. Dress your best at this very elegant and intimate restaurant with only 10 tables. Executive Chef Lance

Repp takes advantage of California farms and purveyors by spoiling guests with local seafood and fresh seasonal produce. Choose from an a la carte menu and be dazzled by Osetra caviar, house-cured salmon, duck confit, or perhaps you prefer the 5-course "tasting" menu, paired with wines hand-selected by the sommelier. More than 1,000 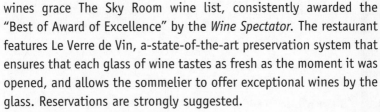 wines grace The Sky Room wine list, consistently awarded the "Best of Award of Excellence" by the *Wine Spectator*. The restaurant features Le Verre de Vin, a-state-of-the-art preservation system that ensures that each glass of wine tastes as fresh as the moment it was opened, and allows the sommelier to offer exceptional wines by the glass. Reservations are strongly suggested.

Specialty Stores, Markets & Producers

Cups La Jolla, 7857 Girard Ave., La Jolla, CA 92037; (858) 459-CUPS (2877); cupslj.com; Desserts; $$. This is an all-organic cupcake store with a full-scale teaching kitchen and party room on Girard Avenue in the village of La Jolla. Freshly baked cupcakes are made in-house with the highest quality local and sustainable ingredients. You can opt for gluten-free, vegan, dairy-free, or low-glycemic cupcakes—who would have thought? Imagine relaxing

Trader Joe's

For over six decades, this neighborhood specialty grocery store has been providing hard-to-find, high-value products with a friendly smile and relaxed attitude. With the staff donned in Hawaiian shirts and the PA system replaced by a code of bell ringing, the entire store is a fresh experience. There are a dozen locations in the San Diego area:

Carlsbad: 2629 Gateway Road, Carlsbad; (760) 603-8473

Chula Vista: 878 Eastlake Parkway, Suite 810, Chula Vista; (619) 656-5370

Encinitas: 115 N. El Camino Real, Suite A, Encinitas; (760) 634-2114

Escondido: 1885 So. Centre City Pkwy., Unit A, Escondido; (760) 233-4020

La Jolla: 8657 Villa La Jolla Drive #210, La Jolla; (858) 546-8629

La Mesa: 5495 Grossmont Center Dr., La Mesa; (619) 466-0105

Oceanside: 2570 Vista Way, Oceanside; (760) 433-9994

San Diego (Carmel Mtn. Ranch): 11955 Carmel Mtn. Rd. #702, San Diego; (858) 673-0526

San Diego (Hillcrest): 1090 University Ste. G100-107, San Diego; (619) 296-3122

San Diego (Pacific Beach): 1211 Garnet Avenue, San Diego; (858) 272-7235

San Diego (Point Loma): 2401 Truxtun Rd., Ste. 100, San Diego; (619) 758-9272

San Diego (Scripps Ranch): 9850 Hibert Street, San Diego; (858) 549-9185

in the Cups lounge and slowly biting into a flourless Chocolate Decadence cupcake that's topped with cinnamon and whipped cream, while sipping on  an ice cold milk "on tap" from Straus Family Creamery, California's first family-owned certified organic dairy. Or how about a Chunky Monkey Banana-Walnut cupcake filled with chocolate chunks with a topping of creamy peanut butter frosting nicely paired with Cups' special blend of organic coffee. It's a Berry Berry Good Strawberry cupcake with creamy strawberry frosting that makes my day complete, but only if I have it with a big glass of the strawberry milk made in-house with Straus milk and organic strawberries.

El Pescador Fish Market, 627 Pearl St., La Jolla, CA 92037; (858) 456-2526; elpescadorfishmarket.com; Grocery/Market; $$. Nearly 40 years ago, El Pescador was opened as a small, fresh seafood market in Del Mar. Within a year, public demand spurred the addition of a seafood deli, offering meals for immediate consumption or carry-out. Now located in the heart of La Jolla just a short walk from the Pacific, this relaxed market displays the freshest fish available. Types of fish will vary depending on the season, but everything is cut and filleted on the premises. If you're in the mood for shellfish, the cooks will prepare them while you wait, if you choose. If you want to dine immediately, many of the daily catches are available sautéed as a meal, or char-grilled and served in a sandwich, salad, or plate with steamed rice and a salad. A very popular item is the El Pescador Salad, with Dungeness crab, medium shrimp, bay shrimp, smoked albacore, and smoked salmon tossed on top of spring mix, romaine, red and white cabbage, tomatoes, and green and red onions, with your choice of dressing.

Homegrown Meats / La Jolla Butcher Shop, 7660 Fay Ave., Ste. C, La Jolla, CA 92037; (858) 454-MEAT (6328); homegrownmeats .com; Grocery/Market; $$. Are you conscious about the meat you're cooking and eating at home? Then you must try Homegrown Meats, only available at the La Jolla Butcher Shop. Their cattle roam free on a large ranch near Palomar Mountain, feeding on the meadow grasses, and without use of antibiotics or hormones. They also offer the finest lamb, poultry, game, and homemade sausages. A very popular item is their grass-fed beef hot dogs, made with only beef and spices. No nitrates, hormones, or fillers. They're delicious! Let them teach you about dry aging, a process that enhances the flavor and tenderness of meat, and is seldom seen outside of upscale steak houses. Best of all, they offer helpful advice and recipes for any cut of meat, making your meal a sure hit with family or friends.

Michele Coulon Dessertier, 7556-D Fay Ave., La Jolla, CA 92037; (858) 456-5098; dessertier.com; Desserts; $$. **Dessert** doesn't have to be a guilty pleasure when it's made from the finest ingredients, including real butter and Belgian chocolate at this cozy bakery in La Jolla. Order a cappuccino and choose from luscious pastries including croissants, cinnamon rolls, and scones as well as delicious pies, cakes, cookies, and more. My favorites are the pecan caramel mini tartes filled with toasted pecans and caramel and drizzled with milk chocolate, and the organic orange butter cookies dipped in white chocolate. Open for lunch; enjoy soups, salads, and sandwiches. Having loved desserts her whole life, Owner Michele Coulon would rather eat a small piece of something incredible than a lot of something not so great. I agree with her philosophy: Dessert is not something you eat every day, so make it worth your while.

Sprinkles, 8855 Villa La Jolla Dr., La Jolla, CA 92037; (858) 457-3800; sprinkles.com; Desserts; $$. I have always been crazy for cupcakes, and Sprinkles in La Jolla is a calming force in my life. Founder Candace Nelson started her cupcake store in Beverly Hills, where customers waited in long lines for these sweet treats handcrafted from the best ingredients. With several locations throughout the United States, Sprinkles has become a household name. From lemon coconut to peanut butter chip, there isn't a flavor you won't find here. My personal favorites are the banana cupcake with bittersweet chocolate frosting and the walnut-studded carrot cake with cinnamon cream cheese frosting.

We Olive, 1158 Prospect St., La Jolla, CA 92037; (858) 551-8250; weolive.com; Olive Oil Market; $$. In support of local growers, We Olive is the perfect place to sample and purchase a retail extra-virgin olive oil from California. A full olive oil tasting bar allows customers to taste and compare olive oils from over 20 olive oil companies in California, and a knowledgeable staff is on hand to educate you about the production process, differences in varietals, harvesting, milling, and storage methods. Whether you prefer flavored olive oils or extra-virgin olive oil for cooking, I'm sure you'll find a favorite to take home. Oils are dated to ensure freshness, flavor, and quality. Choose from handcrafted mustards, pestos, tapenades, balsamic vinegars, and other specialty ingredients as well. Currently there are 10 retail locations around California and an online store.

Ocean Beach, Pacific Beach & Mission Beach

The central beach areas are a vibrant part of San Diego, both day and night. A centerpiece for this cluster of neighborhoods is the Ocean Front Boardwalk, a walkway that runs over 3 miles along the beach from Pacific Beach to Mission Beach, ending at the mouth of Mission Bay in the south. You will find pedestrians, skateboarders, rollerbladers, cyclists, and joggers. A wide variety of shops, bars, coffee houses, and restaurants line the beach, all providing unobstructed views of the wildlife, both in and out of the water.

The beach areas are largely populated by a younger generation, primarily college students, surfers, young professionals, and families. Residences are typically in the form of small cottages, bungalows, single-family homes, and apartment buildings. The nightlife is extremely popular, especially on weekends in the off-season and daily in the summer, when the bars become gathering places for good food, drink, and conversation. Major attractions in the area include Sea World San Diego (opened in 1964) and the historic amusement park Belmont Park in South Mission Beach. Belmont Park was built in 1925 to attract real estate investors and still features the original wooden Giant Dipper Roller Coaster, one of the larger wooden structures of its kind in the US. The park also includes many smaller rides and carnival-type attractions. Adjacent to the boardwalk is Crystal Pier, a public pier and hotel, where you can rent rooms right above the crashing waves.

Across the Mission Bay outlet and right next to Point Loma is Ocean Beach, where the main business activity is along Newport Avenue. Here you will find many restaurants, antiques stores, tattoo and piercing shops, coffee houses, bars, and surf shops. Built in 1966, the Ocean Beach Municipal Pier is the longest concrete pier on the West Coast, measuring 1,971 feet. The pier, and nearly 1 mile of walkway along the beach, is available to the public for walking and fishing 24 hours a day. In the 1960s, surfing became a critical component of this community, which hosts major surfing events year-round. If you're looking for a fun day at the beach and a simple meal, this is the right place.

Baleen, 1404 Vacation Rd., San Diego, CA 92109; (858) 274-4630; paradisepoint.com; California Modern; $$$$. Located among the lush surroundings of the Paradise Point Report, this waterfront restaurant has stunning views of Mission Bay. Choose to sit in the intimate dining room, near the large and bustling exhibition kitchen, or on the outdoor patio with soft breezes and a warm fire pit. Sunsets are especially popular here, with the crimson light shimmering off the water, and sailboats gently crisscross the Bay. It's no wonder Baleen is often noted by national sources as one of the must-see dining destinations in San Diego. Be sure to begin your evening with the pan-seared crab cakes, served with cucumber-mango salad and aioli, or the signature seared diver scallops with a kumquat-chardonnay glaze and microherb and chanterelle salad. For dinner, you can't go wrong no matter what you order. One of the most popular items is the apple brined and glazed pork chop with chipotle sweet potato gratin, smoked bacon, apple-pecan relish, and long beans. Be sure to save room for one of the delectable desserts with coffee, and linger to enjoy the night skyline.

Bo-Beau Kitchen + Bar, 4996 West Point Loma Blvd., San Diego, CA 92107; (619) 224-2884; bobeaukitchen.com; French; $$$. Operated by the Cohn Restaurant Group, this attractive and comfortable Ocean Beach bistro celebrates the spirit and flavors of the Mediterranean with a modern yet rustic cuisine. With "Bo" referring to Bohemian style and "Beau" signifying beauty, this newest neighborhood destination offers old-world charm and new-world polish in a French-inspired setting. A most unique feature includes an entrance into the restaurant through an imported ancient Egyptian gate. Adding to the approachability of Bo-Beau is the Mediterranean-inspired cuisine prepared by Chef Katherine Humphus, who can be spotted preparing a wealth of dynamic offerings from the entryway leading into her kitchen. Choose from soups, salads, and a variety of house-made pastas as well as house-made pâté and various tartines such as the Croque Madame Tartine, which features a delectable combination of sliced pork belly, gruyere cheese, fried egg, and a Parmesan cheese reduction. The menu also highlights flatbreads adorned with flavorful ingredient medleys ranging from roasted brie, beets, and curry onion marmalade to braised short rib, horseradish, smashed potatoes, and chives.

Caffe Bella Italia, 1525 Garnet Ave., San Diego, CA 92109; (858) 273-1224; caffebellaitalia.com; Italian; $$$. Whether you choose the warm and simple interior dining room or the Tuscan-style garden patio, get ready for authentic Northern Italian cuisine. The chef is a native of Milan, and he brings traditional dishes to life in this cute, little free-standing building in the busy neighborhood of Pacific Beach. As a certified green restaurant, they focus on serving only the best local produce and sustainable meats and seafood available. No pesticides, hormones, or preservatives to be found here. Homemade pizza and pastas are their specialty, so no matter what you order, it's bound to be high quality. Take their *chitarra alla pescatora*, an aromatic dish of homemade spaghetti in a fresh chopped tomato sauce with sautéed clams, mussels, salmon, and white fish. Another excellent choice is the wood-fired pizza piccante, with fresh tomato sauce, mozzarella, and hot salami. The restaurant is also available for hosting private events or catering. Its sister restaurant is Solare located in Point Loma.

Dirty Bird's, 4656 Mission Blvd., San Diego, CA 92109; (858) 274-2473; dirtybirdspb.com; American; $$. Situated in the heart of vibrant Pacific Beach, this newer establishment has a rustic interior filled with wooden furniture and wall accents. Chicken wings are a staple at any bar, but adventurous wings lovers know to come here for the notable hot wings paired with craft beers and sports watching. The menu features 23 wing flavors created with house-made sauces. Crowd favorites include the classic Buffalo, Dirty Ranch, Spicy Garlic, Maple Chipotle and Lemon Pepper. House-made ranch and bleu cheese dips, carrots and celery accompany the saucy delights. Baked low and slow before frying, the wings are juicy, meaty, and, quite honestly, irresistible! There are also plenty of other foods on the menu, including sliders, burgers, salads, and popular tater tots. Where else can you enjoy a plateful of potato rounds loaded with chili and melted cheese? They even offer an ostrich burger, made with naturally low-fat meat and served any way you like.

Fig Tree Cafe, 5119 Cass St., San Diego, CA 92109; (858) 274-2233; figtreecafepb.com; American; $$. Open for breakfast, lunch, and brunch on Sunday, break your fast in style with a foamy mug of cappuccino and an egg and bacon sandwich with tomatoes, spinach, and mozzarella cheese on toasted brioche bread. The eggs are 100 percent natural from free-range chickens raised on a local family-owned farm in Ramona. The cozy outdoor patio with checkered green tablecloths and potted fig trees appears to be a magnet for neighborhood regulars craving made-to-order food at a reasonable price. For lunch, I recommend chicken breast cordon bleu panini with smoked ham and bleu cheese on rosemary focaccia bread or the sapphire salad with organic mixed greens topped with turkey, cranberries, goat cheese, and walnuts with lemon-poppy seed dressing. This eatery also welcomes man's best friend, who will love the treats you sneak him under the table! An additional Fig Tree Cafe in Hillcrest is open for breakfast, lunch, and dinner. Consider their growing catering business for your next special occasion or corporate event, as they offer an extensive menu of hors d'oeuvres and larger menu items.

Firehouse American Eatery and Lounge, 722 Grand Ave., San Diego, CA 92109; (858) 274-3100; firehousepb.com; American; $$$. Experience retro-American-chic dining and nightlife experience at this sophisticated, yet approachable restaurant where you can bring the family for breakfast, a business colleague for lunch, or a date for dinner. Standing only a few hundred feet from the beach, this popular hangout is packed year-round, but especially at night when the younger locals are ready to jump-start the evening entertainment. The dining room is cozy but spacious, and the bar is unique, boasting a fiery red hue in the background that makes me feel as if I've entered a fire truck spaceship. An open-air patio and bar upstairs is the best location to enjoy an early morning coffee. Breakfast items include classics like scrambles, waffles, pancakes, and omelets. Their breakfast burrito is especially popular with the locals. Satisfy your craving for something hot and spicy with not one, but three Mini Inferno Burgers topped with pepper jack cheese, grilled jalapeños, and chipotle aioli on sweet Hawaiian bread. And if you're really hungry, opt for the barbecue baby back ribs smothered in Firehouse cider molasses barbecue sauce, and served with fries and slaw on their famous piggy plate.

The Fishery, 5040 Cass St., San Diego, CA 92109; (858) 272-9985; thefishery.com; Seafood; $$. Located in a vintage warehouse just a few blocks from the ocean and in a quieter area of Pacific Beach, the Fishery focuses on products delivered from local artisanal fishermen. Their practices support healthy marine life and sustainability while delivering the freshest seafood available. As such, the menu changes frequently. The daily dinner menu is packed with inspired dishes, like the wild Alaskan coho salmon miso or macadamia-crusted Alaskan halibut. For a special treat, visit during their "Tuesday Tastings," where you will enjoy a catch straight out of the ocean and prepared with local, organically grown fruits and vegetables. It's a great way to take advantage of the chef's creativity. After your meal, be sure to stroll by the glass cases in the central retail seafood market and choose a fresh catch to prepare at home. The staff is extremely knowledgeable regarding cooking styles that fit the product, so don't be shy! The kitchen also prepares delectable side dishes that complement your meal, always made fresh daily.

Hodad's, 5010 Newport Ave., Ocean Beach, CA 92107; (619) 224-4623; hodadies.com; Burgers; $$. "No shirt, no shoes, no problem!" Since 1969, Hodad's is a unique, old-fashioned burger joint located in the heart of Ocean Beach just minutes from where the street meets the water. Re-opening in 1991 at their current location, OB residents have been raving about these infamous burgers. With the interior covered in street signs, surf boards, and license plates, it's a great casual place to grab one of the best burgers in town after a long day at the beach. Don't forget the beer either! Served bottled or on tap, there is a great selection of tasty labels to pair with the juicy burger being grilled fresh to order. The all-around favorite here is the bacon cheeseburger, which includes a high-quality ground meat patty, shredded lettuce, pickles, tomatoes, melted cheese, onion, and bacon that's chopped together to almost create another patty. Pair with their onion rings or french fries, and you'll be very satisfied. If you're not in the mood for alcohol, be sure to try their creamy chocolate malt. Although the lines can get long, especially in summer months, it's certainly worth the wait.

Isabel's Cantina, 966 Felspar St., San Diego, CA 92109; (858) 272-8400; isabelscantina.com; Latin American; $$$. This place is hip and loud, with festive guests filling seats and having some dining fun for breakfast, lunch, and dinner. Only a few blocks from the ocean, the atmosphere is bright and open by day, transforming to a candlelit haven by nightfall. A gargantuan 15-foot Buddha statue staring down at the dining room and an Asian-style bar in the corner sets the tone for Pan Asian and Latin Fusion cuisine. The menu utilizes fresh ingredients whenever possible, including many that are grown at their own Stargazer Farm, which uses only organic farming practices. From spicy pork carnitas to tofu, you'll savor food with bold and unique flavors created by Isabel Cruz, a self-taught chef who believes that clean, simple, and healthy food can also taste delicious. Test out her theory with offerings such as the soy chorizo tacos, veggie torta, crispy shoestring plantains, or the green chile tamales. Or treat yourself to a special breakfast before heading to the beach, with an extensive list of delicious items. For dessert, I don't really know if coconut flan is healthy, but I don't really care. It's too delicious to pass up!

JRDN at Tower23, 723 Felspar St., Pacific Beach, CA 92109; (858) 270-2323; t23hotel.com; California Modern; $$$$. Enter

JRDN at Tower23 Hotel and join the fun at the bar, or take a seat in the sleek and contemporary dining room that includes a massive 70-foot lighted "wave wall" mural. A spacious open-air patio is also the perfect place to enjoy ocean views and watch passersby traveling on the meandering boardwalk. Chef David Warner's distinctively modern menu utilizes hand-selected, all-natural meats, the finest seafood from sustainable sources, and locally grown organic produce. It's a perfect brunch destination. Dine alfresco by the ocean and devour Mama's Baked French Toast with sugar and spice pumpkin, whipped mascarpone cheese, and maple syrup. A local favorite is the chilaquiles and eggs, with chorizo, salsa, queso fresco, avocado, and lime crema. If you dine in the evening, be sure to try one of the fresh catches of the day, or the uber-savory lobster potpie. Open for lunch and dinner daily, brunch on the weekends.

Kafé Yen, 4516 Mission Blvd., Pacific Beach, CA 92109; (858) 373-3936; kafeyen.com; Thai; $$. An inviting respite from the crowded Pacific Beach boardwalk, get comfy and cozy with a warm pot of tea at this Asian haven boasting Thai/Asian Fusion cuisine. Although they have a small outdoor patio, I enjoy sitting in the comfortable couches that line the dining room wall. Hanging tapestries set the mood for relaxed dining. The menu is laid out in helpful sections, making it easy to order. Choose from house specials, fried rice, soups, appetizers, salads, noodle dishes, and desserts. Large portions are served for lunch. The Moo Dang is a unique lunch dish of tender Thai roasted pork with red gravy, presented with boiled egg and cucumbers. The Malaysian pan-fried roti pancakes retain their texture and balance, served with cucumber salad and peanut sauce. I like the sweetness quotient in the butter squash with curry sauce, basil, and bell pepper with a choice of chicken, beef, or vegetables, served with Vietnamese rice noodles. Fried bananas or mango with sticky rice make for a satisfying finish.

Latin Chef, 1142 Garnet Ave., San Diego, CA 92109; (858) 270-8810; thelatinchef.com; Latin American; $$. Take a seat in this small Pacific Beach restaurant and get ready for something different, as Peruvian cuisine is not easy to find in San Diego. Located on busy Garnet Avenue in Pacific Beach, parking can be somewhat of a challenge, but worth the extra effort. The unique blend of flavors incorporates European, African, Asian, and Incan influences. More recently, they have added several Brazilian dishes at the behest of their loyal patrons, who often pack into the dining room on any given day. All of the dishes I've sampled are unique and interesting for my Mediterranean-born palate. One of their specialties is the *seco de carne de res*, a thick beef stew bursting with flavors and served with beans and rice. Another excellent dish is the *aji de gallina*, pulled chicken meat cooked with a creamy aji amarillo sauce and served over boiled potatoes. Be sure to save room for one of their exceptional desserts. Their marketplace includes a variety of Peruvian foods and ingredients available to take home.

The Mission, 3795 Mission Blvd., San Diego, CA 92109; (858) 488-9060; themissionsd.com; American; $$. So what can you expect stepping into a bistro named The Mission, strategically located on Mission Boulevard in the Mission Beach neighborhood? Nothing less than artistic and healthy food served in a bright and busy atmosphere. The bistro uses fresh and seasonal ingredients to create simple meals with complex flavors. It is a rare occasion to be seated without waiting. Focusing on giving back to the community, The Mission is regularly involved in local charities, even using the walls to adorn local artist's works. Their sandwiches and many of the breakfasts utilize fresh baked breads from the kitchen. My favorite is the rosemary loaf, crunchy on the outside and soft inside, the subtle flavor of rosemary and olive oil is superb. Or try the fresh cinnamon bread used for their famous french toast. One of the more unique ingredients is the homemade soy chorizo. You would swear it's identical to the meat variety in looks, texture, and taste. My all-time favorite soy chorizo dish is the breakfast burrito, with black beans, crispy rosemary potatoes, scrambled eggs, jack cheese, cilantro, scallions, tomatoes, and chipotle crema in a large whole wheat tortilla. There are two additional locations in San Diego: downtown in East Village and uptown in North Park.

Poma's Italian Deli, 1846 Bacon St., Ocean Beach, CA 92107; (619) 223-3027; pomasdeli.com; Italian; $. Poma's Italian Deli has been a well-known landmark in San Diego since 1965. Tucked away in the heart of Ocean Beach, this joint is easy to miss if you're not on the lookout. I would consider this place a "hole in the wall" deli; however, don't let the lack of decor fool you; the sandwiches have been raved about for years. As you walk in, you notice the cold case in front of the counter packed with fresh lasagna and cold cut meats. Behind that you have choices of beer or wine as well as soft drinks. There is no waiter service; you simply walk up to the counter and order. All of the sandwiches are made there right in front of you, either hot or cold, and are deliciously done on their famous Solunto's bread. Their classic has been the roast beef sub, which consists of hot, tender roast beef chopped up into bite-size bits over their fryer, provolone cheese melted over the top, and then freshly diced tomatoes, shredded lettuce, and whole pepperoncinis. Other famous menu items include the Torpedo sandwich, which consists of cotto and dry salami, mortadella, and provolone, and the simple, yet delicious, meatball with marinara sub. Lasagna, eggplant parmesan, ravioli, and pizza are also served at this deli. Prices are quite reasonable for the servings you receive.

Red Marlin, 1441 Quivira Rd., San Diego, CA 92109; (619) 221-4868; hyatt.com; California Modern; $$$$. Overlooking scenic

Mission Bay Marina, Chef de Cuisine Danny Bannister places emphasis on sustainable, organic ingredients. Choose from a romantic indoor dining room to the outdoor patio directly over the water. They also have private dining rooms and an elegant communal chef's table encircling a built-in fire pit and extensive wine wall. No matter which area you choose, the views are stunning, especially at sunset. As the signature restaurant for the Hyatt Regency Mission Bay, the Red Marlin is open for breakfast, lunch, and dinner, and includes menu selections thoughtfully designed for patrons of all ages. An excellent choice for dinner is the juniper-brined kurobuta pork chop, served with roasted apple, acorn squash, Weiser Farms baby potatoes, and a Dijon demi-glace. Dessert selections change with the seasons, but I will not soon forget my experience with the warm peach shortcake, a heavenly mix of roasted peaches, bourbon sauce, and a pecan biscuit, topped with house-made whipped cream. They also serve a very popular after-dinner drink called the Key Lime Pie, with Absolut Vanilla Vodka, pineapple juice, and fresh squeezed lime.

Sandbar Sports Grill, 718 Ventura Place, San Diego, CA 92109; (858) 488-1274; sandbarsportsgrill.com; American; $$. For 10 years this two-story eatery has been a popular watering hole and food destination for visitors and the after-work crowd yearning for a relaxed vibe and unfussy food. Since they are open for breakfast, lunch, and dinner, the menu offers hearty omelets, Benedicts, and griddlecakes as well as a simple menu of tapas, burgers, salads, sandwiches, and more. The Sky Bar is the perfect place to watch a sunset and relax with a good draft beer and the popular mahimahi fish taco with chipotle aioli and a secret marinade. Crowd pleasers are the crispy natural wings or tenders that come in buffalo style, sriracha garlic, spicy barbecue, sweet chili, or Jose's secret spicy garlic ranch. Bar food that tips the scale includes hand-dipped beer-battered onion rings, cream cheese-stuffed red jalapeños, and carne asada tater tots, but who's counting calories? The Diablo burger may be the best in Mission Beach: a big, juicy patty with chipotle sauce, spicy jelly, fresh jalapeños, pepper Jack cheese, and crispy onions.

South Beach Bar & Grill, 5059 Newport Ave., Ocean Beach, CA 92107; (619) 226-4577; southbeachob.com; American; $$. South Beach Bar & Grill is located right on the corner where palm-lined Newport Avenue intersects with the Pacific. Whether you choose to sit downstairs or on the second-floor bar, your view of the beach activities can't get any better. Since opening in 1992, this eatery in the heart of Ocean Beach has been home to the famous mahi fish taco. This popular taco delicacy consists of grilled mahimahi topped with cheese and drizzled with a generous amount of house-made white sauce and salsa fresca in a soft tortilla. In addition, choose from a variety of fresh seafood as well as great burgers. Grab a seat at the long wooden bar and catch a game from one of the 10 televisions while sipping on a cold brew or specialty cocktail. Their long list of drafts includes a few local craft breweries. Enjoy a dozen fresh oysters on the half shell or clams and green lip mussels steamed in white wine, lemon, and garlic butter.

Sushi Ota, 529 Mission Bay Dr., San Diego, CA 92109; (858) 270-5670; sushiota.com; Japanese; $$$. Unanimously considered the best sushi restaurant south of Los Angeles, this legendary eatery is nearly invisible from the street. Although many lesser competitors try to compensate with flashy exteriors and attractive crowds, Sushi Ota is simply a great place to eat. Every dish is impeccably prepared with the finest ingredients available. The menu is short compared to similar restaurants, because many of the diners pay most of their attention to the fresh menu, which changes daily based on availability. The baked miso salmon and sea bass appetizers are simply amazing. The flavors and textures of every sashimi dish are spectacular. The toro, albacore, and yellowtail are favorites. At times, the room can be extremely crowded, so reservations are a good choice. You'll also need to be a bit aggressive with the sushi chefs, as they are not apt to linger. And don't let the modest location lull you into thinking that the food is cheap. You'll still pay a price for that meal, but it's definitely worth it.

Specialty Stores, Markets & Producers

Bird Rock Coffee Roasters, 5627 La Jolla Blvd., La Jolla, CA 92037; (858) 551-1707; birdrockcoffeeroasters.com; Coffee/ Tea; $$. Although technically located in the southern portion of La Jolla, this little coffee shop is really closer to Pacific Beach. Don't let the simple interior and street-front patio fool you; this place has received national recognition for its excellence. *Roast Magazine* chose Bird Rock as their 2012 winner for Micro Roaster of the Year. Focusing on organic and sustainable beans, they have built strong relationships with their growers, and it's evident in every cup they serve. Their special roasting techniques bring out the best in every bean variety, and the staff is impressive in their attitude and friendliness. Be sure to ask for a cappuccino or latte in a ceramic cup so that you can marvel at the detail used by each barista to ensure your drink is perfectly cupped and marked by an artistic foam leaf. They also offer a small selection of fresh pastries to pair with your perfect cup. No matter what time of the day you visit, you're bound to find locals filling the seats and chatting at this neighborhood gathering place. Local artists and musicians are frequently featured here.

Old Town, Balboa Park, Mission Valley & Bankers Hill

This section of San Diego is quite diverse, even though the neighborhoods are adjacent to each other in the central part of the county. To really enjoy all of the attractions in this area, you'll need more than one day!

The Old Town area was considered the heart of the city of San Diego until the 1860s, until Alonzo Horton began to develop the downtown and waterfront area. The main attraction for this section of the city is Old Town San Diego State Historic Park, one of the most visited state parks in California. Considering its competition, that's saying quite a lot. Established in 1968, the park commemorates early days of the town of San Diego and includes many historic buildings built between 1820 and 1870. Five original adobes are part of the complex, along with other historic buildings including a schoolhouse, a blacksmith shop, San Diego's first newspaper office, gardens, and a stable with a carriage collection. A number of authentic Mexican restaurants and other quaint eateries are within easy walking distance.

Balboa Park is a 1,200-acre urban cultural park located just north of the downtown area, and attracts over 2 million visitors a year. It was the location of the 1915 Panama–California Exposition and 1935 California Pacific International Exposition, both of which contributed architectural landmarks for future visitors. It was declared a National Historic Landmark in 1977. In addition to open space areas, gardens, and walking paths, it contains a variety of cultural attractions including 16 museums, several theaters, and the world-famous San Diego Zoo. Only one major restaurant is located in the Park, but many others are a short distance away.

Bankers Hill is a well-established uptown neighborhood near Balboa Park, and is literally up the hill from downtown San Diego. It includes many restored Victorian mansions, some of which have been modified into offices for dentists, lawyers, and small companies. Although directly under the flight path of aircraft landing at San Diego International Airport, residents are unaffected by the noise. Many popular restaurants are in the area, including both upscale and casual venues, as well as neighborhood delis.

Mission Valley is a wide river valley just north of Old Town, and was the site of the first Spanish settlement in California, established in 1769. This history may be completely lost when you visit the area, as it now serves as a central shopping and entertainment center for San Diego. Three major shopping malls are located here, including Westfield Mission Valley, Fashion Valley, and Hazard Center. The area is also home to a long street known as Hotel Circle, aptly named for the many hotels and motels lining the road. Farther east is Qualcomm Stadium, home of the San Diego Chargers, and San Diego State University.

Foodie Faves

Andres Restaurant, 1235 Morena Blvd., San Diego, CA 92110; (619) 275-4114; andresrestaurantsd.com; Latin American; $$. Since 1983, this small family-owned and -operated restaurant has a tropical feel complete with fine linen tablecloths, pictures of Cuba on the walls, and Latin American music playing in the background. Although the cuisine is well-seasoned, I don't consider it hot and spicy. Choose from beef, chicken, pork, seafood, and vegetarian entrees all served with rice, black beans, and fried plantains. I like the classic Cuban sandwich with roasted pork, baked ham, mustard, pickle, and Swiss cheese. For dinner, I would recommend the Bistec Empanizado, a Cuban-style breaded top sirloin steak, or the Camarones Enchilados, tender shrimp in tomato sauce with onions, garlic, green peppers, and spices. Be sure to stop by their International Latin Market located next door. Here you will find a large selection of hard-to-find spices, food, and non-food items for the serious chef or casual cook. A large banquet room is also available for a special event.

Avenue 5 Restaurant & Bar, 2760 5th Ave., San Diego, CA 92103; (619) 542-0394; avenue5restaurant.com; California Modern; $$$. It's a skillful cook that can build good food. French trained Executive Chef Colin McLaugin uses European influences, throwing in some Asian and Latin, while keeping his California cool at this culinary spark plug located within walking distance of Balboa Park. Situated on the ground floor of a Bankers Hill office building, the dining room is busy with colors and artwork, and you'll often find a packed crowd conversing and enjoying the signature cocktails like a Cotton Candy Cuban or Cranberry Mojito. The menu moves from the essential to the eclectic, offering anything from burgers to duck confit. Live it up with the house-made pork sausage and short rib tacos. This Italian girl adores the concept of tortellini with grapes, and McLaugin pulls it off with corn, mushrooms, arugula, and Madeira cream. Order the crustless pecan pie with caramel sauce and banana gelato and everyone in the restaurant will look your way; but don't share, they can order their own! An extensive brunch menu is also available Sunday.

Bankers Hill Bar and Restaurant, 2202 4th Ave., San Diego, CA 92101; (619) 231-0222; bankershillsd.com; California Modern; $$$.

Open for dinner only; experience classic and simple New American food at this open and airy contemporary restaurant. Rough wood tables, walls, and beamed ceilings welcome you to a new trend in dining: upscale cuisine that has no item over $20. A rotating seasonal menu offers popular dishes that will excite your senses without emptying your wallet. You'll be surprised to discover deviled eggs as an appetizer, but these aren't your grandma's version: special farmers' market eggs are paired with lemon potato  crisps, arugula salad, and parmesan cheese. Or try the crispy barbecue braised pork tacos, with pepper Jack cheese, avocado, herb-lime cream, and tomato salsa. No matter what you choose, prepare to be astounded. They have plenty of local craft beers available by draft or bottle, and the wine list is equally amazing. Plenty of parking is available nearby.

BUNZ, 475 Hotel Circle S., San Diego, CA 92108; (619) 298-6515; bunzsd.com; American; $$. BUNZ is a casual eatery offering burgers made with Certified Humane Meyer's Natural Angus beef and hormone/antibiotic-free hot dogs. Committed to clean and fair cuisine, Chef-Owner Jeff Rossman uses locally grown produce whenever possible, and even makes his own condiments, including ketchup and beer-thyme mustard. Marvel at a menu that covers breakfast, lunch, and dinner, where no item is over $10. Hands down, the most popular items are in the burger family, and for good reason. The preparations are unique and filled with flavor. Favorites include the Three Li'l Pigs, a burger with smoked bacon, ham, pulled pork, beer-thyme mustard, aged cheddar, lettuce, tomato, grilled onions, and the Cowboy, with smoked bacon, onion rings, house-made beer barbecue sauce, aged cheddar, roasted poblano pepper, lettuce, and tomato. Be sure to ask for extra napkins, because you'll need them to clean up after your culinary rampage. The flat-top hot dog preparations are also delicious, with 100 percent premium Angus beef, split down the middle and grilled to crispy perfection. They offer craft beer, wine, and cocktails, but I suggest you savor their strawberry shake or malt, blended to creamy goodness using locally grown berries.

Cafe Coyote, 2461 San Diego Ave., San Diego, CA 92110; (619) 291-5700; cafecoyoteoldtown.com; Mexican; $$. Margaritas are flowing and the tortillas are made fresh to order at this Mexican mainstay located in the heart of Old Town San Diego's Historic Walking District. For over 20 years, hungry guests have been satisfying their appetites with hearty Mexican flavors in festive surroundings. The portions for all items are impressive. The super-loaded nachos and a chicken, beef, and potato taquito platter make good communal options, and there are also several seafood choices. The massive beef chimichanga with bell peppers, refried beans, and cheese wrapped in a flour tortilla and deep-fried to give it a crispy golden brown is a favorite as is the Famous Old Town Carnitas, with tender pieces of pork slow-cooked in Mexico's traditional style. Select from over 100 tequilas in the Cafe Coyote Cantina, a certified

"Tequila House" by the prestigious Academia del Tequila, Mexico City, and one of only two Tequila Houses in the US. It can get quite busy all day, but the dining room is massive, and typically rotates tables quickly. There are also plenty of shops nearby to keep your attention until your table is ready.

Cucina Urbana, 505 Laurel St., San Diego, CA 92101; (619) 239-2222; cucinaurbana.com; Italian; $$$. This California-inspired Italian restaurant between downtown and Hillcrest has a warm and rustic atmosphere that's a bit understated. The retail wine shop located inside the restaurant allows guests to pick out their own bottles of wine and have them opened at table for a minimal corkage fee. This location is very popular and books up nearly every evening, so reservations are highly recommended. Otherwise, they take first come, first serve walk-ins for the bar, pizza counter, and community table. Ironically, these can be fun options for seating, especially to eat with other people who may just become your best friends. I think what makes this place so popular is great food in good-size portions at an affordable price. The Vasi appetizers are the big hit here, consisting of mini mason jars filled with Tuscan toast and different spreads and cheeses. The pizza and pasta dishes are also big sellers. My favorites are the ricotta gnudi in sage brown butter, the savory short rib pappardelle, or parmesan panko-crusted eggplant. Its location on Laurel near Balboa Park makes it a perfect destination before or after watching a show at the Old Globe Theater.

El Agave Tequileria, 2304 San Diego Ave., Old Town, CA 92110; (619) 220-0692; elagave.com; Mexican; $$. Tequila lovers know to come here, where a Tequila Museum is home to the largest tequila bottle selection in the US. With over 2,000 brands to choose from, you are sure to find one you like, but don't stop there; taste a few to appreciate the many varieties and subtle differences. The selection can be a bit daunting, so feel free to ask the servers, who are happy to assist and help you find the right blend based on your tastes. The authentic taste of Hispanic-Mexico is served in a beautiful and elegant space, with warm lighting and brick walls adding to the ambiance. Varied spices ranging from chocolate and coriander to garlic and cinnamon make for the fabulous made-from-scratch moles (sauces) used for every dish. I like the Mole Rosa de Taxco, with chicken breast served in a creamy and colorful mole made from walnuts and chipotle chili. Assorted bite-size tamales are also fun, stuffed with shrimp, black beans, and roasted poblano peppers, and topped with a trio of sauces.

Hexagone, 495 Laurel St., San Diego, CA 92101; (619) 236-0467; hexagonerestaurant.com; French; $$$. If you are French and crave food from your country, you should visit this intimate dining venue just 1 block from Balboa Park. If you aren't French, but want to eat like the French do, Hexagone is definitely the place for you. A large contemporary menu offers 40 appetizers and entrees at reasonable prices. You'll get prompt and polished service in a cozy and extravagant environment complete with white tablecloths and fine china. From the authentic french onion soup to the beef bourguignon, dining here is like dining in a bistro in France, but without the expensive plane ticket. What emerges from this kitchen is wondrous, especially the grilled beef tenderloin fancily dressed with candied shallots and Cabernet sauce. If you're feeling especially bold, try the classic frog legs Provencale or escargots à la Bourguigonne. Another very popular dish is the Moscovy breast of duck with leg confit and orange sauce. And certainly don't forget to conquer the Crêpes Suzette for dessert!

New Orleans Creole Cafe, 2482 San Diego Ave., #A, San Diego, CA 92110; (619) 542-1698; neworleanscreolecafe.com; American; $$. This cozy eatery is located in the Historic Whaley House Gardens in Old Town. The Wild West–style building was built in the 1890s, with a wonderful outdoor patio to enjoy the Southern California weather. Offering authentic Creole dishes based on recipes handed down through 7 generations, many of the ingredients and most of the beers are imported directly from Louisiana. You will often find the restaurant filled with regular clients who rave about the food and traditional New Orleans–style hospitality. I recommend trying their most genuine dishes: chicken and sausage gumbo, the alligator sausage po'boy, crawfish étouffée, or jambalaya. Each dish is a celebration of the region that will always be known as the Big Easy. And be sure to save room for dessert, because they serve one of the best bread puddings in San Diego.

Old Town Mexican Cafe, 2489 San Diego Ave., San Diego, CA 92110; (619) 297-4330; oldtownmexcafe.com; Mexican; $$.

I've got two words to say about this place: Taco Tuesday. On this special day of the week, you have your choice of chicken, beef, or pork carnitas, fried fish, or potato tacos for a low price. Tuesday seems to be all the rage, especially with the in-house margaritas, Hornitos shots, and Tecate beer priced at only $2.50. This long-standing Mexican restaurant with three dining areas, an outdoor patio, and traditional-style decorations has been a mainstay for food lovers seeking a fun atmosphere and authentic food options. Aside from the overstuffed tacos, the fajita dishes heaped with beef, chicken, shrimp, or veggies are perfect for sharing. Served with guacamole, half order of beans and tortillas, it's more food than you can eat, but do it anyway! Plenty of vegetarian options are also available. They even serve breakfast 7 days a week. Want more excitement? Order the Table Side Shaker Margarita designed to serve two people. Weekend evenings can get packed, so expect a wait.

The Prado, 1549 El Prado, San Diego, CA 92103; (619) 557-9441; pradobalboa.com; American; $$$. Located in the historic house of hospitality, and across from the Mingei and Railroad Museums, the Prado is a must-see tourist attraction. There is blown glass all around the front entrance, and different patterns are painted along the walls and ceiling. In addition to the central bar and lounge, there are two different eating sections inside. Take your pick from the cozy glass room or spacious courtyard. The heated patio is another nice dining option, where you can enjoy a fantastic view of the lush park-like surroundings. A graduate of the Culinary Institute of America in New York, Executive Chef Jonathan Hale never tires of creating dishes in his kitchen. For lunch, choose from great salads, sandwiches, fish tacos, burgers, and soups. The Kobe beef burger and the Kobe beef sushi roll are excellent afternoon choices. For dinner there's a little bit of everything ranging from seafood paella or Thai yellow curry chicken and red pepper pappardelle to your basic grilled bone-in rib eye. The dessert menu boasts several decadent delights, sure to complete your meal on the sweet side.

Saffron, 3731-B India St., San Diego, CA 92101; (619) 574-7737; saffronsandiego.com; Thai; $$. Born in Bangkok, Thailand, to Chinese parents, Chef-Owner Su-Mei Yu opened Saffron Thai Grilled Chicken in 1985 and Saffron Noodles and Saté in 2002 (located right next door). She grew up using cooking techniques handed down from her elders in Thailand, who believed foods have medicinal properties. With this knowledge, Su-Mei Yu made a name for herself with a cuisine specially designed to nourish the mind, body, and soul. The end result is fresh, seasonal, and nutritional fare made on a consistent basis. I recommend the Kung Pao chicken, spicy drunken noodles, and the rad-na wide noodles with beef. All stir-fried noodle and rice dishes can be made with mushroom oyster sauce and/or gluten-free soy sauce upon request for vegetarian and vegan customers. Don't leave without trying the sweet sticky rice with mango for dessert—I might have to eat my dessert first next time! The restaurant is located in a residential neighborhood, so street parking can sometimes be a challenge.

25 Forty Bistro & Bakehouse, 2540 Congress St., San Diego, CA 92110; (619) 294-2540; 25fortybistro.com; American; $$. Located in a quieter side of Old Town just 1 block from the State Park, this new dining destination is quickly gaining a loyal following, especially with a menu and cuisine that deviates from the Mexican influences of its neighbors. New York born and raised, 25 Forty's Chef-Owner Mark Pelliccia worked in top-rated restaurants throughout Italy. His international experience inspired him to create a menu boasting delicacies made with the freshest seasonal produce. From homemade braised duck fettuccine to pork chops with Fuji apples and sautéed spinach, his style has become very popular with the local crowd. Other favorites include bratwurst with homemade sauerkraut, braised pork belly with barbecue sauce, and pumpkin gnocchi with butter and poppy seeds. Admittedly, Pelliccia's true love in the kitchen is pastries. You can experience his love for sweets from a pastry display case located in the front of the restaurant. Choose from luscious cupcakes, vanilla custard turnovers, and apple crisp. After-dinner desserts include caramel panna cotta, chocolate cake with peanut butter custard, and Nutella crème brûlée.

Bertrand at Mister A's, 2550 5th Ave., San Diego, CA 92103; (619) 239-1377; bertrandatmisteras.com; American; $$$$. Located on the 12th floor of the 5th Avenue Financial Center building, experience modern American food with French and Mediterranean influences at this stunning penthouse restaurant just minutes from downtown. The dining room is light and bright with floor-to-ceiling windows boasting panoramic views of San Diego Bay, Balboa Park, Coronado, Point Loma, and even the world-famous San Diego Zoo. Dine alfresco on the heated outdoor patio. Offering a seasonal and revolving menu, Chef de Cuisine Stéphane Voitzwinkler sources all of his produce from Chino Farms in Rancho Santa Fe and varies his seafood use based on what is available from local purveyors. While French ingredients and techniques dominate, Voitzwinkler's German influence makes itself evident in dishes of spaetzel, choucroute, and house-made sausage. Light and simple preparations that offer a refined elegance include the pan-roasted quail salad with fresh herbs or the medley of shellfish "gratinee" with shrimp, scallops, clams, and mussels in Veloute. The flavorful edge of the cognac-lobster sauce is pure and unabashed in the Maine lobster strudel with forest mushrooms. Chef admits there is always plenty of delicious butter used in the creation of Mister A's dishes, even if it isn't always mentioned on the menu. Dress code is high-end, so beach attire and baseball caps are not allowed.

The Cosmopolitan Hotel and Restaurant, 2660 Calhoun St., San Diego, CA 92110; (619) 297-1874; oldtowncosmopolitan.com; American; $$$. The Cosmopolitan Hotel and Restaurant houses a full-service restaurant and bar, and is the only working hotel in Old Town San Diego State Historic Park. After a $6.5-million rehabilitation and restoration, the place still feels like you've stepped back in time. Imagine tying your horse out front and strolling into a fancy 1800s Western saloon and restaurant. Enjoy both indoor and alfresco dining at surprisingly affordable prices. Of course, the food is much better than what you might have received back in the old days. Chef Andrew Lee Sasloe brings his creative energy to this eatery where they grow their own fruits and herbs, make recipes from scratch, and serve hand-crafted drinks. A few special items are the fennel pollen-dusted Scottish salmon, espresso braised Kobe short rib, and apple-cider glazed Berkshire Pork cheeks. Mexican favorites are still on the menu, including traditional taco and burrito plates, enchiladas, and a root beer brined chicken chile relleno. Don't miss the warm and mouthwatering homemade churros! Open for lunch, dinner, and brunch.

El Indio, 3695 India St., San Diego, CA 92103; (619) 299-0385; el-indio.com; Mexican; $$. Founded at the corner of India and

Grape as a tortilla factory in August 1940, this was the place to get handmade corn tortillas and the taquito (little taco). In 1947, they moved to the current location, and you can savor the same Sonora-style Mexican dishes that have been served over the years, with no additives or preservatives. Tortillas are made fresh every day and are frequently used for care packages sent to soldiers stationed all over the world. It's owned and operated by the same family today, and the menu is so diverse, you'll need to visit more than once to experience the many different dishes. Taquito options include shredded beef, shredded chicken, or potato. Other traditional items include burritos, enchiladas, tostadas, quesadillas, chimichangas, and tamales. One of my favorites is the carne asada nachos deluxe, with plenty of guacamole, sour cream, and beans. Certainly not the lowest-fat option on the menu, but splurging every once in a while is one of life's pleasures. Be sure to ask for plenty of hot sauce!

Hob Nob Hill, 2271 1st Ave., San Diego, CA 92101; (619) 239-8176; hobnobhill.com; American; $$. Serving San Diegans since 1944, Hob Nob Hill has been producing breakfast, lunch, and dinner items using the same recipes handed down from the beginning. Nearly everything is prepared on the premises, from the baked items to cured meats. Its popularity has risen to the national stage, as it was featured in the popular Food Network series *Diners, Drive-Ins and Dives*, hosted by Guy Fieri. Sit in a comfortable booth by the window, or pick a stool right next to the kitchen. The menu is extensive and covers all of the great American favorites for a very reasonable price. For example, the old-fashioned chicken 'n' dumpling dinner includes your choice of soup or salad, a potato, vegetable, and fresh homemade bread. I have to confess, the chicken-fried steak with extra gravy is a dish that's hard to share with others at your table, so be prepared to defend yourself! The regulars will tell you it's just like Mom's kitchen, and since most modern moms don't cook this way anymore, it may be the best choice for a special meal from yesteryear.

Specialty Stores, Markets & Producers

Balboa International Market, 5907 Balboa Ave., San Diego, CA 92111; (858) 277-3600; balboamarket.com; Grocery/Market; $$. Located along bustling Balboa Avenue in north San Diego, this popular market offers international foods and products from diverse areas, including Persian, Arabic, Mediterranean, Russian, Eastern European, Turkish, and Spanish. Allow yourself plenty of time to browse through the aisles and gander at the many items available for your next meal. Stop here to purchase specialty ingredients, fruits, vegetables, and spices for a recipe. If you're in a hurry, consider the large list of hot foods available for a snack, meal, or party. I'm especially fond of the many kebabs available with a choice of filet mignon, lamb shank, seasoned chicken, or fish.

Catalina Offshore Products, Inc., 5202 Lovelock St., San Diego, CA 92110; (619) 297-9797; catalinaop.com; Grocery/Market; $$. It all started when professional diver Dave Rudie started diving for sea urchins and seaweed during the day, while wife Kathy processed them in their garage at night. Soon after, the demand grew to a point that fresh deliveries were regular enough to support a business. Rudie rented a processing plant part-time and hired a handful of employees to help him process the sea urchins. Twenty-five years later, Catalina Offshore has become one of the largest seafood import and export companies in California. This is one of the best places to buy fresh seafood from reputable fishermen, including fresh Dry Diver Bay scallops, colossal Baja white shrimp, and sea bass fillets. For beginners

wanting to try their hand at making sushi, there's a sushi-making kit available for purchase, complete with instructions. As for Dave and Kathy, they still run the business, making sure that top-of-the-line seafood and excellent customer service prevail.

Extraordinary Desserts, 2929 5th Ave., San Diego, CA 92103; (619) 294-2132; extraordinarydesserts.com; Desserts; $$. If you are searching for a fabulous dessert location, look no further than Extraordinary Desserts. Owner and Executive Chef Karen Krasne, considered the "Queen of Cakes" according to *Gourmet* magazine, opened her first Extraordinary Desserts in 1988 on 5th Avenue near Balboa Park. Since then, Extraordinary Desserts has become one of San Diego's most prominent and unique dining establishments and has expanded to include a second location in San Diego's Little Italy neighborhood, as well as a line of gourmet products and a robust online store. She uses organic ingredients whenever practical and possible, and always adorns each luxurious dessert with either locally grown fresh flowers, her signature edible gold leaf, stunning seasonal trimmings, or sinfully sweet sauces. It truly makes her unique creations a feast for the eyes as well as the palate. Krasne's cakes have graced the cover of *Bon Appétit* magazine, and Forbes recognized her as one of the country's 10 best pastry chefs. She has been featured in the *New York Times*, *Gourmet*, *Sunset*, and the *Los Angeles Times*, among other publications.

Iowa Meat Farms, 6041 Mission Gorge Rd., San Diego, CA 92120; (619) 281-5766; iowameatfarms.com; Grocery/Market; $$. This is one of the best butcher shops in town, offering USDA Prime and Choice Midwest beef, as well as many other varieties of meats, poultry, seafood, and more. I try to visit at least once a month to buy their phenomenal homemade sausage. From time to time, they also offer more unique meats, such as buffalo, elk, wild boar, and ostrich. The staff is extremely friendly and will help answer all of your questions. Bring in any recipe and they'll provide outstanding advice on the best cut of meat and ideas on how to prepare for optimum enjoyment. Some of their marinated meats, such as carne asada and pollo asado, are very popular. It's a whole new experience, especially if you're used to conversing with less-than-helpful and untrained staff at the local grocery. A full-service deli is also available at the co-owned Siesel's Meats, located on 4131 Ashton St.

Specialty Produce, 1929 Hancock St., Ste. 150, San Diego, CA 92110; (619) 295-3172; specialtyproduce.com; Grocery/Market; $$. As well as supplying fresh produce to local chefs and restaurants for years, this family-owned and -operated retail store is open to the public. Your shopping needs will be fully satisfied at this 32,000-square-foot warehouse, where more than a thousand varieties of produce are carried year-round, including organic, hard-to-find items and a full line of non-produce products. Items in stock include fresh herbs and greens, a variety of fruits and whole wheels of cheeses, quail and duck eggs, popcorn, and chocolate. The organic strawberries were sweeter than anything else I've tasted. Customers can order a weekly Farmers' Market

Bag with local, organic, and sustainably sourced produce from over a dozen farms each week.

Sweet Cheeks Baking Company, 4564 Alvarado Canyon Rd., Ste. A, San Diego, CA 92120; (619) 285-1220; sweetcheeksbaking .com; Desserts; $$. This is not a store but a commercial kitchen. Place an order by phone in advance and pick up your goodies. Bakers like to incorporate a healthy aspect to the sweets here, sourcing locally, cage-free eggs, whole grains, flaxseed, whole wheat flour, and nuts and seeds. They sell cakes for every occasion, breakfast breads, cheesecakes, fruit tarts, cupcakes, and more. The popular European Tosca Cake, an almond tea cake that originated in Sweden, is available by the half-sheet, bars, or mini-bite, also available in lemon, blueberry, and cranberry-orange during the fall. Their tea cake (an almond cake with inspiration from Sweden) is made into little, bite-size bars or larger-size treats. Popular cake flavors include a family recipe carrot cake (featured on Food Network) and fresh banana cake filled with peanut butter and fudge swirl. The chewy chocolate cheek cookies are a big hit!

Temecula Olive Oil Company, 2754 Calhoun St., San Diego, CA 92110; (619) 269-5779; temeculaoliveoil.com; Olive Oil; $$. Temecula Olive Oil Company grows, bottles, and presses all of their oils and balsamic vinegars at their ranch in Aguanga, California. They have 4 locations: Old Town San Diego, Old Town Temecula, Seal Beach, and Solana Beach. They only carry extra-virgin olive oil that is first-pressed and cold-pressed. The most popular brand they

sell, available all year long, is the fresh basil and roasted garlic olive oil. Seasonal flavored oils and vinegars are also available throughout the year. Whole olives are big sellers, especially the olives stuffed with blue cheese, Parmesan, spicy garlic, or oregano and feta cheese. Body products made with the second pressing include soaps, lotions, and shampoos. They also sell herbs, spices, and sea salts from their own ranch or other local growers. A complimentary tasting allows customers to pick and choose different oils, or opt for the full tasting to experience a wider selection.

Hillcrest, North Park, South Park & Kensington

This cluster of neighborhoods immediately north of downtown collectively defines Uptown San Diego. It is a densely populated area that has undergone significant revitalization over the years. Tree-lined streets, compact blocks, and a walkable business district make it a popular choice among locals. It is predominantly a single-family residence area with small apartment buildings and bungalows, and is noteworthy for its varied collection of Craftsman and Spanish Colonial Revival style homes built between 1905 and 1930. It is one of the oldest communities in San Diego, and grew tremendously in the early 1900s, thanks to the new streetcar/ trolley system connecting this area to downtown. The Hillcrest neighborhood includes a large sampling of unique restaurants, trendy stores, salons, medical offices, and two major hospitals.

North Park is an architect's dream, with many styles in view, including Craftsman, California Bungalow, Spanish and Mission Revival, Prairie, and Mediterranean. The main business corridor is along 30th Street (north-south) and University Avenue (east-west). Restaurants, coffee shops, bars, and nightclubs are alive with energy at night. Don't look for chain and franchise businesses in this area, as many independents call it home. A number of national magazines have recognized 30th Street as one of the best boulevards to enjoy locally sourced craft beer. Everything is within easy walking distance.

Foodie Faves

Alchemy, 1503 30th St., San Diego, CA 92102; (619) 255-0616; alchemysandiego.com; California Modern; $$$. This sophisticated, yet casual neighborhood restaurant offers anything but a simple meal. Drawing on different cultures from all over the world, Executive Chef Ricardo Heredia likes to focus on street food and tapas-style entrees meant for sharing. Exclusive signature dishes include the crispy taro tacos stuffed with braised pork belly, spicy cucumbers, bacon, salt, and micro cilantro and the piquillo rellenos, Spanish peppers stuffed with barbecue pulled pork. Interesting theme dinners include a weekly Vegetarian Farm Dinner consisting of three seasonal courses and a monthly Dinner with Six Strangers featuring a surprise menu from the chef. Get your friends together for the Suckling Pig Group Dinner, which serves 8 to 12 people and showcases a whole suckling pig, cooked Cuban style at the restaurant in a La Caja China Roasting Box for 3½ to 4 hours. Choose from 20 wines by the glass as well as local craft beers and old-style craft cocktails with an updated twist. Night owls can enjoy a late night, loungy style scene. Best of all, you won't find a dish priced over $25.

Big Kitchen, 3003 Grape St., San Diego, CA 92102; (619) 234-5789; bigkitchencafe.com; American; $$. A bit of trivia here is that Whoopie Goldberg signed a wall in the kitchen here where she used to work alongside Owner Judy Foreman, better known as "The Beauty" On Duty. All trivia aside, you should pay this place a visit for a darn good breakfast at darn good prices! A counter and booths in this diner-type setting makes for great conversation with the staff and other guests. Mainstays on the menu have kept the locals coming back time and time again. Get your share of biscuit and sausage gravy, bacon, bleu cheese, eggs, and mushrooms frittata, tofu rancheros—sautéed veggies and tofu on a corn tortilla with salsa and cheese. They bake their own muffins and coffeecake. They also honey bake their own hams and fresh roast their own turkey breasts.

Bleu Boheme, 4090 Adams Ave., San Diego, CA 92116; (619) 255-4167; bleuboheme.com; French; $$$. If you're a fiend for French food, this is the place for you! Reminiscent of a French neighborhood bistro with country charm, this blue-tinted Kensington restaurant has a rustic charm all its own. Striving to offer fresh, organic, sustainable, and local ingredients, Chef-Owner Ken Irvine allows the food to speak for itself. Put his Boeuf Bourguignon on your 500-things-to-eat-before-you-die list. This Thunder Ridge Beef simmered in red wine, mushrooms, and smoked bacon is as authentic as it gets. The addition of carrots, baby potatoes, and caramelized pearl onions is so decadent, it's easy to forget you're eating your vegetables. And every bit of sauce begs to be sopped up with a crusty French bread—yes, it's that good! If that entire flavor isn't enough for you, ask for the melted Camembert Fondue cheese in a box. With a pleasant kick of Calvados brandy, sliced apple, and baguette croutons, it'll knock you for a loop—in a good way!

Brazen BBQ, 441 Washington St., San Diego, CA 92103; (619) 816-1990; brazenbbq.com; Barbecue; $$. What just might be the best darn smokehouse in Hillcrest is turning heads and searing tongues with scintillating sauces, homemade rubs, real hardwood smoke, and low-and-slow cooking methods. Entrepreneurial Chefs John Bracamonte and Brad Thomas brought Brazen BBQ Smokehouse & Bar to life after competing against some of the nation's best barbecue chefs on the national barbecue circuit. They received rave reviews from the judges, earning many awards, including the

California BBQ Association's 2009 Top 10 Team of the Year and 1st place Rookie of the Year. Using Southern-style barbecue techniques, these smoke pit experts take their job very seriously, offering up anything from Cajun hotlinks and a Texas-style barbecue Reuben to Louisiana-style catfish, brisket stroganoff, and a bacon-wrapped meat loaf fattie. Two types of barbecue sauce are bottled up on each table, right next to a necessary roll of paper towels.

Busalacchi's A Modo Mio, 3707 5th Ave., San Diego, CA 92103; (619) 298-0119; busalacchis.com; Italian; $$$. The Busalacchi family has been a mainstay in the San Diego restaurant community for decades. Now two generations are working together in presenting the latest white-linen classy eatery in uptown San Diego. Whether you choose the intimate dining room or spacious open-air terrace, you'll find the cuisine and service impeccable. As you would expect, the dishes are prepared with profound pride from a self-taught expert who travels to visit relatives in Italy on a regular basis, learning new ideas and remembering century-old traditions. Don't look for new age or fusion cuisine here. Everything on the menu is created in the style you would expect from nana's kitchen including homemade fettuccine with a beef and pork bolognese ragu, veal with mushrooms, or trout with lemon butter and oregano. Be sure to call ahead if you're planning to visit on a weekend night.

Cafe 21, 2736 Adams Ave., San Diego, CA 92116; (619) 640-2121; cafe-21.com; American; $$. Owners Alex and Leyla, from Baku, Azerbaijan, have put their heart and soul into this diminutive eatery in Hillcrest. Don't be fooled by the worn-down exterior and neighboring businesses, as you'll be pleasantly surprised when passing through the front door. Significant work has led to a modernized interior that provides an upbeat atmosphere. Regulars come here to savor exotic and flavorful foods, as well as attentive staff willing to converse about any subject. The menu is considered "New American cuisine" and includes signature homemade flatbread sandwiches, fresh organic salads, hearty breakfasts, and a wide selection of coffees, teas, wine, and beer. I like to come here for breakfast to enjoy their rendition of french toast "Azeri style," stuffed with a mascarpone and ricotta cream cheese filling. It makes a perfect pair with one of their robust coffees or wide selection of organic teas. For dinner, choose the Azerbaijani-style kabob platter with house-made lamb sausage, Azeri seasoned chicken, and beef kabobs served over curry almond basmati rice pilaf with their special house dip and pickled vegetables. Other popular items are the stuffed cabbage rolls and rosemary trout. Space is limited, so you may need to wait on the busier mornings or evenings.

Caffé Calabria, 3933 30th St., San Diego, CA 92104; (619) 291-1759; caffecalabria.com; Italian; $$. Founder Arne Holt has made his dream a reality for 15 years. Proud to roast the finest coffee on-site for his patrons, the aromas as you enter the door are unmistakable. Coffee is roasted in small batches on-site at this comfortable cafe centrally located in North Park. From espresso extraction to milk texturing, skilled baristas are busy over buzzing espresso machines making you the perfect cup of joe. One taste of my cappuccino convinced me that I would never buy beans in a grocery store ever again. This wonderful little cafe also offers plenty of excellent food to enjoy, including pastries, antipasti, salads, paninis, and desserts, but the biggest draw from the young locals is the authentic Neapolitan pizza and calzone, baked in a wood-fire oven for that distinctive crispy crunch. Italian wine and beer are also available.

Carnitas' Snack Shack, 2632 University Ave., San Diego, CA 92104; (619) 294-7675; carnitassnackshack.com; American; $$. Chef-Owner Hanis Cavin decided to open a shack named after his pet mini pig Carnitas. Funny thing is, he features other pigs on the menu, just not his! Take it from me, one visit to this Snack Shack just isn't enough. With a menu that changes daily, you can go back many times to try items you may have missed days before. Order your food at the walk-up window and enjoy it on a covered patio in the back; heat lamps included. Of course you can get your order to go. All-natural, hormone-free, Vande Rose Farms Duroc pork comes from family farmers in Iowa Falls, Iowa. If you love BLTs, try the extra-special decked-out version with bacon and crispy ham, festooned with an extra-tasty aioli on brioche bread. Other piggy portioned standouts include a juicy pulled pork loin sandwich and pork belly with sweet spicy glaze and an apple and radish frisee salad. If eating Porky Pig just isn't your thing, there are steak, burger, chicken, and veggie options from time to time.

El Take It Easy, 3926 30th St., San Diego, CA 92104; (619) 291-1859; eltakeiteasy.com; Mexican; $$. Take it easy and experience music and Mexican Wine Country cuisine at this neighborhood cantina that's always filled with guests laughing and chatting it up over food made with local produce and seafood, and independently raised pastured meats. There's never a shortage of beverage here with local wines from San Diego and Baja California, local beers, craft cocktails, artisanal mezcal, tequila, American whiskey, and other spirits. Small plates give you a chance to try unusual food suspects like pig ears, fried local rabbit leg, Baja octopus puffs, fried oysters, and duck confit taquitos. The gnocchi with butternut squash sauce is a standout and they offer a tender and juicy grass-fed cheeseburger that's hard to pass up. There are unique specials going on six days a week including Manhattan Monday, Taco Tuesday, Vegetarian Farm Night Wednesday, Oyster Thursday, El Make It Funky Friday offering changing drink specials, and Carnitas Sunday. If you like El Take It Easy, you might also like their farm-to-table, brats-and-beer palace, **The Linkery** (p. 196).

Farmhouse Cafe, 2121 Adams Ave., San Diego, CA 92116; (619) 269-9662; farmhousecafesd.com; French; $$$. This beautiful little bistro in Uptown has everything you would expect from an authentic farmhouse in France, including subtle lighting, softly painted brick walls, old-world wooden table and chairs, and a cozy patio that's perfect on a summer evening. Husband-and-wife team Oliver and Rochelle Bioteau work eagerly to ensure that your experience is perfectly enjoyable. The menu is simple and straightforward, changing seasonally to take advantage of the freshest local ingredients. Whether you choose one of the meat or fresh fish entrees, you're sure to be pleased with the combination of flavors bursting from the plate. During my visit, they offered a wonderful hanger steak with blue cheese butter, caramelized shallots, and Kennebec potato fries. The presentation was stunning. A focused list of wines and beer are also available.

Hash House A Go Go, 3628 5th Ave., San Diego, CA 92103; (619) 298-4646; hashhouseagogo.com; American; $$$. Bar none, this is one of the best places to come if you are really hungry and love gigantic-size portions of twisted farm food with a Southwestern flare. I hate to sound redundant, but it's basically comfort food with a twist. The inside of this restaurant is a great place to watch everything go down. They play really loud music, including rock and roll, and the tables are really close together. Large portions are served on surf board plates and are easily sharable. Farm Benedicts with homemade sauces of chipotle, chili, and barbecue cream are popular for breakfast. Your mama's fried chicken is now Andy's Sage Fried Chicken with a bacon waffle tower drizzled with hot maple reduction and fried leeks. They are well known for their Bloody Marys made with their own house-made spices. Reservations are recommended especially for large groups.

The Linkery, 3794 30th St., San Diego, CA 92104; (619) 255-8778; thelinkery.com; American; $$$. Some restaurants claim that they are "farm to table," but The Linkery epitomizes this philosophy. Nearly all of the produce they utilize is sourced from local farms. Their poultry, chicken, beef, veal, and lamb are pasture-raised and grass-fed animals. All of the fish is wild caught, and the shellfish is either wild-harvested in Baja or farm-raised in Carlsbad. They also prepare their own sausage and cured meats. Can you really tell the difference? Absolutely! A great example is the coq au vin: pastured chicken thigh with red wine reduction, roasted potatoes and carrots, pancetta, mushrooms, and olives. For a truly unique lunch, pick one of their sausage sandwiches, with a choice of Polish, hot Italian, bucyrus bratwurst, kasekrainer, porkstachio, knackwurst, or chicken roasted garlic. They even have a one-page "Linkipedia" on their menu to help describe the ingredients in more detail. The beverage offerings are just as impressive. Ten taps and a cask serve rotating craft microbrews, and a large selection of special bottled beers are also available. Local keg wine is served by the glass and carafe, in addition to an impressive wine list. Even the coffee and tea are sourced from local companies.

Local Habit, 3827 5th Ave., San Diego, CA 92103; (619) 795-4770; MyLocalHabit.com; American; $$. Featuring organic food and local craft beer and wine, look for small, sharable plates and notable pizzas at this eatery in Hillcrest. Utilizing seasonal produce from local farms, Chef and Co-owner Nick Brune likes to add a Creole and Cajun-style touch to his kitchen masterpieces. Specials change nightly or on the chef's whim, and can include anything from a red kale butternut squash pizza with braised bacon to a special gumbo featured monthly or black-eyed peas with stewed tomato. Brune uses Eden Farms pork to make the house-cured bacon and sausages, which are perfectly spiced and flavorful, especially the cured pork loin with roasted cabbage and apple reduction. In addition to all the gluten-free dishes on their menu, they also serve a number of vegetarian and vegan dishes to accommodate individuals with particular dietary restrictions. For a gluten-free pizza, try the California quattro formaggio pizza with Petaluma mozzarella, Spring Hill goat cheddar, and Jack and aged Gouda cheeses. The Cali-Creole Sunday brunch is a big hit!

Mama Testa Taqueria, 1417 University Ave., San Diego, CA 92103; (619) 298-8226; mamatestataqueria.com; Mexican; $$. Get great authentic Mexican food at Mama Testa Taqueria, where they claim to serve a "new generation of old-fashioned cooking." The recipes and presentation are exactly as you would find in taquerias throughout Mexico. Owner Cesar Gonzalez appeared on Bobby Flay's TV show *Bobby Flay's Throwdown* and beat him in a fish taco challenge! Using only high-quality ingredients, Gonzalez makes his fish tacos with catfish. They also serve unique mashed potato tacos that are phenomenal. Although not on the printed menu, I always request the potato taco topped with their house-made chorizo, made from scratch every day, and a flavor combination that is second to none. Another extremely popular item is the unique Tacomal: two corn tortilla tacos filled with nopales and melted cotija and manchego cheese, cooked "tamal style" and covered in warm pasilla salsa. They also have a successful catering option that feeds many businesses and parties in the area. Check out his website for a view of his audition video and portions of the TV episode.

Muzita, 4651 Park Blvd., San Diego, CA 92116; (619) 546-7900; muzita.com; African; $$$. Sharing a traditional Abyssinian (Eritrean/Ethiopian) meal with family and friends at this hospitable neighborhood hideaway in University Heights is nothing short of a tasty adventure. When you enter, you can immediately smell the aroma of spices and homemade cooking coming from the kitchen. Dine inside or on the cozy outdoor patio while listening to African music and discussing the East African decor. Since Owner Abel Woldemichael is from Eritrea, a country in northeast Africa, he offers authentic family recipes reminiscent of the old country. A knowledgeable waitstaff will guide you through the menu. Most of the dishes contain exotic spices such as cardamom, coriander, and cloves. Diners can opt to share large platters of food, served family style. Don't worry about reaching for a fork; use your hands and eat the food the traditional way. An Ethiopian staple, the injera bread is made from a grain called "teff" (one of the smallest grains in the world). It has a spongy, pancake-like texture, and guests tear off the bread, one piece at a time, to scoop up the food. One of the most popular dishes with the guests is the *kitfo*. It is raw (or rare) hand-minced beef with marinade rub in *mitmita* (a spicy seasoning).

Parkhouse Eatery, 4574 Park Blvd., San Diego, CA 92116; (619) 295-7275; parkhouseeatery.com; American; $$$. Parkhouse Eatery is a laid-back, yet well-designed neighborhood eatery closely nestled into the house that once held the St. Vincent de Paul thrift store. Dining options include an outdoor garden patio, a window-lit living room, and what the locals refer to as a comfy and cozy "hearth room" with a wood-burning fireplace. Incorporating free-range eggs and mostly organic vegetables, it's back to the comfort food basics with generous portions of fancy scrambles and blue cornmeal flapjacks offered for breakfast. Well-executed lunch specialties include delicious salads, sandwiches, and entrees. I recommend the griddled turkey meat loaf sandwich with hand-cut russet french fries with homemade chunky ketchup. Straightforward dinner options include steaks, seafood, poultry, and lamb as well as pizza and pastas. The popular five-mushroom polenta cake surpasses all expectations!

The Red Door Restaurant & Wine Bar, 741 W. Washington St., San Diego, CA 92103; (619) 295-6000; thereddoorsd.com; American; $$$. This award-winning bistro in the flourishing Uptown area is quickly gaining a reputation for serving classic American comfort food. Have a seat inside this cozy Cape Cod–inspired cottage eatery and enjoy one of the specialty cocktails or glass of wine from a small production vineyard in California. Harvesting his own ingredients each morning from The Red Door Family Garden on Mt. Helix, Executive Chef Miguel Valdez offers a seasonal menu that's bursting with flavor. To start your experience, be sure to order the homemade corn bread muffins, made with fresh summer corn, mild green chilis, aged white cheddar, and served with their signature rosemary honey butter. One of the most popular dinner items is the savory chicken roulade, an organic breast of meat stuffed with prosciutto and sautéed spinach and served with cauliflower puree, roasted marble potatoes, baby carrots, and pearl onions, finished with a port wine reduction.

Sabuku Sushi, 3027 Adams Ave., San Diego, CA 92116; (619) 733-0430; sabukusushi.com; Japanese; $$$. Nestled in Normal Heights, this contemporary neighborhood sushi bar continues to surprise diners with time-honored sushi rolls and a unique blend of Japanese cuisine with an American flare. In addition to classic nigiri, sashimi, and rolls, Proprietor and Chef Bob Pasela has developed a knack for pairing fresh and unique ingredients that exhibit a wide range of flavors. Two standout examples are the Bacon and Scallop Roll, and the signature Chillaxin Roll, made with shrimp tempura, spicy crab, a spicy ginger aioli glaze, and baked Chilean sea bass. In addition, Sabuku Sushi makes it a point to carry traditional filtered and unfiltered sakes, along with flavor-infused versions with hints of plum, Asian pear, and coconut lemongrass. Even the cocktails are infused with sake, like the Mimosa Ke, a combination of sparkling sake and orange juice. Visually, Sabuku Sushi takes a minimalist approach with a modern atmosphere designed to calm and soothe. Sleek metal accents, dark wood tables, and large windows provide a panoramic view of the street and allow natural light to flood the space.

Sea Rocket Bistro, 3382 30th St., San Diego, CA 92104; (619) 255-7049; searocketbistro.com; California Modern; $$$. On a corner in North Park lies this little restaurant with a big heart for supporting local farmers, anglers, and ranchers that raise their animals responsibly and humanely. Executive Chef Tommy Fraioli, who comes from a large, multigenerational Italian family, is passionate about his profession, keeping the restaurant menu breathing with live sea urchin with lavender sea salt, sardines al' Italiano with broccoli rabe, Mediterranean-style fisherman's stew, and the infamous sea-rocket grass-fed burger. The very cool and locally sourced oysters on the half-shell are served with a lavish house-made mignonette sauce. Award-winning local craft beers and California wines will enhance your experience here even further, and the conspicuous sea urchin gelato for dessert is definitely something you'll want to write home about! See Chef Fraioli's recipe for **Mac n' Blue** on p. 356.

The Smoking Goat, 3408 30th St., San Diego, CA 92104; (619) 955-5295; thesmokinggoatrestaurant.com; French; $$$. Small in stature and surrounded by plenty of choices in the North Park area, this cute bistro stands tall. Trendy artwork adorns the walls, and soft lighting helps set the mood. Serving what they call "French & American countryside fare," the meals are made from fresh, simple ingredients, but prepared with modern influences. No matter what you order, be prepared to enjoy the highest quality meats and produce. The local organic beet salad and butternut squash ravioli that I enjoyed one night were tremendous. There are usually a few uncommon meat dishes available for the adventurous. The wine and beer list changes regularly and include some interesting labels worth trying.

Taste of Thai, 527 University Ave., San Diego, CA 92103; (619) 291-7525; tasteofthaisandiego.com; Thai; $$$. Opened as one of the first vegetarian restaurants in San Diego, Taste of Thai was instantly home in the eclectic Uptown area. Established when Thai cuisine in Southern California was still in the fledgling stages, its popularity has increased significantly, resulting in numerous awards nearly every year. With a bright and elegant dining room, you'll find the service prompt and courteous. However, it can be very crowded on any given day, and for good reason. Locals are in love with cuisine that is fresh, spicy, and full of flavor. You'll notice the quality and freshness of ingredients in every dish. Their fresh spring rolls are a perfect example. Light-as-air rice paper is stuffed with lettuce, bean sprouts, mint, vermicelli noodles, and shrimp (or tofu) and served with a special house sauce. Two of my favorite entrees are the vegetarian/tofu hot basil, with green pepper, onion, chili, and garlic; and the spicy duck, a half duck topped with green pepper and green beans, served in a sweet and spicy curry sauce. After all of that delicious spicy food, don't forget to order the classic fried banana and ice cream. A perfect ending to the meal!

Urban Eats Plates + Bar, 3850 5th Ave., San Diego, CA 92103; (619) 729-4588; urbaneatspb.com; American; $$. Combining all-natural meats and locally sourced ingredients, Owner and Executive Chef Chris Sayre likes to focus on classic dishes as well as putting his own unique twist on traditional comfort food entrees. Good eats include Angus meat loaf with wild mushroom jus, Kobe beef tacos, pork sliders, sesame-crusted ahi with wasabi smashed potatoes, and the steak + blue sandwich. A relaxed atmosphere at this urban-industrial-inspired restaurant lends natural wood tones and historical artwork from the San Diego Historical Society. A great happy hour offers a nice selection of house red and white wines and local craft beers. Urban Eats also offers a kids' menu with classics including grilled cheese, quesadillas, and turkey and peanut butter + jelly sandwiches.

Urban Solace, 3823 30th St., San Diego, CA 92104; (619) 295-6464; urbansolace.net; American; $$$. With acclaimed Chef-Owner Matt Gordon at the helm, Urban Solace has gained a following that makes this North Park eatery a star among its peers. The building design is reminiscent of a New Orleans French Quarter hideaway, with narrow, wrought-iron balconies and an internal open-air courtyard dimly lit at night with sprinkling lights throughout the space. Equally impressive is the philosophy for sourcing every ingredient used in the cuisine. From the meat and seafood to the produce, and all the way down to the condiments, everything is natural and locally produced whenever possible. The wine and craft beer offerings are extensive and highlight many of the superb West Coast labels. Lunch and dinner items concentrate on traditional American cuisine with a unique flair. On any given night, nearly every table will start with one of the most popular items, the warm cheese biscuits with orange-honey butter. The menu changes seasonally but concentrates on familiar American comfort food dishes. They also serve an entertaining brunch every Sunday, with live bluegrass music in the courtyard and plenty of tasty menu items, including butter-pecan french toast with maple sausage and fresh fruit, biscuits 'n' gravy with sausage, brown sugar slab bacon and eggs, and the Brandt Farms Beef Cheek Hash with poached eggs and ancho chili hollandaise. Dinner and Sunday brunch get very crowded, but it's certainly worth the wait.

URBN Coal Fired Pizza, 3085 University Ave., San Diego, CA 92104; (619) 255-7300; urbnnorthpark.com; Pizza; $$$. Joe Mangini opened the doors to URBN Coal Fired Pizza in Vista in 2008 and, most recently, a second location in the progressive North Park neighborhood. Taking up a 5,000-square-foot space, this restaurant specializes in coal-fired thin-crust pizzas, local craft beers, Italian wines, and a selection of fine tequilas. The pizzas come with toppings you've most likely never eaten before. White pies are topped with anything from fresh clams and Parmesan cheese to mashed potato and pancetta. I also love the red pies, especially one topped with gorgonzola-stuffed cherry peppers and fresh mozzarella or the meatball pie with sautéed red onion and ricotta. Of course the coal-fired wings aren't too shabby either!

The Wellington Steak and Martini Lounge, 729 W. Washington St., San Diego, CA 92103; (619) 295-6001; thewellingtonsd.com; Steak House; $$$$. This small and intimate space is perfect when you're looking for a romantic night in a supper club. Located in the vibrant Uptown district, this establishment balances the local energy with stylishness of a classical steak house. Sink into your seat in the dining room and get ready for a special meal. Be sure to start with one of the many martinis available, from all-time classics like the Manhattan and Bombay Dirty, to new versions like the Jose Suave, a combination of Serrano-infused vodka, Tabasco olive juice, and olives. The wine list has representatives from around the globe, including well-known to more obscure labels. For dinner, start with my favorite, the house wedge salad: iceberg lettuce, crispy pancetta, sun-dried tomatoes, house-made croutons, crumbled blue cheese, and Maytag blue cheese dressing. Of course, if you've made the trek to this quaint eatery, you must try their most popular namesake dish, the beef Wellington. Although not seen regularly in any restaurant these days, it's easy to see why it was a staple in older days. The current preparation starts with an organic filet mignon and cremini mushroom duxelle, then is wrapped in puff pastry and finished with a madeira-shiitake mushroom sauce and garden vegetables. Truly special.

Specialty Stores, Markets & Producers

Bite San Diego, 770 11th Ave., San Diego, CA 92101; (619) 634-8476; bitesandiego.com; American; $$$. Owner Rebecca Bamberger is the genius behind Bite San Diego, Hillcrest's only food walking tour. The food tasting and cultural walking tour, led by experienced tour guides, covers some of the neighborhood's best restaurants. Taste great food while learning about the history and reasons San Diego is quickly becoming a food fantasy mecca for locals and visitors alike. With tours scheduled every Saturday and Sunday starting at 1 p.m., Bite San Diego–Hillcrest will take up to 15 guests on a 1.5-mile tour of 6 noted restaurants. Each restaurant will offer a generous taste of a dish and/or beverage, and guests will be treated to an overview of the establishment's highlights and cuisine. Tickets are $45 per person and must be booked in advance and online through Bite San Diego's website. Additional "Bite" Tours are held in Downtown San Diego, Coronado, Old Town, and La Jolla San Diego.

Bread & Cie, 350 University Ave., San Diego, CA 92103; (619) 683-9322; breadandcie.com; Bakery; $$. Established for nearly 2 decades, Bread & Cie was the first artisan bread bakery in San Diego. As a testament to their high-quality product, they are now baking daily for over 150 dining and shopping venues in the county, and offer bread and pastries to restaurants, markets, caterers, and hotels. It's hard to resist the luscious pastries and fresh-baked bread aroma that this specialty bakery provides. For breakfast, sip on a tall cappuccino paired with a cream cheese Danish, or the decadent french toast panini stuffed with mascarpone fruit compote. Soups, salads, and specialty sandwiches are available for lunch. My husband's fave is the roasted portobello mushroom sandwich served on rosemary-olive oil bread, packed with portobellos, zucchini, onions, and Parmesan cheese.

Cafe Bassam, 3088 5th Ave., San Diego, CA 92103; (619) 557-0173; cafebassam.com; Coffee/Tea; $$. Since 1991, Cafe Bassam has been a well-known wine and tearoom as well as coffee bar. As you walk in, you first notice the atmosphere and decor, which is very old-fashioned. Many antiques to look at and very rustic; you almost feel like you are taking a peek into the 1920s era. There are chairs with tables and a couch to lounge on while you drink a large beverage of your choice. Secondly, you see the pastry case filled with delicious sweets that are paired very well with any drink you choose. Located on 5th Avenue and nestled away in Hillcrest San Diego, it's the perfect place to grab a hot drink or a decadent pastry and socialize while being in the city. Ordering the raved-about chai latte, the first thing you'll notice is how huge the cup is. The chai is foaming and delicate tasting, not too sweet yet not over powerful with flavor. Other favorites are their dark hot chocolate as well as their very wide range of teas that they provide. Come here for a great, dimly lit atmosphere that's perfect for a pit stop on the way to a movie or somewhere to just simply relax.

Chocolat Bistro—Creperie—Cremerie, 3896 5th Ave., San Diego, CA 92103; (619) 574-8500; chocolat-hillcrest.com; Desserts; $$. Born in Milan, Italy, with its debut American location in San Diego, Chocolat entices patrons with authentic Italian gelato, warm and delicious homemade crepes, wood-fire pizza, handmade pastas, and paninis. Alessandro Minutella, the founder of the US Chocolat concept, showcases authentic recipes and time-honored traditions of Italy's gelato and pastry artistry. Two dozen gelato flavors made from top-of-the-line ingredients include amaretto chocolate, nutellone, honey and poppy seed cream, and fruit flavors like mango, lemon strawberry, wild strawberry, basil lemon, and chocolate pear. Available daily, a new all-day brunch features a wide variety of offerings, including sticky macadamia and apples, consisting of grilled panettone stuffed with baked apples, honey, macadamia nuts, and mini marshmallows. There is an additional location in the heart of the Gaslamp Quarter. See the recipe for **Sticky Macadamia and Apples** on p. 353.

Eclipse Chocolat, 2121 El Cajon Blvd., San Diego, CA 92104; (619) 578-2984; eclipsechocolat .com; Desserts; $$. Driven by high standards, Eclipse is a special company with exquisite products. Just read their mission statement: "to provide premium artisan foods & confections with a unique culinary perspective while maintaining sustainable & ethical operations and contributing to our local community." They source all of their chocolate from the famed Guittard Chocolate of San Francisco,  a family-owned company in business for 150 years. Quality and sustainability are paramount, as the company does its part to give back to the farmers and environment. In addition to being avid recyclers, they only use corn-based and post-consumer paper products for their consumer containers. They pride themselves in preparing and packaging all of their products by hand. Entering their small cafe is an experience akin to a child's dream. Enjoy a variety of drinking chocolates, dessert trays, and espresso drinks.

Their most popular items are the creme fraiche cupcakes in 24 different flavors with either dark chocolate or vanilla butter cake, a special filling, and chocolate ganache glaze. Once a month they also offer a full-service three-course tasting dinner that incorporates chocolate, vanilla bean, or caramel in each plating. Wine and beer are available to pair with your dishes. Be sure to reserve a table in advance. Many of their products are available online or at exclusive retail stores in several states.

Heaven Sent Desserts, 3001 University Ave., San Diego, CA 92104; (619) 793-4758; heavensentdesserts.com; Desserts; $$. Located in North Park, Heaven Sent Desserts offers a varied dessert and coffee menu, provides catering, and creates custom specialty cakes of any size and shape to perfectly match the clients' needs. Everything is baked and prepared at the Heaven Sent Desserts kitchen, and only the freshest and finest quality ingredients are used. This contemporary bakery takes pride in each item on the menu, which changes constantly with seasonal trends and flavor, such as the vanilla lychee sponge cake with lavender icing in the spring. Visiting the glass case will make you feel like a small child in a candy store—so many choices and not enough room to eat them all. Old-time favorites include bourbon bread pudding and red velvet vixen cake. They can create any cake you desire; just ask.

Coronado, Harbor Island, Shelter Island & Point Loma

Although not technically part of the downtown core, this cluster of coastal communities resides in a unique area between the Pacific Ocean and San Diego Bay.

Harbor Island and Shelter Island are located on the north and west sides of San Diego Bay. These man-made peninsulas are lined with marinas, hotels, restaurants, and an exclusive yacht club. Views from every possible location are absolutely stunning, looking across the bay at downtown San Diego. Situated between the centrally located International Airport (Lindberg Field) and the Coronado Naval Air Station, you're bound to see (and hear) a variety of aircraft zooming overhead. This is an amazing opportunity to sample upscale cuisine on the waterfront. Don't be surprised to see boaters mooring at specially designed landings right next to your balcony table. Daily charter fishing boats are also available, if you're interested in catching your own dinner.

At the most western end of the bay is the long, hilly peninsula of Point Loma, which is sandwiched between the bay and Pacific Ocean. Often described as "where California began," this area was discovered by the first European expedition to land in 1542. Don't miss the Cabrillo National Monument and Old Point Loma Lighthouse at the very southern tip. Liberty Station is a modern retail and commercial center built on the site of the former Naval Training Center. Several excellent restaurants are located in this area as well as a large waterfront park.

Located on a small peninsula directly across the bay from downtown is Coronado, an oasis that can be accessed via the landmark Coronado Bridge, or along the thin isthmus dubbed the Silver Strand that leads to the South County area. This is one of the most expensive places to live in the US, and for good reason. No matter where you reside in this town, you're within walking distance of the Pacific Ocean as well as San Diego Bay. When the legendary Hotel del Coronado opened in 1888, this town officially became a major resort destination. Orange Avenue is the main street through the town and is lined with restaurants, shops, theaters, and hotels. For a real treat, take the ferry between downtown San Diego and Coronado, where you can easily travel by foot (or bike) to all of the major attractions.

Candelas, 416 3rd Ave., San Diego, CA 92101; (619) 702-4455; candelas-coronado.com; Mexican; $$$$. With stunning views of the San Diego skyline through floor-to-ceiling windows, this romantic and elegant hacienda on Coronado serves "Mexico City" cuisine, just steps from the Coronado Ferry Landing. The blending of French techniques and Mexican ingredients makes this a unique dining destination for upscale food, especially paired with the impressive wine list. A great example on the appetizer menu is the Crema Fabiola, a wonderfully creamy poblano chile soup surrounding a tiny half lobster tail and mashed potatoes. Or the main entree Langosta Baeza, a lobster tail flambéed in tequila and placed atop a sauté of bacon, mushrooms, and jalapeños. Happy hour is quite popular at this location, both for the quality of items on the menu, as well as decent prices.

Corvette Diner, 2965 Historic Decatur Rd., San Diego, CA 92106; (619) 542-1476; cohnrestaurants.com; American; $$. If you're looking for a quiet, romantic evening, this is certainly *not* the place to visit! But I have to admit, it's one of my secret indulgences when I am craving good, 1950s diner food with plenty of free entertainment. Lots of chrome, flashing lights, waitresses with bouffant hairdos and poodle skirts, and plenty of singing and laughing. This destination is as much about the atmosphere as the food. My recommendation? Go for the chocolate-peanut butter-banana malt and Dante's Inferno Burger, with jalapeño mayo, pepper jack cheese, lettuce, tomato, onion, and jalapeños. Another option is to forget dinner and just order the gigantic brownie hot fudge sundae or banana split boat. Either one will blow your calorie count for the week, but what a way to go! This is definitely a great spot for families, especially during a birthday celebration.

Devine Pastabilities, 3545 Midway Dr., #E, San Diego, CA 92110; (619) 523-5441; torpasta.com; Italian; $$. Located in the Point Loma area, Devine Pastabilities has reinvented the conventional sandwich and turned it into an extraordinary Italian creation. This winner of "Best Sandwich Shop in San Diego" features its signature dish, Torpasta, a delicious Italian roll that is hollowed, perfectly toasted, and stuffed with amazing Italian entrees. It's hard to beat a sandwich made with Italian sausage, onion, bell pepper, and penne in marinara stuffed into a large torpedo roll. Most menu items are also available as traditional Italian meals, served on a plate. Other unique combinations offered daily include fettuccine Alfredo with broccoli, spaghetti and meatballs, vegetarian favorites, and more. Also choose from traditional torpedo sandwiches and pizzas, or one of the unique Torsalads served on a roll. There is also a small selection of wine and draft or bottled beer.

Gabardine, 1005 Rosecrans St., San Diego, CA 92106; (619) 398-9810; gabardineeats.com; Seafood; $$$. Gab at the bar and dine at this lively coastal hub, boasting an old wood barn ceiling and sultry light fixtures crafted from dozens of antique fishing poles. Serious seafood enthusiasts come here to get their fill from a Portuguese-inspired seafood bar offering a hybrid of ocean specialties categorized by preparation style. There are over 35 menu items. Appetizer options include Cold Bar (oysters and such), Hot Bar (steamed choices), Aged Bar (meats and cheeses), and Gab Bar (olives and other small bites). Larger fresh and fried dining options are enough to satisfy any craving. In addition to regular menu items, a chalkboard-style menu features imaginative creations changing daily based on ingredients readily available. Don't miss the smoked swordburger with apple-currant jam, jalapeño aioli, and onion confit. A frozen dessert concoction of sea urchin roe, cream, sugar, and liquid nitrogen tastes like vanilla ice cream and pumpkin pie all rolled into one. Fun libations include an extensive selection of local craft brews, wine-based spirits, and boutique sodas.

Humphreys by the Bay, 2241 Shelter Island Dr., San Diego, CA 92106; (619) 378-4281; humphreysrestaurant.com; California Modern; $$$. With stunning views of the marina and a casual-but-upscale vibe, Humphreys is a great destination. Unlike most other restaurants in San Diego, this location is also host to major concerts from April through September right on the hotel property. There's no better way to spend a warm summer evening than dining under the stars and enjoying top-tier entertainment. Some of the biggest acts to visit San Diego will use Humphreys as their venue. But what about the food? The menu is packed with items that celebrate many global cuisines and flavors. Their brunch is considered one of the best in San Diego, offering everything from the traditional breakfast, carving station, pastas, and dessert fare to upscale choices including ceviche, sushi rolls, steamed mussels, and oysters. The dinner menu is extensive and offers something for everyone. One of the more popular dishes is the blackened jidori chicken, with piccholine olive potato puree and pancetta-blue cheese sauce.

Ikiru Japanese Restaurant, 2850 Womble Rd., San Diego, CA 92106; (619) 221-1228; ikirusushisd.com; Japanese; $$. This quaint little Japanese restaurant is located in the heart of Liberty Station and offers a relaxing break from the hustle and bustle of shopping nearby. Lunchtime is especially crowded, with many of the businesspeople stopping by for a quick sushi fix or lunch special before heading back to work. In addition to the items you would expect, such as sushi/sashimi, hand rolls, and specialty rolls, the broad menu includes many other traditional Japanese meat and seafood dishes, such as Teriyaki, Yakisoba, Udon, Katsu, and Ramen. Their full bar features a variety of sake and Japanese beers. They even offer an online ordering and delivery menu for convenience.

Island Prime/C-Level Lounge, 880 Harbor Island Dr., San Diego, CA 92101; (619) 298-6802; islandprime.com; American; $$$$. Resting on stilts atop San Diego Bay overlooking the city skyline and Coronado, this is one of my favorite restaurants. Not just for the view, but mainly because I am a huge fan of Executive Chef and Partner Deborah Scott. I've visited many restaurant kitchens in my career, and they often get messy and chaotic, but not for Scott. She runs a tight ship, and her kitchen is the cleanest I've ever seen. She has a unique flare for making guests feel at home. The C-Level is a more relaxed dining experience, primarily on an open patio, offering both lunch and dinner. Island Prime is the more sophisticated sibling, offering upscale indoor dining focused on high-end meats. No matter which side you choose, the meals are excellent in quality, presentation, and taste. One of my favorites is the Island Prime double pork chop with brown sugar crust, gruyere au gratin potatoes, apple pearl onion chutney, wild boar bacon, and apple-mustard demi. One of the most popular C-Level items is the crusted ahi tuna, with Chinese black rice, pineapple salsa, wasabi, and soy-ginger reduction.

Jimmy's Famous American Tavern, 4990 N. Harbor Dr., San Diego, CA 92106; (619) 226-2103; j-fat.com; American; $$$. Come here for a bottle of Old Rasputin Imperial Stout and a *big* burger (so big that you'll hardly finish). Located on the Marina, it's a great place to relax and enjoy the view. More than just a neighborhood tavern, this local hot spot has some innovative food to go with their great drinks. Plenty of excellent beer choices are available on tap and by the bottle, as well as a selection of wines by the glass or bottle. One of the more popular signature drinks is Jimmy's Bramble, with True lemon vodka, fresh squeezed lime and grapefruit juices, simple syrup, and muddled blackberries. Since early childhood, Jimmy has been learning to create simple foods that he describes as "authentic, real, delicious comfort food for the foodie." His burgers are some of the best in town. The Spicy California burger, a half-pound of Creekstone Farms Black Angus Beef, with Jack cheese, avocado, pickled jalapeños, and herb aioli is amazing. Every burger is served with wonderfully seasoned french fries, peanut slaw, or simple greens. The burger is so big, it comes to your table with a huge steak knife driven though the center. Also tops is the buttermilk fried chicken breast, served crispy on the outside and juicy on the inside, with mashed potatoes and famous thyme cream gravy. Delicious!

Leroy's Kitchen and Lounge, 1015 Orange Ave., Coronado, CA 92118; (619) 437-6087; leroysluckylounge.com; American; $$$. This newbie in Coronado is reasonably priced for the normally expensive Coronado location. Grab a seat in the open-air dining room or at the busy bar and lounge. Specializing in seasonal, farm-fresh food from local and sustainable sources, the food at Leroy's is prepared in a way that highlights the ingredients without masking flavors. Discover and enjoy the many pleasures of a globally influenced menu with unique flavor pairings, such as grilled local yellowtail with arugula pesto, porter-braised short ribs with creamy polenta or Duroc bone-in pork chop with maple bourbon glaze and ginger pears. Experience irresistible local craft beers, and craft cocktails made with unique ingredients, including ginger beer, chipotle vodka, and rose water.

Mistral, Loews Coronado Bay Resort, 4000 Coronado Bay Rd., Coronado, CA 92128; (619) 424-4000; loewshotels.com; French; $$$$. Chef Patrick Ponsaty takes the concept of farm-to-table to a whole new level at this captivating restaurant where his menu matches our Mediterranean climate. Fittingly named after the wind that blows through the Rhone Valley, Mistral is located just inside Loews Coronado Bay Resort. It is an unrivaled secret not to be missed. Starting with a captivating view of the city skyline across San Diego Bay and ending with a dining experience that is unsurpassed in presentation and flavor. Ponsaty relies heavily on same-day picked ingredients from a 3,800-square-foot on-site garden, hearkening back to a time when food was prepared in the kitchen on the farm where it was grown, perfectly fresh, perfectly sustainable. His progressive French cuisine speaks for itself with melt-in-your-mouth delicacies including lobster consommé, pork cheeks, moulard duck breast, and squid ink risotto. The wine list is constructed in tandem with the menu, thus making the selection of a wine to pair with dinner an easy task! See Chef Ponsaty's recipe for **Dungeness Crab Salad Appetizer** on p. 351.

Old Venice, 2910 Canon St., Point Loma, CA 92106; (619) 222-5888; oldvenicerestaurant.com; Italian; $$$. Family owned and operated for 30 years, this venerable restaurant gives you a taste of Old Italy but is located in the heart of Point Loma and just minutes from Shelter Island, the airport, and major freeways. The warm Venetian decor features stark white walls, hanging chandeliers, flickering candlelight, and a covered brick patio in the back of the restaurant. The patio is especially romantic in the evenings, when small lights flicker along the walls, on your table, and around a large tree. Love is always in the air, where you'll see couples feeding each other pasta while sipping on Chianti, or large families reveling in conversation. The bolognese sauce features an earthy and garlicky richness that's perfect over rigatoni. I have a soft spot for cheese-filled ravioli, which taste like the ones from my mother's kitchen. Other local favorites include the veal saltimbocca and chicken cacciatori. Live music is offered on weekend nights, making it the most popular time to visit, so be sure to call ahead for reservations.

Peohe's, 1201 1st St., Coronado, CA 92118; (619) 437-4474; peohes.com; Seafood; $$$$. Located on the water's edge in the Coronado Ferry Landing Marketplace, this is one of the most romantic restaurants on Coronado. In a casual, elegant dining room with views of the downtown skyline and San Diego bay through floor-to-ceiling windows, diners savor fresh tropical seafood dishes influenced by Pacific Rim flavors. The natural essence of the sea is evident in unexpected menu offerings such as crab-stuffed tilapia with a caper butter sauce, pan-seared jumbo scallops finished in a ginger-orange sesame glaze, and crispy wok-fried whole bass served with a hot and spicy Thai sauce. A sushi bar entices patrons with inventive rolls and contemporary sushi creations. Peohe's is easily accessible by land or water—just a 5-minute trip from downtown via private yacht or water taxi, and a 10-minute automobile ride over the Coronado Bay Bridge.

Pomodoro Ristorante Italiano, 2833 Avenida De Portugal, San Diego, CA 92106; (619) 523-1301; pomodorosd.com; Italian; $$$. Taking inspiration from a primary ingredient, Pomodoro Ristorante boasts a decor that features more than one nod to that master fruit, the tomato. With curtains hanging over the dining room's large windows and accent pieces that could have come from Grandmother's home, Pomodoro is both casual and comfortable. Fresh house-made pastas and sauces drive in that home-away-from-home feeling, while the full menu of sumptuous steak, seafood, and chicken specialties confirms you're in a special place indeed. One of the better menu items is the Gamberi Pomodoro, a wonderful mix of shrimp sautéed with artichokes and mushrooms in a light tomato sauce. The heated patio makes dining alfresco a possibility any time, especially with the Point Loma breezes beckoning us out to play.

Restaurant at The Pearl, 1410 Rosecrans St., San Diego, CA 92106; (619) 226-6100; thepearlsd.com; American; $$$. This restaurant is located in a vintage, 1950s boutique hotel in the heart of Point Loma. Cocktails are a specialty, where the mixologist takes classic drinks to a whole new level. The menu features a variety of regional styles that utilize seasonal ingredients and an imaginative mix of flavors. One of my favorite appetizers in the city is right here: blue cheese and bacon-wrapped California Medjool dates with almonds. The flavors are phenomenal! For dinner, be sure to try the stout-braised short ribs, with parsnip and celery puree, peas and carrots, and a port reduction. The Pearl also offers semi-private poolside dining options, with a full menu and cocktail service available inside luxurious cabanas. It's a perfect location to enjoy the "Dive-In Theater" on Wednesday evenings, when the pool area is turned into a movie venue with large screen and popcorn!

Slater's 50/50 Burgers by Design, 2750 Dewey Rd., San Diego, CA 92106; (619) 398-2600; sandiego.slaters5050.com; Burgers; $$. If you are a burger lover, head straight into the heart of the happiest burger place on earth! No frills here, just a wide-open and modern burger joint that offers novelty burgers that are hard to beat. Best of all, guests can design their own burger in a variety of creative ways. Choose from patties made with beef, turkey, or their signature 50/50 (50 percent ground beef and 50 percent ground bacon) patty. The veggie patty is also extremely good. Slater's also showcases an abundance of accouterments, including 12 cheeses, 30 toppings, and 20 sauces. Don't miss the Flaming Hot Burger; a fiery beef patty compressed in between a ciabatta roll with fire-roasted green chilies, pepper jack cheese, and chipotle mayo, seductively topped off with beer-battered onion rings. With 111 brewskies on tap, you'll have no trouble cooling off your tongue. On any given day there are about 40 craft brews from San Diego, with the remainder coming from all over the world.

Tender Greens, 2400 Historic Decatur Rd., San Diego, CA 92106; (619) 226-6254; tendergreensfood.com; Organic/Health Food; $$. This is a cafeteria-style first come, first serve organic restaurant where you order your food at one end and pay at the other end and seat yourself. One of seven in California, Tender Greens relies on fresh-picked produce from small local farms, namely Point Loma Farm, located right across the street. The menu offers big salads, comforting soups, fresh sandwiches, and grilled meats. Breads are made fresh daily by artisan bakeries and the finest quality ingredients are used in the food, including cold-pressed olive oils, ground spices, mustards, vinegars, and cheeses, as well as desserts made on-site. Executive Chef Pete Balistreri is known for his rotating house-cured meats, especially his handcrafted salamis and prosciutto. The beef comes from grain-fed hormone/antibiotic-free cows and free-range chickens. Even the tuna is line caught from the Pacific. Savor wines from local boutique wineries, as well as great microbrews and organic teas.

Landmarks

Bali Hai, 2230 Shelter Island Dr., San Diego, CA 92106; (619) 222-1181; balihairestaurant.com; California Modern/Asian Fusion; $$$. Located on the northern tip of Shelter Island, Bali Hai was opened in 1955 by San Diego restaurateur Tom Ham. It's been family owned and operated for over five decades. It was the island's first "tiki temple," named after the song popularized by the musical *South Pacific*. Two famous tiki icons were created for the structure: *Mr. Bali Hai,* a large wood sculpture at the front entrance greeting guests, and *The Goof,* a playful and mysterious remnant that has stood guard on the restaurant roof for over five decades. Ham's vision continues through his daughter, Susie Baumann, and her husband, Larry. Sons Grant and Andy Baumann, representing the third generation, have added a fresh, youthful influence. This iconic Shelter Island dining spot—known for its sweeping bay front views, oversized Mai Tais and distinctive Pacific Rim cuisine—boasts approachable fresh flavors. Don't miss the coconut curry steamed mussels, blackened albacore, char siu glazed duck, and Kalua pork tenderloin.

1500 Ocean, Hotel del Coronado, 1500 Orange Ave., Coronado, CA 92118; (619) 522-8490; hoteldel.com; California Modern; $$$$. Everyone agrees that the Hotel del Coronado is a legendary landmark in San Diego. That places a lot of pressure on its signature restaurant, 1500 Ocean, to deliver unparalleled excellence. No visit to this city would be complete without dining at this upscale eatery, mere steps from the Pacific Ocean, and offering both indoor and terraced seating. There's something special about dining in a location that has become a flagship picture for the city, not to mention the view is hard to duplicate. Garnering outstanding reviews from national publications, this culinary paradise offers only the freshest cuisine, primarily sourced from local farmers and producers. The wine and craft beer list is extensive, offering an endless list of options from every major region of the world, ranging from reasonable to extravagant. The menu is filled with items that will appeal to all of your senses. Their daily selection of oysters is one of the best in the city. The black spaghetti starter is outstanding, with Dungeness crab, jalapeño sea urchin and gremolata crumbs. For dinner, choose one of the daily fresh fish offerings, or the tasting menu to sample four items and a dessert for one reasonable price.

Specialty Stores, Markets & Producers

Con Pane Rustic Breads and Cafe, 2750 Dewey Rd., San Diego, CA 92106; (619) 224-4344; Bakery; $$. With a spacious location in the ever expanding Liberty Station area, this bustling bistro is truly carb heaven! Owner Catherine Perez says that the word "companion" derives from *con pane* (with bread), and this is the perfect choice for enjoying a meal with friends or family. This bakery offers several tables by sunny windows, a large patio area, and an endless variety of freshly baked bread to enjoy. The popularity of this establishment can be measured by the typically long lines of patrons waiting to order their favorite breakfast or lunch. Everything is made from scratch, with a menu offering over 20 flavors of handmade artisan breads, decadent morning pastries, inventive sandwiches, and aromatic coffee and espresso drinks. The savory loaves are by far the most popular item and include favorites such as rosemary olive oil, kalamata olive, gorgonzola, and roasted red onion. So pull up a chair, order a big mug of foamy cappuccino and one (or two) of the now-famous cinnamon rolls, and enjoy a break from the hectic day!

Cupcakes Squared, 3772 Voltaire St., San Diego, CA 92107; (619) 226-3485; cupcakessquared.com; Desserts; $. Owner Robin Wisotsky offers one-of-a-kind "square" gourmet cupcakes made from top-of-the-line, natural ingredients including Cacao Barry chocolate and fresh Hawaiian vanilla shipped in weekly. No preservatives or stabilizers in these delicious cakes. Wisotsky even grinds fresh almonds to make almond flour. Cupcakes are baked from scratch fresh daily and come in over 28 flavors. My faves are the Not So Red Velvet with mild cocoa and vanilla cake with cream cheese frosting, the pistachio cake with pomegranate butter cream, and the Mocha Baileys with rich chocolate and coffee flavors and Bailey's Irish cream frosting. Most cupcake flavors can be ordered gluten free and a baker's choice of gluten-free cupcakes are available every day.

Moo Time Creamery, 1500 Orange Ave., Coronado, CA 92118; (619) 435-2383; nadolife.com/mootime/main.html; Desserts; $. Some things remain the same throughout the years—one of those things is my love of ice cream. I can't think of a better place to enjoy that creamy frozen treat than on the lawn of the Hotel del Coronado in a lounge chair just steps from the Pacific Ocean. Over 40 flavors of hand-crafted ice cream, sorbet, and low-fat frozen yogurt are available. They also have great seasonal flavors during the holidays, like pumpkin, peppermint stick, and my favorite egg nog. Once you've chosen the base, you can also personalize your taste, with plenty of mixes available to create a unique flavor or crunch. The waffle cones are cooked and rolled while you watch, and melt in your mouth. They also have plenty of cake and pie choices, like Kahlua brownie or strawberry cheesecake. It's a sinful indulgence that must be satisfied!

Point Loma Seafoods, 2805 Emerson St., San Diego, CA 92106; (619) 223-1109; plsf.com; Seafood; $$. In 1963 Kelly Christianson and his wife, Marie, started selling the finest catches from the sea out of their small store. Over the years, business grew tremendously and they become known for their slogan, "The freshest thing in town," selling seasonal fish purchased directly from local fishermen. Today, their recently remodeled restaurant and fish counter is a must-see. An ideal waterfront location with a view of the Marina allows diners to feast inside or on a spacious outdoor patio. The large menu offers seafood plates, sandwiches, salads, chowders, sushi, and sashimi. They also provide a full-service retail case of the freshest seafood around, most locally caught, available

for taking home. Feel free to ask for recipes and tips on the best cooking methods to create a phenomenal meal. Their special smoking process results in some of the best-tasting seafood I've sampled outside of the Pacific Northwest.

Downtown: Little Italy

This compact district along India Avenue in downtown was once home to nearly 6,000 Italian families that worked to establish San Diego as the center of the tuna industry. Since the decline of this industry in the mid-1900s, Little Italy has now become the largest and oldest continuous ethnic neighborhood in San Diego. Centrally located between the waterfront and I-5, this urban district is easy to access, with plenty of street parking available. The streets are lined with vintage and modern buildings that house ground-floor restaurants, shops, and boutiques, anchoring multiple levels of condos, townhomes, and businesses.

Although the area has a variety of cuisines available, it primarily serves the visitor looking for everything Italian. From bakeries to delis, take-out pizza to high-end dining rooms, you'll find a taste to please every craving. Park yourself in one of the bistro tables, order an espresso with a pastry, and watch the bustling street-life pass by.

The Neighborhood Association is well-known for its engagement, hosting regular events to support this vibrant community. The Mercado is a weekly farmers' market that draws huge crowds, including many of the local chefs who pride themselves with including local produce and freshly caught fish on their menus. Although a number of festivals are hosted throughout the year, none is more popular than the Little Italy Festa in October, one of the largest Italian festivals outside of New York City. You can enjoy endless food options, entertainment, arts and crafts, street painting, stickball, and bocce ball tournaments.

Foodie Faves

Anthology, 1337 India St., San Diego, CA 92101; (619) 595-0300; anthologysd.com; California Modern; $$$. It's a culinary opus where "fine dining meets song" at this contemporary restaurant suggestive of the great supper clubs of the '30s and '40s. With three levels of seating, you're bound to find the right spot, whether it's on the ground floor next to the stage, or one of the comfortable booths overlooking the balcony; every seat has a great view. Food lovers and music lovers are able to combine their passions, trying out seasonal fare while listening to their favorite live music. Whether it's jazz, rock, classical, or the blues, you will see some of the finest artists in the world from a stage that is up close and personal. Culinary composer Executive Chef Todd Allison fits the bill, taking center stage with his sustainable and market-driven menu. In support of local farmers and fishermen, Allison gets my seal of approval with his Asian pear and wild arugula salad, octopus carpaccio, Szechuan pepper-crusted local albacore, and all-natural beef short rib sliders. Most nights, you can choose a fixed menu including the show for a great price.

Bencotto Italian Kitchen, 750 W. Fir St., San Diego, CA 92101; (619) 450-4786; lovebencotto.com; Italian; $$. Located in the new "Q" building in the heart of Little Italy, a young generation of Italians, motivated from their experiences from the restaurant business in Milan, Modena, New York, and San Diego, succeeded in creating a modish, relaxed, and appealing kitchen-restaurant. "Bencotto" means and refers to a meal "done well," or perfectly cooked, and that is exactly what you'll get. Menu items are designed to share, so that guests can casually pick and choose from a nice variety of home-style dishes. I've eaten Italian food all my life, and given that pastas are their signature dish, I am happy to report that the pasta here is the real deal. Nothing overwhelming, just simple handmade "home style" pasta straight from the heart of Italy. Get *Pasta A Modo Tuo* (pasta your way) by opting for either pasta *fatta a mano* (daily hand-made) for a smooth consistency, or pasta *artigianale* (artisanal) for an "al dente" texture. With a variety of pasta sauces to choose from, my favorite is the pesto with basil, parmesan, pecorino, pine nuts, and garlic. Craving a little risotto with a lot of cheese? Make a reservation in advance for your special occasion or private party to get a taste of Chef Fabrizio Cavallini's creamy risotto recipe served tableside from a carved-out wheel of Parmigiano Reggiano.

Buon Appetito, 1609 India St., San Diego, CA 92101; (619) 238-9880; buonappetito.signonsandiego.com; Italian; $$$. It's an Italian celebration of food, wine, and art at this alluring eatery in Little Italy. Original art pieces are featured on the walls from a special artist every other month. They've sweetened up the escarole, a somewhat bitter lettuce, ever so slightly with an insalata (salad) combination of sliced pears, gorgonzola, and raspberry vinaigrette. I am a big fan of any kind of meat sauce, typically known as ragu, so I always choose the fusilli pasta topped with a slow-simmered homemade ragu of duck. They also make a fantastic cioppino with fresh clams, mussels, calamari, scallops, fresh fish, and shrimp in a zesty tomato broth. A wine bar attached to the restaurant features a nice selection of vino from around the world.

Cafe Zucchero, 1731 India St., San Diego, CA 92101; (619) 531-1731; cafezucchero.com; Italian; $$$. If you're looking for authentic Italian pastries, this is the place to visit, especially in the morning when all of the delicious treats are fresh out of the kitchen. Everything is handmade in this cute little coffee shop that includes adequate seating inside and plenty of espresso steaming behind the counter. A long glass case lining an entire wall is the centerpiece, showcasing some of the best Italian confections in San Diego. It's nearly impossible to pick just one item, but if I had to choose, it would be the creamy-smooth Strawberry Napoleon. Breakfast and lunch are the busy hours, but they are also open for a casual dinner, offering salads, pizzas, and pastas. Live music is common, and on any given night you'll find a number of the regular patrons stopping by to sing their favorite Italian melody. Unlike the typical karaoke bar, no one reads lyrics on a screen while squawking off-tone. The gentlemen here sing every song by heart, and in a manner that will have you dreaming of gondola rides in Venice.

Craft and Commerce, 675 W. Beech St., San Diego, CA 92101; (619) 269-2202; craft-commerce.com; American; $$$. The outside of this restaurant is covered in ivy and inside there's a country-meets-modern house feel with very dim lighting and candlelight. The ceiling is made from restored wood, with restored wood tables and bright orange steel chairs. Inside the walls there are piles and piles of hardbound classic novels, definitely giving you something to think about. I couldn't find any cookbooks here, but was very pleased that Executive Chef Craig Jimenez's contemporary take on seasonal American cuisine focuses on quality-driven fare and a flavor-unique concept. You won't find ketchup here because he believes that ketchup covers up the flavors in food. You will, however, find house-made sauces of garlic aioli, spicy aioli, and whole-grain mustard, to name a few. You haven't lived until you've tried the dry-rubbed smoked ribs with jalapeño spoon bread or the fried chicken with buttermilk slaw. If you feel like vegetarian, order the Farmers Plate, a selection of market vegetables and grains that changes weekly. Choose from various craft beers from all over the world with almost 30 rotating taps. A weekend brunch showcases cocktails available in punch bowls and plates designed for sharing.

Davanti Enoteca, 1655 India St., San Diego, CA 92101; (619)-237-9606; davantisandiego.com; Italian; $$$. Yes, there is such a thing as casual fine dining, and it's happening at this Italian restaurant and wine bar in Little Italy that's slowly but surely building a following and changing my long-held belief that good Italian food can exist in America's Finest City. A dimly lit ambiance, a full bar, semi-loud rock n' roll playing in the background, wood tables adorned with wine glasses begging you to take a sip of vino—all looks good to me! The wide-ranging menu embraces salumi and formaggi (cheese), pizza, pasta, and seafood and meat entrees. Among the dishes, the Ligurian-style baked focaccia with fresh soft cow cheese and honeycomb is the number one seller. Bold flavors are crammed into the Davanti burger with its special blend of beef made in house and you'll get a nice jolt of spice from the giant rigatoni and sausage. The kitchen delivers further with grilled swordfish *alla siciliana* and the oven-roasted wagyu tri tip. Finish off with an exceptional goat cheese cheesecake with salted caramel.

Filippi's Pizza Grotto, 1747 India St., San Diego, CA 92101; (619) 232-5094; realcheesepizza.com; Pizza; $$. In 1950, Vincent DePhilippis and his wife, Madeleine, opened a deli grocery on India Street, aptly named Filippi's Cash and Carry. This was the beginning of what has become a successful line of family restaurants. Today, Filippi's Pizza Grottos are owned and operated by family members of the original founders. This Little Italy restaurant is expansive, with checkered red-and-white tablecloths and wine bottles hanging in woven baskets on the ceiling. Everyone comes here for the straightforward Italian food in big portions at reasonable prices. Heed this warning: The pasta dishes are hearty and hefty, filled with meats, sauces, and cheese. So if you're counting calories, this may not be the best place for you. The pizzas here are fabulous, with a crispy crust and plenty of toppings. Other popular favorites include lasagna with meat sauce, fettucine Alfredo, veal scalloppini with mushrooms and wine sauce, or chicken parmigiana. Entrees are served a la carte or as a dinner, including soup, salad, and garlic bread. Great desserts include spumoni, cheesecake, and cannoli. A small retail grocery store is located just inside the front door, and offers a deli with Italian meats, a variety of imported olive oils, pasta, Italian cookies, and much more. There are several Filippi's locations throughout San Diego.

Glass Door, 1835 Columbia St., San Diego, CA 92101; (619) 564-3755; portovistasd.com/dining/glass-door.cfm; California Modern; $$$. Situated on the fourth floor of the Porto Vista Hotel, this restaurant offers magnificent views of the downtown waterfront and San Diego Bay. Elevated chairs are situated around communal tables and along the open west wall, which is essentially a lengthy "perch" offering 180-degree views. Colorful glass lanterns of various sorts hang from the ceiling, and enhance the mood when lit in the evenings. This destination is extremely popular in the late afternoons, as patrons collect together to enjoy spectacular sunsets and blinking lights from the nighttime skyline. The menu has California flair but is influenced heavily from several international culinary styles. A great example is the simple but stunning Luca Brasi, a whole fried tilapia served with corn puree, baby carrots, and jalapeño chimichurri. For a Middle Eastern touch, try the tandoori skewer, with spice marinated chicken, pickled vegetables, and fried dough. There is also a long list of small plates, salads, and burgers to satisfy any appetite/palate. Don't forget to sample one of the many signature drinks, featuring house-infused liquors and creative recipes. Also open for brunch on the weekends.

Indigo Grill, 1536 India St., San Diego, CA 92101; (619) 234-6802; indigogrill.com; California Modern; $$$. Although this compact neighborhood is lined with excellent choices to satisfy your Italian fix, there are a few exceptions. Indigo Grill is a perfect example, drawing its influences from Alaska to Mexico and settling on an identity of Southwestern Fusion cuisine. Stepping past the front door, you'll be greeted by American Indian totems and ancient Mexican runes, off-set by modern touches of glass and mosaics. The restaurant is almost always overflowing with patrons eager to taste the unique blends of flavors in the drinks and food. A good example is the cucumber black pepper martini, a spicy mix of gin, muddled kiwi and lime, and melon liqueur. For dinner, try the Vera Cruz maize tamale or pecan-crusted rainbow trout, both excellent choices to savor the special blend of flavors that only a bright-minded chef like Deborah Scott can create.

Landini's Pizza, 1827 India St., San Diego, CA 92101; (619) 238-3502; landinispizzeria.com; Pizza; $$. Nestled in the heart of San Diego's historic Little Italy you'll find Landini's Pizzeria. Serving New York–style, hand-tossed pizza, this is a great spot to pick up a few slices and enjoy during your walk through the neighborhood. They also serve paninis layered with imported meats and cheeses, Florentine-inspired pastas, baked dishes, and a fine selection of beers and wines. A very popular item is the stromboli: pizza dough rolled like a sandwich and stuffed with ham, green pepper, pepperoni, mozzarella, and marinara.

Mimmo's Italian Village, 1743 India St., San Diego, CA 92101; (619) 239-3710; mimmos.biz; Italian; $$. Established for nearly 4 decades in Little Italy, this destination is more than just a restaurant. Step inside and be transported to a small village in Sicily, with a cobblestone walkway and storefronts, complete with faux balconies, lamp posts, and planter boxes. The experience is reminiscent of a simpler version of a Las Vegas indoor walkway, sending you to a faraway city without the plane fare. There's also a very generous patio in the front, if you prefer to watch the action along India Street. Lunches are ordered deli style and include a vast array of sandwiches, salads, pastas, and pizzas. The baked eggplant sandwich is a guilty pleasure and the Italian sausage and peppers are delicious. For dinner, it's a great alternative to the higher-priced and fancier establishments in the area. Buy a bottle of wine, a couple of hearty Italian dishes, and enjoy some good conversation. Live music is often scheduled at night, especially on the weekends.

Petrini's, 610 W. Ash St., San Diego, CA 92101; (619) 595-0322; petrinisitalian.com; Italian; $$. Chef-Proprietor David Petrini keeps family and friends at his Italian table with generations-old, tried-and-true family recipes. His "La Famiglia Mangia" ("the family eats") philosophy keeps the diners happy at his warm and welcoming restaurant. There are plenty of windows to enjoy the hustle and bustle of San Diego, but the warm light and candles make you feel at home. The open kitchen adds to the ambiance, and Petrini is often seen wandering through the dining room talking to patrons and enjoying the conversation. Petrini's Italian peasant cuisine is offered three times a day. For breakfast it's a fig loaf with butter for my Italian coffee and me. For lunch, try the smoked salmon served atop thin-crust pizza dough that's lightly brushed with pesto sauce and topped with fresh sliced Roma tomatoes, red onions, capers, and freshly grated Parmigiano Reggiano. For dinner, try the baked penne noodles (ziti) smothered in meat sauce and topped with melted provolone and mozzarella.

Zia's Bistro, 1845 India St., San Diego, CA 92101; (619) 234-1344; ziasbistro.com; Italian; $$$. Experience the flavors of Sicily with an American twist and this romantic Italian restaurant in Little Italy where celebrity Food Network chef Giada De Laurentiis dined during the annual Sicilian Festival. Open for lunch and dinner, the atmosphere is fun and stylish both indoors and on the outdoor patio. Choose from countless appetizers, salads, and notable pastas as well as delicious seafood, chicken, beef, and veal entrees. Stone-fired gourmet pizzas are delicious, especially the "In Bianco" with mozzarella, parmesan, and goat cheeses. Finding a great vino from their reputable wine list is never a problem. They offer great deals for their happy hour, and it can get very busy, especially on the weekends.

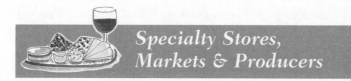

Specialty Stores, Markets & Producers

Assenti's Pasta, 2044 India St., San Diego, CA 92101; (619) 239-5117; assentispasta.com; Grocery/Market; $$. Handmade pasta is the big seller at this Italian shop in Little Italy. Umberto and

Adriana Assenti's pastas are made of a combination of semolina, durum, and wheat flours, water, and eggs (*pasta al'ouvo*), which makes the flavor and texture very delicate. There are no artificial flavors, colors, or preservatives in any of their homemade food products. All pasta is sold by the pound, which serves approximately three people. All of the sauces are homemade, and I love their pesto sauce over fettuccine. Choose from a fresh selection of deli meats, sliced to your satisfaction. Assenti's also carries a wide variety of imported Italian olive oils, anchovies, biscotti, imported olives, and other specialty items. Be sure to also taste their homemade desserts—tirimisu and cannoli, especially around the holiday season (when eating sweets is deemed acceptable) are divine.

Mona Lisa, 2061 India St., San Diego, CA 92101; (619) 234-4893; monalisalittleitaly.com; Grocery/Market; $$. I like to frequent this popular store and restaurant in Little Italy. The deli has a nice selection of authentic Italian meats including proscuitto bresaola, cappicola, coppa, Genoa salami, pancetta, pepperoni, and sopresatta. My favorite cheeses are always available, especially Parmagiana Reggiano, buffalo mozzarella, and cambozola. I can always find what I am looking for when it comes to Italian cookies, olive oil, Italian wines, and fresh pasta. A limited selection of produce includes tomatoes, apples, lemons, pears, bananas, rapini, lettuce, celery, carrots, mushrooms, eggplant, garlic, onions, avocado, and potatoes. An adjoining restaurant offers a full bar, extensive wine list, and great service in a relaxed and comfortable atmosphere. The restaurant's menu includes pizza, antipasti, hot and cold sandwiches, pasta and ravioli, and house specialties including veal and chicken dishes, lasagna, manicotti, seafood, and more.

Gaslamp Quarter, East Village & Seaport Village

This area is hands-down the heartbeat of San Diego tourism. With hundreds of restaurants, nightclubs, shops, boutiques, and major hotels within an 8-block radius, you would never need another destination for the San Diego experience. Encompassing the lower-downtown area and stretching to the bay, a good pair of walking shoes will allow you to journey through the action, both day and night. Victorian-era buildings are densely packed along the street and intermingle with modern hotel entrances, compact restaurant patios, nightclubs, and shop fronts. It is truly a place to lose yourself in the action.

Born in the mid-1800s, this area along the waterfront was a centerpiece of what was to become San Diego. However, it wasn't until the mid-1900s that a major renovation took place, transforming what had become a neighborhood of ill repute into a shopping and entertainment mecca. In more recent times, the Gaslamp is an epicurean's paradise, with virtually every international cuisine available in high-end dining rooms to budget hole-in-the-walls. Parking can be a challenge, but the Horton Plaza (named after one of the first land owners, Alonzo Horton) offers 3-hour validation in a high-rise parking garage adjacent to the largest shopping mall in downtown. Better yet, stay at one of the fine downtown hotels and bypass the parking headache. Everything you need is within walking distance.

Seaport Village encompasses 14 acres of waterfront shopping and dining, with cobblestone pathways intertwined among lush landscapes and some of the best Bay views in the city. Waterfront eateries are a popular destination year-round.

East Village is one of the largest and fastest-growing neighborhoods in the downtown area, primarily fueled by the opening of Petco Park, a uniquely centered baseball stadium that is home to the San Diego Padres. Once an old warehouse district, it has quickly become a destination for visitors and residents who crave living in a vibrant urban environment.

Foodie Faves

Analog, 801 5th Ave., San Diego, CA 92101; (619) 233-1183; analogbar.com; American; $$$. Decorated to mimic a recording studio from the 1970s, this intimate restaurant/club hearkens me back to my youth, as vintage vinyl album covers and cassette tapes adorn the walls. Essentially divided into two areas, the dining room and the bar area, where visitors enjoy karaoke, DJ, or dancing. The specialty drinks will catch your attention, with concoctions that are reminiscent of simpler days, but adding a modern twist, like the Mr. Rogers, with Jim Beam Black label, double wood smoked cherry reduction, and a bottle of real Mexican Coca-Cola on the side; or the popular rosemary Manhattan, with rosemary-infused Makers Mark 46, maple reduction, Carpano Antica, and a garnish of rosemary rock candy. The appetizer menu has interesting choices such as lobster corn dogs, barbecue pork "banh mi" street tacos, and short rib sliders—succulent meat stuffed into wonderfully soft mini brioche buns, with spicy tomato jam and shoestring fries tossed in parsley-garlic oil.

BICE, 425 Island Ave., San Diego, CA 92101; (619) 239-2423; bicesandiego.com; Italian; $$$$. From the modern and elegant ambiance to the extraordinary Italian fare, this is a restaurant you don't want to miss. Relying heavily on local and seasonal ingredients, Executive Chef Mario Cassineri has created a diverse menu of items that he likes to eat. You'll immediately notice that it highlights a more sophisticated style of Italian cuisine, tapping into his experience from an upbringing in Milan, and changing on a weekly basis. Don't look for any deep-fried calamari or gooey lasagna here! Begin your experience with a selection from the tempting cheese and salumi bar, emphasizing traditional styles, and paired with olives, jams, and honeys. All of the meals are thoughtfully prepared and meant to savor every wonderful bite. Take the subtle and tender grilled octopus salad, with baby fennel and fresh artichokes. Another excellent meal choice is the homemade fettuccine with asparagus and smoked salmon in a light and flavorful tomato-vodka sauce. The dolce selections are equally magnificent, ranging from light and subtle to darkly sweet. A perfect ending that must be enjoyed with a double espresso.

Bolillo Tortas, 417 4th Ave., San Diego, CA 92101; (619) 255-6268; bolillotortas.com; Mexican; $$. When Stefano Pezzotti and business partner Luis F. Zuber were unable to find a fast-casual restaurant to enjoy a real, authentic Mexican torta, they decided it was time to open Bolillo Tortas. Now guests can enjoy flavorful and reasonably priced fresh, made-to-order tortas, soups, salads, salsas, and desserts. The comfortable and modern dining area is complete with an open kitchen, bar seating, and a covered outdoor patio. My favorites are the carne asada, shrimp, or pork loin, served on a fresh torta bun with all the fixings. Be sure to ask for the bacon-wrapped cheese-stuffed jalapeños on the side. The restaurant also offers a selection of 20 international and handcrafted beers and list of wines. It's the perfect spot to stop for a quick bite over lunch, or before and after a baseball game.

Cafe Chloe, 721 9th Ave., San Diego, CA 92101; (619) 232-3242; cafechloe.com; French; $$$. A little French culture with a lot of French taste is what you'll get at Cafe Chloe in the East Village, a charming neighborhood bistro where you can enjoy a nice cappuccino for breakfast, a quick lunch, and linger on with wine and beautiful food for dinner. Executive Chef Katie Grebow, who completed the Cordon Bleu program with top honors at the California School of Culinary Arts in Pasadena, CA, lends a rustic approach to culturally rich, regional ingredients. The menu changes seasonally and daily featuring sustainable seafood and all-natural meats and chicken. The produce comes from local farms including Crows Pass, Sage Mountain, and Suzie's Farms. The lunch crowd comes in for smoked trout salad with apple vinaigrette and the Jidori chicken crepe with mushrooms, spinach, and truffle oil. Dinner is all about the Moules Belgique, local mussels cooked in Belgian ale and cream, and the lamb cassoulet with house Merguez sausage, braised lamb, pork belly confit.

Cafe Sevilla, 353 5th Ave., San Diego, CA 92101; (619) 233-5979; cafesevilla.com; Latin American; $$$. First opened in 1987, Cafe Sevilla is easily one of the most entertaining establishments in the San Diego area. A $2.7-million renovation gives this three-level Spanish restaurant a spacious and stunning new look. An exhibition kitchen, tapas bar, and underground club adds to the fun. Once you browse the menu, you'll quickly realize that multiple visits will be necessary to sample the extensive tapas selection. Every dish has its own personality, and the flavors are exceptional. I highly recommend the braised basque rabbit and black paella en su tinta, with Bomba black rice, mixed seafood, and aioli drizzle. But no visit would be complete without enjoying the weekly Flamenco dinner show, including authentic Flamenco and gypsy musicians and dancers. In addition, the nightclub is open 7 days a week with live music and dancing.

Croce's Restaurant & Jazz Bar, 802 5th Ave., San Diego, CA 92101; (619) 233-4355; croces.com; American; $$$. Restaurateur and owner/operator Ingrid Croce, wife of the late singer-songwriter Jim Croce, continues to pay tribute to her husband and his music at this casual restaurant adorned with high ceilings and pictures of Jim, family, and records on the walls. Savor prime meats, fresh fish, and pastas in the main dining area, loft, or outdoor patio where an efficient waitstaff offers amiable and consistent hospitality, even when the place is packed. Patrons gather here for the chocolate coconut martini and the small plates of baked brie and honey, roasted garlic with toasted baguette, and Jamaican Jerk braised baby back ribs with roasted corn polenta. Judicious choices include filet mignon, New York steak, a hearty pork chop, or the grilled duck breast. A great meatless alternative is the seared scallops with lobster-scented risotto. Live music is offered nightly in the jazz bar.

The Dragon's Den, 315 10th Ave., San Diego, CA 92101; (619) 358-9332; thedragonsdensd.com; Chinese; $$. Across from Petco Park and within walking distance of the San Diego Convention Center, this fashionable restaurant in downtown's East Village offers shrewd cocktails, unique appetizers, authentic Japanese sushi, and generous portions of Asian fusion cuisine. The boiled pork and chive dumplings and the pork potstickers are a big hit here. I like the crispy aromatic duck tostadas shell, a unique small-bite appetizer with salad. The crispy duck is actually quite similar to a traditional Peking duck. The duck is cooked for 3 to 4 hours to melt the fat, and then deep-fried to melt even more fat, after which it is finely chopped and served tostada style. Another exceptional entree is the spicy ginger garlic sole fillet that's breaded with Japanese bread crumbs (panko) and served over baby bok choy and rice. A little bird told me that diners come from near and far to have the sesame-crusted and lightly seared ahi salad with wasabi aioli. In addition, a pet-friendly patio means Fido will be happy too!

Gaijin Noodle + Sake House, 627 4th Ave., San Diego, CA 92101; (619) 238-0567; gaijinsd.com; Asian Fusion; $$. No, you're not in Tokyo's red light district, but you might as well be at this restaurant boasting red and black colors, a massive street-art styled mural, and an eye-catching lounge that's anchored by a massive bird's nest. Executive Chef Antonio Friscia and Chef Komei Nishiyama

Slurp offer noodles and favorites from the yakitori grill, along with other authentic Asian fusion cuisine showcased on the weekly rotating chalkboard-style menu. Great starters include the blistered shishito peppers, clam miso, and yellowtail crudo. Ramen offerings include hot and cold noodles, and from the yakitori grill, top savory bites include Duroc pork kimchi, Mexican white shrimp, and Nueske bacon-wrapped jumbo asparagus. Choose from a selection of rare jizake sakes as well as an extensive list of Japanese beers.

Greystone the Steakhouse, 658 5th Ave., San Diego, CA 92101; (619) 232-0225; greystonesteakhouse.com; Steak House; $$$$. Located in the historically landmarked Rivoli Theater building from the 1920s, this award-winning steak house was renamed The Bijou Theatre and operated by Pussycat Theatres, which screened adult films in the early 1970s. Today, this spacious, multilevel restaurant features a suave and sophisticated ambiance perfect for any occasion. A nightly dinner menu features aged steaks, fresh seafood, and homemade pastas, along with an extensive wine list. More than a steak house, exotic game selections include roasted elk chop and buffalo tenderloin. Other great choices include a slow simmered Kobe beef short rib, bourbon brined pork chop, and lamb chops. Pair your meat with a nice selection of sauces including béarnaise, bordelaise, truffle zabayon, armagnac and green peppercorn, and whole-grain mustard Chardonnay.

J-Six Restaurant and Lounge, 616 J St., San Diego, CA 92101; (619) 531-8744; jsixrestaurant.com; California Modern; $$$$. This upscale eatery is built for style, from the white linen tablecloths to contemporary fixtures. Award-winning Chef Christian Graves weaves his slow-food philosophy in every aspect of the kitchen. Nearly everything is created from scratch, including the breads, condiments, charcuterie, and herbs from the rooftop garden. Although his plates are usually prepared with only a few simple ingredients, the flavors are outstanding. Nearly all of the produce is local and organic, so the menu changes seasonally to reflect availability and freshness. The meats and seafood are carefully selected from the most earth-friendly sources, a difference that can be tasted in every bite. Adjacent to the Hotel Salomar, J-Six is open for breakfast, lunch, and dinner. For a most special meal, be sure to visit in the evenings, when the conversation and energy reach a crescendo. I would suggest the "Chef's Mercy," a 5-course tasting menu chosen by the kitchen to highlight some of the best dishes available. They also offer an excellent wine list that includes local and well-known international labels.

The Kebab Shop, 303 W. Beech St., Suite C-2, San Diego, CA 92101; (619) 550-5481; thekebabshop.com; Middle Eastern; $$. A.J. Akbar and Tony Farmand took over the successful eatery in San Diego's East Village in 2008. The owners opened the next location in Mira Mesa in 2009, a third location in Encinitas in fall of 2011, and a final location in Little Italy in February 2012. Break away from your daily routine and escape to this European getaway offering a delectable array of healthy and authentic options including Turkish Döner kebabs, originally from Turkey, offered in spiced lamb, marinated chicken, or falafel with a mix of fresh vegetables, a creamy garlic yogurt sauce, and homemade spicy sauce. Choose from shawarma sandwiches on soft, fluffy rolls, and sides including hot french fries and saffron rice. Other popular favorites include shish kebab plates, rotisserie plates, and Iskender kebab (rarely found in the US). A selection of fresh salads includes the Bebe Caprese, Tabouli, and Algerian Eggplant salad.

Lotus Thai, 906 Market St., San Diego, CA 92101; (619) 595-0115; lotusthaisd.com; Thai; $$$. If you're looking for a more tranquil destination among the hustle and bustle of downtown, this is definitely the place. Lotus serves upscale Thai cuisine in a dining room meant to create a soothing and relaxed environment. Take your seat next to a Buddha statue and enjoy the warm wood accents and tropical plants. The extensive menu offers something for everyone, whether you're a vegetarian or meat-lover. I am a sucker for their fresh and tasty spring rolls to start my meal, but another great choice is the Lotus Platter appetizer, which includes a sampling of their 5 most popular starters. Other favorites include the spicy eggplant, with Thai basil, onions, carrots, and a white bean sauce; or the flaming-hot Crying Tiger, with charcoal-broiled marinated prime steak, a spicy lime dipping sauce, and mixed greens. To cool your palate, consider the luscious fried banana and ice cream for dessert. There is also a second location on 6th Avenue in Hillcrest.

Lucky's Lunch Counter, 338 7th Ave., San Diego, CA 92101; (619) 255-GRUB; luckyslunchcounter.com; American; $$. Situated in the expansive and famed Culy Warehouse in Downtown San Diego, Lucky's Lunch Counter offers nostalgic eats in an easygoing atmosphere, just steps away from Petco Park in the East Village. Built to evoke memories of the old-style ballpark counters from the early 1900s, their most popular fare are overstuffed sandwiches and vintage hot dogs. Fast casual cuisine is the name of the game here. Breakfast is served all day, including a build-your-own omelet or burrito. Their hot pastrami or crispy pork tenderloin over-stuffed sandwiches are spectacular! No visit would be complete without tasting their original fire dog or bratwurst, split, grilled, and just waiting for you to dress up any way you like. Plenty of salad choices are also available. Be sure to stop in before or after one of the San Diego Padres home games, when Lucky's will reward you with a game-day special.

The Merk Bistro, 820 5th Ave., San Diego, CA 92101; (619) 814-6375; themerk.com; American; $$$. The Merk Bistro is located inside The Keating Hotel, which features a modern Pininfarina design within the exposed brick architecture of the historic 1890s

Mercantile Building. Michelin-starred Chef Gordon Ramsay and Executive Chef Brian Rutherford created a menu based primarily on seasonal and locally grown produce. Specials on a chalkboard menu are updated and customized regularly. Anything goes from roasted corn fritters or huevos rancheros to salads, sandwiches, pizza, and creative dinner entrees. I highly recommend the lasagna with béchamel or the chile relleno filled with quinoa, roasted corn, black beans, and goat cheese. A delightful new drink menu features a wide variety of unique specialty cocktails, including their "Rainforest on the Rocks" with VeeV Acai Liquor, mint, Agave Nectar, watermelon, and fresh lime juice. Choose from a unique selection of domestic and Italian wines, or purchase a bottle from the new Pininfarina wine collection. Nightly happy hour at the bar, and weekend champagne brunch on the patio.

Nobu, 207 5th Ave., San Diego, CA 92101; (619) 814-4124; noburestaurants.com; Asian Fusion; $$$$. Located inside the Hard Rock Hotel San Diego, Nobu launched in November 2007. Executive Chef-Owner Nobu Matsuhisa currently has 25 restaurants in 21 different cities around the world, spanning across five continents. Acclaimed actor, director, producer, and two-time Academy Award-winner Robert De Niro is a co-founder, instrumental in providing creative direction for all Nobu Restaurants. The menu offers cold dishes, hot dishes, tempura and kushiyaki, sushi and sashimi, and desserts. Off the cold menu, I love the yellowtail tartare with caviar and the oysters with Nobu sauces. My favorite hot dishes are the black cod with miso and the king crab tempura with amazu ponzu sauce. If you want to experience the true essence of Chef Nobu Matsuhisa's cuisine, I suggest his multicourse Omakase menu.

The Oceanaire Seafood Room, 400 J St., San Diego, CA 92101; (619) 858-2277; theoceanaire.com; Seafood; $$$$. The Oceanaire Seafood Room lives up to its name by offering only the finest and freshest sustainably caught seafood from prompt and professional servers. With its sprawling, dark-wood dining room and tables adorned in white linen, you'll feel as if you've stepped back in time to a classic 1930s ocean liner. A sizeable menu provides regionally inspired and seasonal offerings that are based on market availability. Fish is flown in daily from around the world, and one of the most famous items on the menu is the baked Maryland blue crab cake. California dover sole emerges from the oven stuffed with spinach, blue crab, and shrimp, and the classic beer-battered fish-and-chips is deep-fried to a light and golden crunch on the outside, yet tender and juicy inside. The prosciutto-wrapped Scottish Loch Duart salmon with roasted red pepper relish is wildly delicious. Seasoned wine stewards are always on hand to answer questions and help you chart a course for the wine selection that best complements your meal.

Osetra Fishhouse, 904 5th Ave., San Diego, CA 92101; (619) 239-1800; osetrafishhouse.com; Seafood; $$$$. Taking great pride in supporting local seafood farmers, Osetra Fishhouse serves dinner nightly, offering a gourmet seafood menu along with "Wine Angels" (pretty girls) who fly to retrieve your fine wine selection from their extraordinary three-story collection. With culinary inspirations from Europe, the Americas, and the Pacific Rim, the menu offers some of the finest and freshest seafood around, as well as aged meats and homemade pastas. An impressive oyster bar offers local oysters, caviar, sashimi, shrimp cocktail, and more. Up to four types of oysters are offered daily, including kumamoto oysters, kumai oysters, Bahia Falsa oysters, and, very rare, Huma Huma oysters. An ice bar offers an extensive collection of vodkas. Great choices off the new sushi menu include the Double Double Tuna Roll, Tempura Lobster Roll, or the Spicy Diego Roll.

Osteria Panevino, 722 5th Ave., San Diego, CA 92101; (619) 595-7959; osteriapanevino.com; Italian; $$$$. Experience fine Italian cuisine in a setting reminiscent of a small bistro dotting the hills of Firenze and the Tuscan region of Italy. Your meal is served in a farmhouse setting complete with terra-cotta floor tiles, large paintings and murals on the walls, colored tablecloths, and a full-marbled bar. Choose the intimate dining room or open-air patio where the Gaslamp pedestrians are shuffling along busy 5th Avenue. They operate a fine bakery producing fresh breads, pastas, and desserts daily. Be sure to review their extensive and award-winning wine list featuring a wide variety of California and Italian labels. Your entire meal could be spent tasting the many varieties of fresh mozzarellas available in the antipasti section, served in several savory presentations. The pasta menu is equally impressive. A great example is the *strozzapreti emiliani*, a twisted pasta with roasted pork loin, portobello mushrooms, and sun-dried tomatoes, tossed in a tomato sauce infused with rosemary. This is one eatery that will require multiple visits to sample the variety of offerings.

Quality Social (Downtown), 789 6th Ave., San Diego, CA 92101; (619) 501-7675; qualitysocial.com; American; $$. Located in the heart of the Gaslamp Quarter, this luxury dive bar strives to provide a mix of elements that cater to locals and visitors alike. Believing strongly in farm-to-table cuisine, Chef Jared Van Camp maintains a close relationship with local farmers who source many of his culinary ingredients, including produce, seafood, and meats. His cuisine is described as "blue-collar fare that's both approachable and honest." The interior is spacious and playful, with plenty of seating options at the bar or in one of the comfortable couches. Although Friday and Saturday nights can be crowded, the atmosphere is more subdued than many of the nearby dance clubs. This is the place for enjoying good food and conversation. Try one of their most refreshing cocktails; simply called "H," it includes Square One Organic Cucumber Vodka, St. Germain, lime, and cucumber. From the menu, a must-try is the homemade charcuterie plate, with a choice of a dozen rotating meat and artisanal cheeses. An excellent, and simply prepared, salad is the duck prosciutto and organic pear, with local green and roasted shallot vinaigrette. For a light but heartier meal, try the grilled organic salmon with roasted spaghetti squash, braised greens, and pumpkin seed pesto. The flavor combination is amazing.

Rama Restaurant, 327 4th Ave., San Diego, CA 92101; (619) 501-THAI (8424); ramarestaurant.com; Thai; $$$. The sense of place emanating from this humble restaurant is sweet home, Thailand, where award winning Executive Chef Pannuwat Soukjai offers a note-perfect rendition of authentic Thai dishes in an elegant and serene setting studded with unique works of art. Savvy foodies have found this modest spot to be a tranquil escape from the mundane, stopping in for lobster potstickers, drunken noodles, and coconut lemongrass shrimp off the traditional charcoal grill. Specialties of the house include the five-spice braised pork belly and the maple leaf roast duck in red curry. I like the pineapple fried rice with Chinese sausage and Japanese eggplant with Thai basil. Seafood offerings are plentiful and never boring.

RA Sushi Bar Restaurant, 474 Broadway, San Diego, CA 92101; (619) 321-0021; rasushi.com; Japanese; $$$. With its first location opened in Scottsdale, Arizona, in 1997, RA Sushi successfully combines distinctive sushi with a trendy, hip atmosphere. Fresh sushi is served sliced to order along with outstanding Japanese fusion cuisine in a fun and lively environment. Utilizing a wide variety of fresh fish including crab, shrimp, tuna, and salmon, the chefs at RA know how to make all the flavors come through and pop in your mouth. The thinly sliced chile ponzu yellowtail with jalapeño, cilantro, and sautéed cashews, served with a Kochjan chili ponzu sauce, is so fresh it could jump off your plate. Another one of my favorites is the grilled teriyaki salmon topped with a sautéed Fuji apple glaze and served with wasabi mashed potatoes. RA has 25 locations across the country.

Red Pearl Kitchen, 440 J St., San Diego, CA 92101; (619) 231-1100; redpearlkitchen.com; Chinese; $$$. All red and black inside with low dim lights and booths, this decent-size restaurant combines authentic Chinese/East Asian recipes with an all-the-rage bar scene. Guests come here for happy hour and the full bar with an Asian movie showing at all times. The far-reaching menu is ideal for family-style dining, and offers a redefined Pan-Asian flare for vegetable and wok-fired dishes, as well as dim sum, curry, and noodle entrees. Specifically known for their hot pots, don't miss the seafood hot pot in a spicy lemongrass broth. The Kung Pao prawns get a whopping burst of flavor from pineapple and asparagus, and the strawberry miso spareribs are worth a reservation in advance, especially on the weekends.

Richard Walker's Pancake House, 520 Front St., San Diego, CA 92101; (619) 231-7777; richardwalkers.com; American; $$. Imagine taking a bite out of a massive and sugary baked apple pancake with imported Saigon cinnamon and clarified butter! There's quite a bit more to like about this whimsical restaurant, cleverly decorated

with stained-glass windows and hand-blown glass fixtures. An extensive menu of gourmet pancakes, waffles, crepes, and omelets are the stars here. First-time visitors beware of the long lines, especially on the weekends, but hang in there, the "wow factor" when the food arrives at your table is worth the wait. The blueberry and sour cream crepes are pure comfort. Richard Walker, who owns and operates two larger pancake houses in Illinois, refers to his San Diego restaurant in the Marina District as "the little diamond of downtown." There's also seating on a busy outdoor patio.

Royal India, 329 Market St., San Diego, CA 92101; (619) 269-9999; royalindia.com; Middle Eastern; $$$. With awards including "Best Indian" and "Most Romantic Restaurant" in San Diego, there is no doubt that Royal India sets the standard for San Diego's Indian cuisine. Royal India treats its guests like royalty with its richly colored and plush architectural design in a tranquil setting complete with imported items directly from the palaces of India, including the royal chandeliers that dangle above a custom-carved wood bar. A diverse and assorted menu focuses on home-cooked family recipes that incorporate fresh herbs and spices with top-quality vegetables, seafood, and meats. I highly recommend the spicy tandoori wings and the chicken coconut pineapple curry. See

Sam Kambo and Jag Kambo's recipe for **Royal Chicken Tikka Masala** on p. 354.

Sally's Seafood on the Water, 1 Market Place, San Diego, CA 92101; (619) 358-6740; sallyssandiego.com; Seafood; $$$$. "Where Passion Meets the Plate" is the slogan at Sally's Seafood on the Water. Bordering Seaport Village, this modern-looking restaurant, decked out with high ceilings, numerous windows, and granite countertops, is further complemented with dark woods, black accents, and work from local artists adoring the walls. Grab a seat at one of the high-top tables with an up-close and personal view of the marina. The menu is seafood-dominated, with vibrant ocean flavors in every entrée—particularly the sushi and sashimi offerings. The Canadian lobster potpie is an irresistible marriage of pungent lobster with assorted seasonal veggies, linguica, and Boursin cheese, all underneath a blanket of puff pastry. The chili-crusted Maine diver scallops with preserved lemon raviolis, pine nut relish, and a velvety white wine butter sauce gets equal billing. A 3-course prix-fixe menu that changes from week to week is another nice option. Reservations are strongly recommended.

Saltbox Dining & Drinking, 1047 5th Ave., San Diego, CA 92101; (619) 515-3003; saltboxrestaurant.com; California Modern; $$$. This Kimpton restaurant is a new American gastro-lounge pairing seasonally inspired cuisine with artfully designed cocktails. Executive Chef Simon Dolinky draws inspiration from local San

Diego purveyors and farmers for an ingredient-driven "social plates" menu designed to be accessible and inspiring for under $25. There is an extensive selection of hors d'oeuvres on the dinner menu including crazy pickles, brisket sliders, and shrimp ceviche tacos. The bar and cocktail program, created by in-house master mixologist Erin Williams, previously from renowned Pegu Club in New York City, offers options from Prohibition-era classics to Saltbox original cocktails, local beers, food-friendly wines, and satisfying nonalcoholic options; our bar has just the spirit you need.

Searsucker, 611 5th Ave., San Diego, CA 92101; (619) 233-7327; searsucker.com; California Modern; $$$$. Created by celebrity Chef Brian Malarkey and hospitality visionary James Brennan, this chic and sexy restaurant attracts a young and hip crowd craving fancy cocktails and an innovative and classic New American cuisine. The food remains a stylish and sincere interpretation of Malarkey's imagination. The menu changes daily and can feature anything from spicy shrimp and bacon grits and mahimahi with chipotle to hanger steak or diver scallops with pumpkin, brown butter, and foie molasses. Searsucker is open for lunch, dinner, and Sunday brunch. Malarkey and Brennan have opened several restaurants in the San Diego area, including **Burlap** (p. 67), **Gingham** (p. 272), and **Gabardine** (p. 215).

Serenity Restaurant & Lounge, 201 J Street #101, San Diego, CA 92101; (619) 450-4201; serenitysd.com; Asian Fusion; $$$$. Nestled in the Marina District, experience a delicate balance of flavors and aromas from a mouthwatering array of Asian Fusion cuisine served in a modern and intimate environment complete with a large wall fountain as its focal point. A visually stunning glass-enclosed ceiling upstairs makes a meal here truly distinctive so that during the day, soft warm sunlight pours in over the lunch crowd, while soothing moonlight bathes dinner guests in the evening hours. The open kitchen allows you to watch Executive Chef Josh Hernandez and his crew passionately craft each and every one of Serenity's flavorful signature dishes. Standouts include the Caramel Pork Belly with cucumber and chili bamboo relish, Seafood Ramen with Pork Cheek and Caramel Apple Tart for dessert.

Landmarks

Grant Grill, 326 Broadway, U.S. Grant Hotel, San Diego, CA 92101; (619) 744-2077; grantgrill.com; California Modern; $$$$. This is fine dining at its best, with attentive service and classic touches of wood paneling, cream linens, and soft candlelight. The Grant Grill served its first mock turtle soup in 1951. Still serving it today, every bite of this rich and beefy tomato-based soup, with a touch of sherry poured tableside, is a sumptuous journey through time. Breakfast, lunch, and dinner are available daily. The large bar area is a perfect location for after-work relaxing or setting the mood for a great evening. Live music is playing regularly, and the happy hours can get very crowded. Executive Chef Mark Kropczynski and

Chef de Cuisine Chris Kurth highlight their ever-evolving menu with local produce, fresh seafood, and prime meats. For dinner, I would strongly recommend you splurge on the tasting menu, a rotating combination of 3 to 5 chef specialties paired with fantastic wines. It is truly a special experience. See Chef Kurth's recipe for **Poached Hen Egg with Sweet Onion Bullion** on p. 348.

Westgate Room, 1055 2nd Ave., San Diego, CA 92101; (619) 238-1818; westgatehotel.com; French; $$$$. Built over 40 years ago, the Westgate Hotel has an elegant interior and decor reminiscent of French nobility. Executive Chef Fabrice Hardel of the award-winning Westgate Room is consistently pleasing diners with his creative and delicate gourmet French cuisine offered in a graceful and European-inspired atmosphere. Staying away from the old-world style of creating French cuisine, Hardel has left heavy cream and butter behind for a new lease on lighter fare. For lunch try the milk-fed veal picatta with Yukon potato gnocchi or the Alaskan halibut cheeks with sweet yellow corn risotto. Start your evening with a creative cocktail from the Plaza Bar and relax and unwind with live entertainment. The dinner menu changes with the seasons to take advantage of the freshest ingredients. A few of the most popular year-round items include British Columbia king salmon, Black Angus beef tenderloin with German butterball potato, and

Colorado lamb chop mascarpone polenta. The dessert menu is a special creation that exudes indulgence. Two of my favorites are the fragrant Tonka Bean Creme Brulee and creamy Honeycomb Panna Cotta.

Specialty Stores, Markets & Producers

Cowboy Star Restaurant & Butcher Shop, 640 10th Ave., San Diego, CA 92101; (619) 450-5880; thecowboystar.com; Steak House; $$$. Experience an inimitable cuisine that embodies the spirit of the American West while utilizing the season's freshest offerings in a warm and welcoming atmosphere complete with exposed beam ceilings, cowboy accents, and classic landscape photography. A display kitchen allows guests to get an up-close and personal view of Executive Chef Victor Jimenez in action, and an adjoining walk-in retail butcher shop is the source for the signature meat served in the restaurant. All meats are brought in from farms and ranches that adhere to the highest integrity farming practices, include 100 percent grass and corn-fed, USDA Prime, 35-day dry-aged beef along with several free-range poultry and game options. Cowboy Star sources only the freshest ingredients for each and every dish, utilizing farmers' markets to find the best produce available. Their seafood program also follows the strict Monterey Bay Aquarium's "Seafood Watch" to ensure total sustainability in an effort to save the oceans. I am crazy about their signature hand-chopped steak tartare prepared to order with capers, shallots, and parsley then topped with a quail egg and served with toasted baguette.

Cremolose, 840 5th Ave., Ste. 100, San Diego, CA 92101; (619) 233-9900; CremoloseSD.com; Italian; $$$. Cut right to the good stuff at this Italian cafe and specialty dessert restaurant featuring authentic Italian gelato imported from Italy. With 40 locations throughout Europe, this is the first Cremolose location in the US. The decor is bright red and beige with display cabinets imported from Italy, and campari pendants used for lighting over the bar. Featuring 24 flavors of Italian gelato and 24 flavors of the Italian imported cremolose, a new type of gelato that is fresh-fruit based with a creamy texture, they also serve espresso drinks, paninis, salads, pizzas, and hot and cold Italian dishes. An extensive dessert menu features 40 cakes made in-house in individual serving sizes as well as larger cakes, available to go. A full bar includes an extensive selection of 55 whiskeys, 19 domestic and microbrewed beers, a wine selection, and several specialty drinks using cremolose as a base. Delicious cremolose-based specialty cocktails include the Lemonade di Jack (Jack Daniels and lemon cremolose), Tuscan Berry (El Jimador rosemary-infused blanco tequila, fresh lemon and lime juices, and black mulberry cremolose), and Sparkling Pear (Hanger One Spiced Pear, Berentzen pear liqueur, ginger liqueur, muddled cucumber and basil, served with a Prosseco float).

Frosted Robin Cupcakes, 859 W. Harbor Dr., Ste. B, San Diego, CA 92101; (619) 702-7188; frostedrobincupcakes.com; Desserts; $$. Frosted Robin Cupcakes is a unique gourmet cupcake, coffee, and tea cafe in Seaport Village with a sister location in Grand Cayman. Guy and Sheree Harrison opened Frosted Robin Cupcakes in February 2011 after moving to San Diego from Sheree's home country, Grand Cayman, in 2010. The atmosphere is shabby chic, boasting a vintage French country style decor. They have more than 40 cupcake flavors that rotate monthly. Some of the more unique flavors include Cayman Spice (cinnamon, nutmeg, cornmeal, and coconut milk), Lavender, English Sticky Toffee, and Lychee Rose. Every month they feature between 12 and 18 flavors. They also specialize in artisan loose-leaf teas and organic coffees.

National City, Chula Vista, La Mesa & El Cajon

This area of San Diego is large and diverse, spanning much of the south-coastal communities between San Diego and Mexico and stretching to the easternmost borders of the county. Primarily settled by ranchers in the 1800s, this area was also frequented by workers traveling between San Diego and gold mining operations in the mountains. Major growth was seen in these communities after World War II in the 1940s and '50s.

National City is home to a 3-mile port area along the San Diego Bay, including the Naval Base San Diego, one of the largest US Naval bases on the west coast. One of the first "auto malls" ever built in the world is located on a strip dubbed "the Mile of Cars," and Highland Avenue is considered one of the more popular cruising routes for auto enthusiasts. Listed as a California Historical

Landmark, the National City Depot was built in 1882 and served as the first Pacific Coast terminus station of the Santa Fe Railway system's transcontinental railroad. Also a large attraction for South County residents is the Westfield Plaza Bonita shopping mall, which includes a large cinema complex and plenty of unique and chain department stores.

Chula Vista earned its name due to the scenic location between San Diego Bay and coastal mountain foothills. It is the second largest city in San Diego County, and home to one of Americas few year-round US Olympic Training centers. Other popular tourist destinations include a large outdoor amphitheater used for concerts year-round and Knott's Soak City USA. A large marina is home to the Chula Vista Yacht Club, and sports fishing and whale watching charters operate daily. The Nature Center is home to interactive exhibits describing geologic and historic aspects of the Sweetwater Marsh and San Diego Bay. The Center has exhibits on sharks, rays, waterbirds, birds of prey, insects, and flora.

El Cajon is located in the eastern portion of the county, along the I-8 corridor between San Diego and the Cleveland National Forest. Several interesting museums call El Cajon home, including the San Diego Aero-Space Museum and Heritage of the Americas. A number of popular golf courses are open daily. Both Sycuan and Viejas Indian Reservations and casinos border the eastern end, and attract professional and casual gamblers alike.

Andiamo Ristorante Italiano & Bar, 5950 Santo Rd., San Diego, CA 92124; (858) 277-3501; andiamo-ristorante.com; Italian; $$$. Located in a charming strip mall in the quiet Tierrasanta neighborhood, this wonderful restaurant serves mainly Northern Italian cuisine. The dining room is charming and elegant, and they have a spacious patio for enjoying the great outdoors. When seated, you'll receive a warm and aromatic rosemary focaccia bread and tomato-basil dipping sauce. Their menu is simple and very authentic. Just ask the regulars who frequent the dining room on any given night. For beginners, try the delicious meatball appetizer with a roasted pepper cream sauce. It pairs well with the bread on your table. The pizzas are perfectly prepared, with a crunchy crust right out of the oven. A unique flavor combination is the prosciutto, fig, and gorgonzola pie, topped with a fistful of fresh arugula. The pasta selections are lengthy and varied. Specialties that will catch your eye include veal piccata and fileto albese.

The Barbeque Pit, 920 E. Plaza Blvd., National City, CA 91950; (619) 477-2244; thebarbecuepitrestaurant.com; Barbecue; $$. Established in San Diego over 60 years ago, the Texas-style recipes have been handed down for generations. The interior hasn't changed much over the years, with plenty of wood throughout the dining room and animal heads hanging on the walls. You simply order your meal at the front, then sit at the communal tables and enjoy some of the best barbecue in town. Nothing fancy here, just a large selection of timeless favorites at an extremely reasonable price. The sauce is a blend of flavors, ranging from savory to sweet, with just the right tang to tickle your taste buds. Obviously, the chicken and ribs are the most popular items, but I really enjoyed the ham dinner with coleslaw, potato salad, and old-fashioned baked beans. The sliced barbecue beef sandwich is also an excellent choice. This is a great choice for catering a business gathering or special occasion. There is also a second location on Fletcher Hills Parkway in El Cajon.

Blue Print Cafe, 1805 Newton Ave., San Diego, CA 92113; (619) 233-7010; blueprint-cafe.com; American; $$. Tucked away on a quiet street in the Barrio Logan neighborhood, Blueprint Cafe exudes a spirited ambiance. Bold colors, stainless steel, and strategically located lighting set a mood for fun conversation. Passionate about food her entire life, New York native Gayle Covner draws inspiration for this friendly neighborhood eatery from her hometown and travel experiences. A fresh and seasonal comfort food menu is offered for lunch, dinner, and late-night enjoyment. Favorites include the classic tuna melt on rye, with melted Swiss, caramelized onions, and shoestring fries, and the peanut noodle salad, with spinach and greens, cucumber, veggies, grilled spicy chicken, and Thai dressing. On the lighter side, they offer the 440 cal plate, a black bean burger with avocado, fried egg, chipotle, and tomato on a thin whole-wheat roll. Craft beers by the bottle and a short list of wines are also available. And no visit would be complete without ordering a slice of their now-famous cream cheese carrot cake. Heaven on a plate! Take note: They are closed on the weekend, so be sure to plan ahead.

Cafe La Maze, 1441 Highland Ave., National City, CA 91950; (619) 474-3222; cafelamaze.com; Steak House; $$$. This legendary restaurant has been serving locals and visitors for over 70 years. Best of all, they've kept the interior reminiscent of the Golden Era of Hollywood, with comfortable booths and decor that will make you feel like you're dining in a classic 1940s and '50s era steak house. During the Prohibition years, many of Hollywood's elite would travel to Tijuana for gambling at the Caliente racetrack, but the trek was significantly longer than our modern times, as interstate highways were only beginning to take shape. Marcel Lamaze, a legendary and influential restaurateur and maître d' in Los Angeles, was challenged by his connections to establish a halfway house near the Mexican border, as a pit stop for rest (and gambling). All of Marcel's acquaintances still adorn the walls, and take you back to an influential and entertaining time in American history. Cafe La Maze's famous prime rib steak is still the most popular dish on the menu today, but many seafood selections are also tempting to the palate. And unlike recent trends at most fine dining restaurants, all meals still include a choice of soup or salad, seasonal vegetables, and a starch. Open daily for lunch and dinner, oftentimes with live music in the evenings.

Casa de Pico, 5500 Grossmont Center Dr., La Mesa, CA 92142; (619) 463-3267; casadepico.com; Mexican; $$. Take part in the true spirit of Mexico by tasting regional and traditional food in a colorful dining room with hand-painted artwork and wrought-iron chandeliers. A heated patio offers a fountain, tropical plants and colorful flowers, frosty margaritas, and strolling mariachis. This is certainly not the right place for a quiet, romantic interlude! This location is perfect for a family or office gathering where you're looking for plenty of entertainment. Their handmade tortillas are served warm off the griddle and prepared for you right in the front lobby area. Be sure to try their most popular item, the Cheese Crisp Special, a crisp flour tortilla topped with refried beans, two kinds of beef or shredded chicken and melted cheese, avocado slices, tomato wedges, guacamole, and sour cream. It's been on the menu for over 40 years!

Gingham, 8384 La Mesa Blvd., La Mesa, CA 91941; (619) 797-1922; ginghameats.com; American; $$$. Dubbed the first "urban cowboy diner" and offering "meat market cuisine," Gingham offers low and slow-roasted meats with the price point as nothing over $20. Nightly offerings are divided into categories including "Not From a Can," "Baked," "Oil Boil," "Low and Slow," "Smoked," and "Charbroil." Choose from an array of salads, sandwiches, dogs, and sausages. For lunch, try the fried green tomato salad with burrata or the wild boar bratwurst with stewed onions and peppers. Standout dinner dishes include pork shoulder made with "Julian Cider" and fried kale; milk butter chicken and collards topped with smoked corn gravy; venison osso bucco made with stout, chipotle, and chocolate; and brisket with "Momma's Dry Rub" and hot link; and whole catfish with lavish and house condiments. Specialty cocktails infused with an assortment of ingredients ranging from fresh pressed juices to Serrano chilies are offered. Gingham also features a noteworthy selection of whiskeys, local craft brews, and California wines paired perfectly with Gingham's meaty fare.

Luna Grill, 2275 Otay Lakes Rd., Ste. 119, Chula Vista, CA 91914; (619) 656-5862; lunagrill.com; Middle Eastern; $$. Make a better fast food choice at Luna Grill, where eating on the go can be a healthy and affordable experience. Specializing in Near East and Mediterranean cuisine, the menu focuses on grilled-to-order kabobs. They offer all-natural beef, lamb, and poultry paired with marinades and dressings made from scratch daily. There are also plenty of vegan and vegetarian choices to satisfy any craving. A couple of excellent starters include the spicy cilantro hummus with whole-wheat flatbread, or traditional Persian Eggplant dip with pita bread, and topped with yogurt and sautéed mint. Or try their traditional spanakopita: baked phyllo dough filled with spinach and feta cheese. All of the kebabs can be served in a sandwich, as a salad topping, or as an entree with basmati rice, pita bread, cucumber yogurt dip, fresh green salad, and a grilled tomato or carrots. Multiple locations available throughout San Diego.

Ono's Cafe, 4154 Bonita Rd., Bonita, CA 91902; (619) 470-6667; onoscafe.com; Islands; $$. Ono's Cafe offers an Asian Fusion, Pacific Rim cuisine with Hawaiian and Philipino influences. Located in a mall near the Chula Vista Municipal Golf Course, this restaurant has limited seating inside and additional tables on the outdoor patio. Prominent Hawaiian decorations will greet you, including a large tiki and 750-gallon fish tank as a centerpiece. Well-known for their sushi, they also offer plenty of other seafood and chicken options. One of their best specialty rolls is the Onolicious, with smoked salmon, crab, and cream cheese deep-fried in tempura batter. Two excellent entrees include the Seafood Dynamite, a little tower served on top of rice with a soy vinaigrette salad, and the macadamia nut-crusted salmon with unique cranberry coleslaw. But the best-kept secret is the Malasaza—a Portuguese doughnut-sweetbread baked to order with sugar or cinnamon.

Pinnacle Peak Steakhouse, 7927 Mission Gorge Rd., Santee, CA 92071; (619) 448-8882; pinnaclepeaksteakhouse.com; Steak House; $$$. No city slicker wearing a tie is allowed at this long-standing steak house, reminiscent of an old barn with tables covered in red and white tablecloths. Story has it that back in the day, some businessmen came in a bit overdressed in their suits and ties. Since this place is very casual, one of the servers (a friend of one of the businessmen) came up and explained there are no city slickers allowed. With no hesitation, he cut off the tie and hung it on the wall. Since then, guests have intentionally entered the dining room wearing ties. Doing so will trigger a loud cow bell, followed by an amusing display of surprise from your server, and the tie-cutting ceremony culminating in a display on the wall. Each server has their own special speech prepared for guests. When you enter the dining room, you'll see the cooks searing steaks in The Cook Shack on a flaming mesquite grill. All dinners include a salad, traditional Cowboy baked beans, and plenty of bread and butter. If you're a little intimidated by the 28-ounce Porterhouse, rejoice in the list of smaller cuts, including a 12-ounce Cattleman's Rib Eye, or 10-ounce Flat Iron cut. Barbecue chicken and pork ribs are also favorites here.

Romesco Baja Med Bistro, 4346 Bonita Rd., Bonita, CA 91902; (619) 475-8627; romescobajamed.com; Mexican; $$$. Well-regarded Chef-Owner Javier Plascencia has taken his successful family restaurant business north of the border, and we are all better off because of that decision. For three decades, the family has sought to change the culinary landscape in Tijuana, operating 10 distinctive eateries and serving cuisine that has garnered international attention. They have taken traditional Mexican fare to a new level, which is wonderfully evident at the Romesco bistro. The main dining room is subdued and relaxing, or you can choose the separated tapas bar that's open late and much livelier.

In either case, you're sure to enjoy a meal that will tantalize your senses. The tapas menu is extensive, making your decisions more difficult, but the staff is happy to understand your tastes and make appropriate recommendations. My eyes were drawn to the *favada con almejas*, Spanish white fava beans with chorizo, garlic, white wine, tomatoes, saffron, and clams. Although I've enjoyed fava beans my whole life, it was a new taste for me, with wonderful aromas and textures. For dinner, the lamb asada was a colorful and amazingly complex mixture of flavors. Plascencia also serves some Mediterranean specialties on the menu, including the beef Milanesa Napolitana, a lightly breaded steak stuffed with ham and mozzarella and topped with marinara. I can honestly say that my Italian mother would have been impressed! Even the wine and craft beer lists highlight the Baja area, although there are plenty of other options to suit your taste.

Sammy's Woodfired Pizza & Grill, 8555 Fletcher Pkwy., La Mesa, CA 91942; (619) 460-8555; sammyspizza.com; Pizza; $$. Known for its award-winning gourmet pizzas, tapas, salads, and pastas, Sammy's menu is constantly evolving and expanding with unique dishes and an expansive gluten-free menu that caters to a wider audience. Sammy's conveys a healthy, fresh, and organic approach with dishes including the tabouli and quinoa salad, featuring organic cucumber, parsley, mint, red onion, tomato, carrot, lemon juice, extra-virgin olive oil, and romaine. Or try the Redwood Hill Farms smoked goat cheddar artisan thin-crust pizza, made with oven-roasted tomatoes and fresh organic rosemary. A new vegan menu keeps ingredients fresh and light with delicious selections that exclude meat, eggs, dairy products, and all other animal-derived ingredients. Appetizing items include tapas such as the oak-roasted asparagus with vegan mozzarella, extra-virgin olive oil, and balsamic vinegar, various salads with dressings made from scratch, and delicious pizzas made on whole-wheat or gluten-free crust with dairy-free mozzarella. Sammy's also adds sophistication to its dessert menu with salted butterscotch pudding and orange-infused whipped cream. Sammy's has multiple locations throughout San Diego.

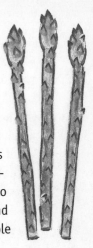

South Bay Fish & Grill, 570 Marina Pkwy., Chula Vista, CA 91910; (619) 420-7234; southbayfishandgrill.com; Seafood; $$$. This is a spacious restaurant located on the bay with expansive views of the Chula Vista Marina. The dining room features nautical antiques and yacht club memorabilia, and is the perfect location for a special occasion or office party. The lunch and dinner menus include all of your favorite dishes and feature some of the freshest seafood available. Selections can be grilled or sautéed, and include soup or salad and two side dishes. The hazelnut-crusted scallops are especially delicious and topped with tropical fruit salsa. Sunday Jazz brunch is a popular choice, so reservations are recommended. Their in-house pastry chef creates all of the desserts, including crème brulee and lemon meringue pie. They also have live evening entertainment Tuesday through Saturday.

Terra American Bistro, 7091 El Cajon Blvd., San Diego, CA 92115; (619) 293-7088; terrasd.com; American; $$$. Boasting a bar in the shape of a horseshoe and a captivating chandelier over the chef's communal farm table, this cozy New American bistro reverberates with a style all its own. The restaurant decor offers warm colors of tan and brown, with brick, wooden beams and polished concrete. Executive Chef-Owner Jeff Rossman offers a seasonal menu, focused on local, organic, and sustainable ingredients, even pulling herbs off his wall garden from time to time. Homemade soup of the day may include anything from white chili bean to vegetable bisque or seafood chowder. Flatbread pizzas and ginger chicken potstickers are great to share. Build your own burger or opt for the barbecue sliders, which may seem small, but are extremely filling. Great lobster options include the lobster BLT with smoked bacon or the lobster macaroni n' cheese. Grilled yellowtail or rock cod are some of the fresh catches of the day that you may find here. One more thing—don't miss the pumpkin ravioli! Terra welcomes vegan, vegetarian, and gluten-free guests. Rossman's cookbook, *From Terra's Table: New American Food, Fresh from Southern California's Organic Farms,* is the recipient of several awards.

TJ Oyster Bar, 4246 Bonita Rd., Bonita, CA 91902; (619) 267-4577; tjoysterbar.com; Seafood; $$. Started over 30 years ago on a corner in Tijuana, Mexico, the current location continues with the same traditional-style menu that made the business so popular. Don't let the diminutive size fool you, as the menu includes some heavy-hitting favorites that make this place a popular hangout for many of the locals, as well as the astute readers who circulate the positive reputation. Clearly, oysters on the half shell are a signature item, but don't pass by the unique flavors of the *aguachile en molcajete*, a bowl of raw shrimp drowned in lemon juice and hot chilies to create a ceviche, and served with onions and cucumbers. Other traditional favorites include smoked marlin or stingray tacos, and a whole fried fish that has a crispy crust and tender meat.

The Vine Cottage Wine Bar and Kitchen, 6062 Lake Murray Blvd., Ste. 101A, La Mesa, CA 91942; (619) 465-0138; thevinecottage .com; American; $$. Offering food and wine from all over the world, the Mediterranean-inspired menu focuses on seasonal, all-natural, organic, locally sourced, and sustainably produced ingredients whenever possible. The spacious dining room feels like a country cottage, with wood-beamed ceilings and rock walls. There is also a heated outdoor patio for alfresco dining. A good choice for dinner would be any of the daily specials, which change frequently and take advantage of seasonal or readily available ingredients. A popular favorite among the locals in the neighborhood is the charcuterie and artisanal cheese board, served with Epi Demi-Baguette; a 3 wheat-shaped half-baguette baked locally by the Sadie Rose Baking Co. They serve an excellent take on fish-and-chips, with craft beer-battered Lingcod and house-made remoulade sauce. Another popular item is the Vine Cottage grass-fed beef burger, with a high-grade "Paso Prime" California beef patty, roasted Anaheim chilies, Drunken Goat cheese, wild arugula, and Yukon gold fries. The flatbread pizza choices are outstanding.

Landmarks

Anthony's Fish Grotto, 9530 Murray Dr., La Mesa, CA 91942; (619) 463-0368; gofishanthonys.com; Seafood; $$$. For more than 60 years, Anthony's Fish Grotto has been pleasing multiple generations of regulars. Kids who once dined in diapers are returning with their own families. It's no surprise that they're voted one of the best seafood restaurants in San Diego. Located in a scenic area with a beautiful man-made lake in the background, you can choose a seat with a view. The lobby is decorated like an underwater paradise, complete with rock walls and plenty of fish seemingly floating in the air. Here you will find the freshest seasonal catches, including shrimp, crab, albacore tuna, cod, sole, and more. The most popular items are their oyster shooters, creamy clam chowder, and crispy calamari. I love the crab stuffed mushrooms and Crab Louis salad, but the fresh catches of the day are always a sure bet. They also have a full-service fish market.

Chicken Pie Shop, 2633 El Cajon Blvd., San Diego, CA 92104; (619) 295-0156; American; $$. What was started in 1938 by owner

George B. Whitehead as a tiny eatery on the corner of Fifth and Robinson Avenues in Hillcrest, has moved not once but twice to accommodate demand. The current location in North Park on El Cajon Boulevard is definitely big enough for everyone to enjoy old-fashioned chicken pie and gravy. The inside dining room is not fancy by any means, offering a laid-back country-style atmosphere with plain wooden tables and chairs and old photos and memorabilia adorning the walls. The chicken pie dinner is a dirt-cheap deal served with soup, salad, coleslaw, mashed potatoes and gravy, veggies, warm roll, and a slice of pie for dessert. Take one of the delicious home-made pies with you! Great choices include blueberry, peach, lemon, coconut and pineapple cream. This home-style restaurant with a come-back-soon hospitality offers food a la carte as well as a take-out menu. No checks, no credit cards, no debit cards. It has been a cash-only business since the beginning.

D.Z. Akins, 6930 Alvarado Rd., San Diego, CA 92120; (619) 265-0218; dzakinsdeli.com; American; $$. Since 1980, D.Z. Akins has expanded their restaurant five times to accommodate diners clambering at their door for down-home, New York–style deli food in massive portions. Open at 7 a.m. for breakfast daily, choose from 3 dozen selections including french toast, Belgian waffles, omelets, steak and eggs, smoked salmon (lox), and more. For lunch, the menu boasts 134 unique sandwiches, including Triple-Deckers, piled sky-high with top quality deli meats such as corned beef, pastrami, turkey, and roast beef. Complete dinner entrees include historical favorites like corned beef and cabbage, roast brisket of beef, and stuffed cabbage rolls. Old-fashioned desserts include sundaes, shakes, malts, and sodas. They say they make the best cheesecake in San Diego . . . guess what, they are right!

Specialty Stores, Markets & Producers

Frubble, 9628 Carlton Hills Blvd., Santee, CA 92071; (619) 270-1230; frubble.com; Coffee/Tea; $. If you have ever had boba tea, or would like to try something new and unique, stop at Frubble where they have their own take on these Taiwanese-style drinks that first originated in the 1980s. Boba, also known as bubble tea, are typically tea- and milk-based drinks that contain tapioca pearls at the bottom that are sipped through a large straw. These tapioca pearls are chewy and virtually tasteless balls that take on the flavor of the drink you choose. The menu offers drink flavors of vanilla, coconut, mango, honeydew, and banana as well as green tea and my favorite, chai. Choose to have your drink blended or over ice with a big helping of the boba at the bottom. There are many tables and chairs as well as black leather couches to relax in. There is also a little stage in the middle of the shop where local bands play on occasion for entertainment.

Hans & Harry's Bakery, 5080 Bonita Rd., Bonita, CA 91902; (619) 475-2253; hans-harry.com; Bakery; $$. Since 1991, customers have been raving about the gourmet cakes, strudels, and pastries from this retail bakery in Bonita. Trained in the fine art of European cake design and baking in their native country of Holland, business partners and skilled Pastry Chefs Hans Zandee and Harry Eijsermans have been luring customers to their bakery for an assortment of elaborate confections made with the finest and freshest ingredients available. Combining over 5 decades of experience, they have been able to achieve the best of the Old-World European cake styles, with the current creations of quality crafted cakes. Today, they are still hard at work putting their finishing touches on one-of-a-kind, sugary masterpieces. Surprise the chocolate lover in your life with a Belgian chocolate truffle cake, walnut fudge brownies, or a Black Forest strudel. Hans and Harry will inspire you to try all of their creations— just not in one visit of course!

The Wine Scene

Although Northern and Central California have historically been considered two of the finest wine-growing regions in the world, industry professionals are recognizing the contribution from all points south, including the Santa Ana, Temecula, and San Pasqual Valleys. Given the right environmental conditions, excellent varietals are being produced and consumed in areas within close driving distance from San Diego. Whether it's a day trip to wineries in the valleys, or a quick drive to a local wine bar, enthusiasts have a wide diversity of choices, ranging from budget to extravagant. All of the wine shops, bars, and bistros offer a great selection of local, domestic, and international wines to enjoy. Some of these proprietors also offer an exceptional menu of culinary favorites, with plenty of advice on pairing flavors to reach the ultimate tasting experience. In this chapter, I have also included several local wineries that are either within, or a short driving distance from, downtown San Diego. Enjoy!

The Barrel Room, 16765 Bernardo Center Dr., Rancho Bernardo, CA 92028; (858) 673-7512; thebarrelroomsandiego.com; Wine Bar; $$. The Barrel Room is a vintage retail wine bar and bistro offering food and wine connoisseurs a perfect place to dine and relax. The atmosphere is sophisticated, yet comfortable, featuring black leather couches, a cozy indoor dining space, and a small outdoor patio. Born and raised in France, Executive Chef Marc Liautard prepares Mediterranean-inspired fare, paired with specific wines. Sip on a Pinot Gris and be prepared to dive into warm and glutinous brie wrapped in a puff pastry and topped with raspberry preserves and lightly candied pecans. If that's not your style, than try a Pinot Noir and dig into a pork shank that's been slowly roasted in red wine and served over a bed of imported fettuccine sautéed in butter, better known as the Osso Bucco Milanese. Delicious! Weekends can be crowded, so it's a good idea to call in advance and reserve a table.

Bernardo Winery, 13330 Paseo Del Verano Norte, San Diego, CA 92128; (858) 487-1866; bernardowinery.com; Winery; $$. Producing red wines in the Italian tradition they are known for, step back in time to one of the oldest operating wineries in Southern California. Established in 1889, it was purchased by Vincent Rizzo in 1927, and is still owned by the family today. Take a tour of the wine-making process from beginning to end, enjoy a wine tasting, or wander the grounds filled with flowering trees and olive gardens. Enjoy coffee, sandwiches, and scones from the coffee shop while browsing through the specialty shops, or savor a seasonal fresh menu from Cafe Merlot. This is the perfect setting for a wedding, social gathering, or corporate event.

Cordiano Winery, 15732 Highland Valley Rd., Escondido, CA 92025; (760) 469-9463; cordianowinery.com; Winery; $$. This family-owned and -operated vineyard has southern Italian roots, evident in the passion used to create special varietals for over a decade. The views are spectacular, beckoning you to stay and relish the sunset while picnicking with a fine wine. In fact, the Cordiano family encourages visitors to spend time conversing and laughing with each other, the way it was meant to enjoy life. The tiled indoor/outdoor tasting patio is an excellent option for special occasions or corporate gatherings. There's even a bocce ball court to add to the ambiance. Among the several varietals available, try the deep and complex Cabernet Sauvignon, Syrah, or Zinfandel. Join the Primo Amore Wine Club and take advantage of additional savings on your purchases, either online or in person.

Dolce Pane E Vino, 16081 San Dieguito Rd., Rancho Santa Fe, CA 92091; (858) 832-1518; dolcepaneevino.com; Wine Bar; $$. Located in the heart of Rancho Santa Fe, this cozy wine bar offers inside seating at large tables carved from tree trunks, situated between racks of fine wine. There is also a moderate-size outdoor patio, with seating next to inviting fire pits. The wine list is extensive, with offerings that span most varietals from domestic and international locations. Their Formaggeria is open daily for market fresh Italian meats, artisan cheeses, or made-to-order paninis. For the perfect picnic, include a bottle of your favorite wine. Full lunch and dinner menus have been created to satisfy any craving. A local favorite is the grilled veal chop with porcini reduction, Chino Farm's vegetables, and whipped potatoes. I'm a sucker for the simple things, like the Caprese salad, with delicious vine-ripened tomatoes, Burrata cheese, aged balsamic, micro basil, and sea salt. Pair it with a special blended red wine. Catering is also available.

Enoteca Style, 1445 India St., San Diego, CA 92101; (619) 546-7138; enotecastyle.com; Wine Bar; $$. Across the country of Italy, enotecas are the gathering place for reveling in great food, wine, and conversation. Inspired by these traditions, the Enoteca Style wine bar is a home-grown illustration located in the heart of the landmark Little Italy neighborhood. Seating is available indoors or on a small patio where you can enjoy the busy street-life passing by. The menu includes popular bistro items, including paninis, salads, marinated olives, cured meats, and specialty cheeses. One of my favorites is the vegetarian Hawthorn panini, with portobello mushroom, goat cheese, avocado, tomato, roasted red peppers, caramelized onion, and a creamy marinated artichoke spread. A large selection of international and domestic wines is available by the taste, glass, or bottle, and is sure to satisfy anyone's palate.

ENO Wine Room, 1500 Orange Ave., Coronado, CA 92118; (619) 522-8546; enowinerooms.com; Wine Bar; $$. Located in the historic Hotel del Coronado, this intimate wine lounge is just steps from the Pacific. Don't let the cozy interior lull you into thinking the selection here is limited. With a 2,800-bottle inventory, you're likely to find something for any taste. A large glass case highlights the other two delightful offerings, international artisan cheeses and handmade chocolates. Perfect pairs are only a moment away, as the attentive staff is always available to assist in matching your desires with the right combination of savory or sweet. This is a picture-perfect location for an after-hours meeting with the office staff, or a romantic interlude for two next to the warm fire pit. My visit always includes a special bottle of California red, a savory charcuterie plate paired with a cheese flight, and a selection of marinated olives. And, of course, a few locally crafted Dallmann Chocolates to complete the experience!

Firefly Grill & Wine Bar, 251 N. El Camino Real, #B, Encinitas, CA 92024; (760) 635-1066; fireflygrillandwinebar.com; Wine Bar; $$. Hidden in a strip mall along the business center of Encinitas, this little gem is a favorite among locals. Modest in size, the dining room is quaint and inviting. There is also an outdoor patio perfect for enjoying wine and conversation in predictable southern California weather. The Wine Bar is impressive, with 30 wines available by the glass, representing popular favorites, unique finds, and truly extraordinary values. All wines are grouped by flavor category for simplicity, but the staff is always available to lend advice based on your personal taste. The dining menu is created specifically to pair with certain varietals, and changes seasonally to match the freshest local ingredients available. A new tasting menu is created weekly to make the choice even easier. They also host Winemaker Dinners, where you have the chance to converse with the experts and savor a specially designed menu.

Mosaic Wine Bar, 3422 30th St., San Diego, CA 92104; (619) 906-4747; mosaicwinebar.com; Wine Bar; $$. Considered one of San Diego's best new wine bars, Mosaic is located in the heart of North Park. It has a hip atmosphere, with plenty of artwork lining the walls, and comfortable chairs and couches ready to provide respite from a busy day. They offer unique and eclectic wines, with many varietals offered by the glass or bottle. They are a licensed retailer, so you can enjoy your wine in-house or take it home. Their Sangrias are all made in-house with a perfect combination of fresh fruit that leaves you refreshed. Their tapas and salad menus are extensive, but the flatbreads and gourmet pizzas have garnered the most attention. A favorite is the buffalo chicken pizza, with chicken breast, buttermilk ranch, red onions, mozzarella and blue cheeses, hot buffalo sauce, and diced celery. For a lighter choice, try the exotic herb olive flatbread, with thyme, oregano, marjoram, ground sumac, roasted sesame seeds, kalamata and cerignola olives, and fresh tomato.

Orfila Vineyards and Winery, 13455 San Pasqual Rd., Escondido, CA 92025; (760) 738-6500; orfila.com; Winery; $$. The Orfila family has roots in Argentina, where they have been in the wine-making business for four generations. With over 1,300 medals awarded in major national and international competitions, this local winery has the experience to create impressive vintages. Perched on a hill overlooking the picturesque San Pasqual Valley, this estate focuses on Rhone-style wines. The spacious facility and surrounding grounds are a perfect location for that special occasion or celebration. They host the highly popular Grape Stomp every August, which has become a tradition for locals and visitors alike. Two of my favorite whites are the fruity Lotus and oaky Chardonnay, but my heart is always longing for the smooth and complex characters of the Estate Sangiovese or Cabernet Sauvignon. At noon every day you are invited to join a complimentary tour of the cellar and winemaking process.

Sogno DiVino, 1607 India St., San Diego, CA 92101; (619) 531-8887; sognodivino.signonsandiego.com; Wine Bar; $$. This beautiful little gem in Little Italy will transport you to another country. The interior is very colorful and inviting, with tables and couches that beckon you to stay and enjoy good conversation under warm fixtures and natural light from the large windows. You're also welcome to sit on the outdoor patio and watch the world pass by. An array of reasonably priced domestic and international wines are available by the glass, half-carafe, or bottle. They also offer a number of delightful small plates, salads, and paninis to accompany your wine. Consider keeping it simple, and order the cured meat and artisan cheese plate with crusty bread and crackers. Be sure to leave room for dessert, because they have a delectable homemade strawberry tiramisu that is heavenly!

Solana Beach Winery on Cedros, 320 S. Cedros Ave., Solana Beach, 92075; (760) 207-5324; wineryoncedros.com; Winery; $$. Adam Carruth's artisan coastal winery located in the Cedros Design District of Solana Beach produces some of the finest red wines California has to offer, and since wineries in the city are rare, this is a real "wine find." The wine-making process begins with premium grapes from premiere California vineyards located on the Northern and Central Coast of California, including Mendocino County, Lake County, Sonoma Valley, and Napa Valley. September and October are busy for the small facility, where the grapes are crushed, barreled, aged, and bottled before shipping to the local wine stores in San Diego, Orange County and Los Angeles. One of my absolute favorites is the rich, smooth, and velvety 2006 Barbera, using Barbera grapes harvested from St. Olof Vineyards near Clear Lake in Northern California.

Splash Wine Lounge, 3043 University Ave., San Diego, CA 92104; (619) 296-0714; asplashofwine.com; Wine Bar; $$. This warm and welcoming wining and dining space in North Park is as comfortable as it gets. With 72 wines offered by the 1-ounce taste or glass from self-serve Enomatic machines, guests are allowed the freedom to try new and different wines at an affordable price. Sip and savor rare and expensive wines by the glass, as well as "value" labels. With 72 wines dispensed from the machines, find a style that will suit your taste. The nice selection of Italian wines is a pleasant surprise; Splash boasts the famous and fabulous Rosso di Montalcino, Brunello di Montalcino, Barbaresco, Barolo, Chianti, and other fun and interesting whites and reds from Italy. This was the first wine bar I ever visited that offered a Barolo and Brunello by the glass, much less a "splash," as well as a tasting of a variety of olive oils dispensed from the machines. I love the made-to-order flatbread pizzas, especially the Mediterranean with pesto sauce, peppers, onions, olives, sun-dried tomatoes, artichokes, mozzarella, and feta.

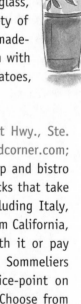

3rd Corner Wine Shop and Bistro, 897 S. Coast Hwy., Ste. F-104, Encinitas, CA 92024; (760) 942-2104; the3rdcorner.com; Wine Bar; $$. This is a very charming retail wine shop and bistro in Encinitas. Tables are placed all around the wine racks that take center stage. Wines are from all over the world, including Italy, Spain, France, and South America, as well as wines from California, Oregon, and Washington. Buy a bottle and leave with it or pay the $5 corkage and enjoy it for lunch and dinner. Sommeliers are on-site to answer any questions. With a low price-point on the bistro menu, nothing is too fancy or expensive. Choose from delicious pastas, salads, and sandwiches. For dinner, try pairing a California Zinfandel with either the braised short rib or juicy New

York steak. 3rd Corner has two locations in San Diego and one in Palm Desert.

Toscana Cafe and Wine Bar, 238 5th Ave., San Diego, CA 92101; (619) 231-5788; toscanacafe.net; Wine Bar; $$. Located on a corner in the historic Gaslamp Quarter, this beautiful bistro will make you feel like you're in the center of an Italian town. The brick walls and warm colors are inviting any time of day. They are open for breakfast, lunch, and dinner, serving European-style foods that pair perfectly with your beverage of choice. In my case, that would be a velvety Italian red, side by side with either the linguine marinara or lasagna alla bolognese. Located only 2 blocks from Petco Park, this is a great destination before or after enjoying a Padres game. If you're looking for a quiet, romantic evening, be sure to visit during the week, or early evenings on the weekends. Friday and Saturday nights are packed with patrons enjoying the downtown entertainment.

Vin de Syrah, 901 5th Ave., San Diego, CA 92101; (619) 234-4166; syrahwineparlor.com; Wine Bar; $$. You know you're stepping into something special at this subterranean lounge, as the front door is a wall of ivy with a nearly hidden handle. Unique in design, this upscale gathering place has plenty of soft high-back couches, ivy and brick-laden walls, colorful murals of forest pathways, large grape vines, solid wood tables, and some of the most eclectic chandeliers I've ever seen. Setting a warm and inviting mood to the interior, lights are created from wine barrels, umbrellas, and intertwined antlers. They offer over 20 wines by the glass and an extensive list of domestic and new world wines by the bottle, as well as beer and cocktails. There is also a menu of small bites to enjoy with your favorite drink. It is very popular on weekend nights, and is frequently used for private parties. Interactive wine tastings are offered every Friday and Saturday, but call in advance to ensure a seat.

Wet Stone Wine Bar & Cafe, 1927 4th Ave., San Diego, CA 92101; (619) 255-2856; WetStoneWinebar.com; Wine Bar; $$. You'll immediately feel welcome as you enter this cozy and friendly wine bar located off the beaten path near Balboa Park. Plenty of room, with dark wood accents, padded couches and chairs, and lots of foliage. The wine list is dotted with a number of small-production domestic and international selections. No matter what you choose, the staff is always happy to provide suggestions on the best food pairing. This is one wine bar that also offers patrons a diverse and tempting food selection. The menu is designed by Chef Christian Gomez, a native San Diegan with culinary inspirations from the Mediterranean and Latin America. A great starter that exhibits this style is the crostini with Chinese 5-spiced braised pork belly, fennel slaw, aji amarillo aioli, and pickled red onions. Be sure to also try the popular churrasco, a mixed grill of flat iron steak, Merguez lamb sausage, and chicken breast with chimichurri and bleu cheese crostini.

The Wine Pub, 2907 Shelter Island Dr., No. 108, San Diego, CA 92106; (619) 758-9325; thewinepubsd.com; Wine Bar; $$. Hidden in the Shelter Island Village 2 blocks from the San Diego Bay and Marina, this spacious wine bar has plenty of seating both inside and outside. The dog-friendly patio includes a bubbling fountain, warm fire pit, and plenty of overhead heat lamps, making it the perfect spot to enjoy a glass of wine with friends. The atmosphere is especially romantic at night with the stars overhead. At least 25 hand-selected domestic and international wines are available by the glass, including a wide selection of bubblies, dessert wines, and ports. They also serve a broad range of menu items, including smaller sharing plates such as the stuffed portobellinis or bruschetta trio, and larger meals like the stuffed chicken breast or Kobe beef meat loaf. Be sure to call ahead to hear about the daily specials. See the Wine Pub's recipe for **Cajun Shrimp Cakes** on p. 359.

Wine Steals, 1953 San Elijo Ave., Cardiff-by-the-Sea, CA 92007; (760) 230-2657; winestealssd.com; Wine Bar; $$. This is one of the more picturesque locations to enjoy a glass of wine and relax after work on the weekend. Plenty of space both indoors and on the outside patio overlooking the Pacific Ocean. The owner likes to focus attention to the boutique-style California wines in smaller cases, but also offers a small selection of international wines from

Spain, Portugal, Italy, Argentina, South Africa, and Australia. Their wine list is always changing as new labels arrive every couple of months, but 300 to 500 labels are always available. Happy hour and wine tastings are available throughout the week, including 38 wines by the glass. You are also free to purchase a bottle for home, or pay a small corkage fee to enjoy on the premises. Meal choices cover all of the best pairing options, including artisan cheeses and meats, salads, and specialty pizzas. Wine Steals has four locations in San Diego.

Wine Vault & Bistro, 3731 India St., # A, San Diego, CA 92103; (619) 295-3939; winevaultbistro.com; Wine Bar; $$. Hidden away on north India Street in Mission Hills, this wine bar is easy to miss from the street. You'll need to wind up a narrow set of stairs to the second floor, where you'll be surprised to step into a cozy cottage interior. There is also a very nice outdoor patio with a fire pit, but I prefer the simply decorated tables inside, nestled next to walls filled with art and wine bottles. It is very important that you plan ahead before visiting, as the restaurant is only open on select nights when they offer a winemaker dinner or special event. A calendar is updated frequently on their website, announcing the multicourse dinner and wine pairing for the evening. Although the quality of each meal is impressive, the price is extremely reasonable. A typical 3- to 5-course meal will run around $20 to $35 total, with a nominal extra charge for wine pairing. Street parking can be somewhat of a challenge in this crowded neighborhood, but the metered parking is free after 6 p.m.

Witch Creek Winery, 2906 Carlsbad Blvd., Carlsbad, CA 92008; (760) 720-7499; witchcreekwinery.com; Winery; $$. This award-winning boutique winery is located a block from the beach in the Carlsbad Village neighborhood, with plenty of restaurants and shopping within walking distance. They produce special, hand-crafted wines on a small scale, focusing on the rare varietals produced domestically, such as Nebbiolo and Montepulciano. As a testament to their quality, they earned 20 medals in the last 3 years at the *San Francisco Chronicle* Wine Competition. Their grapes are sourced locally from the Guadalupe region in Baja and smaller vineyards in California. All of the production activities, including barreling and bottling, are located in Carlsbad. There is also a quaint tasting room located in Julian. All of their wines are available only in the tasting rooms and online, and well worth the visit!

The Beer Scene

San Diego is considered one of the fastest-growing beer scenes in America, and possibly the world. Nearly 40 breweries now call San Diego home, with a reputation that is quickly becoming comparable to what Napa Valley is to wine. This isn't the place to look for pale, fizzy beers churned out of large manufacturing plants by the thousands. Let's face it, would you rather drink mass-produced wine out of a 3-liter bottle, or savor a special vintage from a small-volume, family-owned estate? Many local brewers believe it's the healthy competition that has elevated San Diego to stardom among beer aficionados. Regular communication and camaraderie is evident throughout the region. The result? Visit any national or international website devoted to the craft, and you will be amazed at the sheer volume of awards bestowed to local breweries. If you're yearning for specialty craft brews with endless flavors, styles, and techniques, then look no further. In the following pages, I highlight a small cross section of the many breweries nearby, as well as a number of brewpubs that offer a nearly endless variety of specialty beers on tap and in the bottle.

AleSmith Brewing Company, 9368 Cabot Dr., San Diego, CA 92126; (858) 549-9888; alesmith.com; Brewery; $$. Primarily inspired by the brewing styles of Great Britain and Belgium, this craft brewery produces a variety of beers, many of which have high alcohol content and are strongly hopped. One of my favorites is the Speedway Stout, a jet-black brew aged in bourbon barrels, with an alcohol level in the low teens. If that isn't enough, it has a heap of coffee added for an extra kick. Sold in a number of retail locations throughout much of California, their beers are found in 22-ounce bottles or 750ml champagne bottles. Their tasting room, which is open Thurs through Sun, offers growler fills, bottles, and official AleSmith merchandise for sale. They also host free tours of the brewery on the last Saturday of every month. As a testimonial to their experience, AleSmith's brewmaster, Peter Zien, is the only San Diego County brewer to be named a BJCP "Grand Master level 1" beer judge.

Ballast Point Brewing & Spirits, 10051 Old Grove Rd., San Diego, CA 92131; (858) 695-2739; ballastpoint.com; Brewery; $$. In the early 1990s, founder Jack White opened the Home Brew Mart, a paradise of supplies and ingredients for the home brewer. Soon after, he teamed up with Yuseff Cherney, an award-winning local brewer, to move his backyard brewery into the store. Ballast Point Brewing was born. As demand grew over the years, the brewery was moved to a separate location, but the Mart is still open for business. The staff is extremely knowledgeable and willing to help the novice or expert with a dream for creating the ultimate brew. All of their beers are named and labeled after fish, a tribute to one of their favorite pastimes. Don't miss out on the Sculpin IPA, inspired by the fish with tasty meat but poisonous spikes on the fins. A gold medal winner at the World Beer Cup in 2010, this brew has bright fruit aromas that make it easy and refreshing to drink. The main brewery and Brew Mart are open 7 days a week, with tours available daily.

Breakwater Brewing Company, 101 N. Coast Hwy., Oceanside, CA 92054; (760) 433-6064; breakwaterbrewing.com; Brewery; $$. Located right on the scenic Coast Highway in Oceanside, the Breakwater has become a local favorite. Owned and operated by California natives, this beach area location serves over a dozen of their own house brews, as well as 30 guest brews on tap. Don't miss trying their DMJ IPA, which won a gold medal at the 2010 San Diego International Beer Festival. If you're looking for something really

different, try the Rasbiscus Mead, a semi-sweet, sparkling honey wine flavored with raspberries and hibiscus flowers. It is also a hot spot for great food, including salads, sandwiches, and pizzas. Open every day for lunch, dinner, and late-night munching.

Coronado Brewing Company, 170 Orange Ave., Coronado, CA 92118; (619) 437-4452; coronadobrewingcompany.com; Brewery; $$.

Perfect for a quick lunch or a relaxing dinner, or as a hangout for sports fans who want to enjoy a game or two from one of many HDTVs, the Coronado Brewing Company offers a nice selection of year-round and specialty beers. One of the more popular beers is the Coronado Golden, a light and crisp golden-colored ale, comparable to a European-style pilsner. My favorite is the Mermaids Red Ale, a medium- to full-bodied beer, boasting a beautiful red color and slight caramel-roasted flavors that come from generous amounts of caramel malts and a touch of chocolate. Choose from fresh seafood, steaks, and pastas as well as signature pizzas and calzones from a wood-fired oven. Personally, I like to pair my brew with the corned beef Reuben sandwich with sauerkraut and Swiss cheese on rye and lots of Thousand Island dressing. The fish-and-chips and the Philly cheese steak are also popular items.

Green Flash Brewing Co., 6550 Mira Mesa Blvd., San Diego, CA 92121; (858) 622-0085; greenflashbrew.com; Brewery; $$. Former pub owners Mike and Lisa Hinkley founded this hugely successful local brewery in 2004, along with Brewmaster Chuck Silva. One of their most famous creations is the West Coast IPA, a National IPA Challenge Champion in 2008. As a testament to their multiple award-winning beers, you can find their product available by draft or bottle in bars, restaurants, and retail outlets throughout the US. To support this demand, they recently opened a new

45,000-square-foot brewery, including a beautiful 4,000-square-foot tasting room and beer garden that is open to the public Wednesday through Sunday. The tasting room serves a full array of available beer styles, some of which are only available at the tasting room. Guests may purchase merchandise and beer to-go via growler, 4-pack, keg, or case. They currently brew 12 styles of beer regularly as well as a growing lineup of seasonal and special offerings, including several barrel-aged beers, throughout the year.

Karl Strauss Brewing Company, 5985 Santa Fe St., San Diego, CA 92109; (858) 273-2739; karlstrauss.com; Brewery; $$. This is the beer that started the microbrew revolution in San Diego. In 1989 Chris Cramer and Matt Rattner fulfilled a dream to bring locally handcrafted beer back to San Diego. Partnering with Chris's cousin was the one-and-only Karl Strauss, a renowned master brewer for over 50 years. Starting in a small location downtown, the original location offered 3 beers. Twenty-three years later, they now brew over 30 beers a year, including 6 core beers and a host of specialty beers and seasonals. They can be found in bars, restaurants, liquor stores, and grocery stores throughout Southern California. You can also enjoy their beer and a full menu of items at one of their 6 Brewery Restaurant locations in San Diego, Orange County, and Los Angeles. One of my favorite pairings is Karl's most famous Amber Lager with a Big Beer Burger, a juicy patty basted with KS Amber Lager, topped with

Red Trolley Ale onions, IPA mushrooms, Woodie Gold-brined bacon, gruyere, tomato, lettuce, and fries.

Lightning Brewery, 13200 Kirkham Way, Poway, CA 92064; (858) 513-8070; lightningbrewery.com; Brewery; $$. Spending most of his adult life in biotech research, founder Jim Crute decided to merge his scientific knowledge and decades of home-brewing experience to open Lightning Brewery. Claiming that they brew "better beer though science," you can now find their products in stores, bars, and restaurants throughout the San Diego area. Although their tasting room is modest in size and only open to the public for a few hours on Friday and Saturday, their brews are far from modest. Be sure to try their Old Tempest Ale, an award-winning UK strong ale with hearty maltiness and a slightly spicy flavor. Another excellent choice (and also winner of many awards) is the Black Lightning Porter, a full-bodied blend that is smooth and creamy with a dark chocolate character.

Mission Brewery, 1441 L St., San Diego, CA 92101; (619) 544-0555; missionbrewery.com; Brewery; $$. Located right next to Petco Park in an old brick building that once housed the Wonder Bread Bakery, the Mission Brewery is taking the beer world by storm, garnering multiple award-winners in only a few years. Visiting the tasting room is an experience unlike most craft breweries. The high-ceilinged warehouse is essentially one large room, where you are situated only a short distance from the stainless steel brew house, and have an opportunity to watch the work taking place on a future batch. Taking their inspiration from the old Mission Brewery first established in the early 20th century, there are five main beer styles currently in production. One of the most popular is the Mission IPA, an American-style Pale Ale that won a bronze award at the Great American Beer Festival in 2007, during the first year of operations. The tasting room is open daily, but be prepared for large crowds during home games for the San Diego Padres.

Port Brewing Company, 155 Mata Way, Suite 104, San Marcos, CA 92069; (800) 918-6816; portbrewing.com; Brewery; $$. In the early 1990s, Vince and Gina Marsaglia had a brilliant idea. As co-owners of Pizza Port in Solana Beach, they yearned for sharing their home-brew passion with their loyal customers. What started out as a 7-barrel brewery in the back of their pizza joint quickly expanded into two additional locations. However, demand was far larger than their capacity, so in 2006 they moved into their current facility, which now houses over 800 barrels. Using a noteworthy process for aging in oak bourbon, brandy, sherry, and wine barrels, this brewery has won acclaim for their Belgian-style Lost Abbey label. Scarcely 1 year after their move, they won the coveted Great American Beer Festival Small Brewery of the Year and head brewer, Tomme Arthur, won Small Brewer of the Year. A year later, they were again honored as Champion Small Brewery and Small Brewer at the 2008 World Beer Cup competition, making them one of the youngest breweries ever to win back-to-back honors. The tasting room is open Fri through Sun and offers over 20 taps of Port Brewing and Lost Abbey Beers.

San Marcos Brewery and Grill, 1080 W. San Marcos Blvd., San Marcos, CA 92078; (760) 471-0050; Brewery; $$. Located right along Old California Restaurant Row in the middle of San Marcos, this establishment is highly popular with the local crowd. Their tasting room offers several of their craft beers on tap, all created on-site in their state-of-the-art microbrewery. One of my favorites is the Wild Clover Honey, a specialty beer that has most of the sweetness from added honey removed during fermentation, but creates a wonderful aftertaste and aroma in the finished product. Their Old English Ale and Oatmeal Stout are dispensed through a traditional hand pump, creating a distinct likeness to an authentic English Ale. They also have a very popular All-American Grill, a full-service steak and seafood restaurant with a distinctive old California rustic charm. Open daily for tastings, lunch, and dinner.

Stone Brewing Company, 1999 Citracado Pkwy., Escondido, CA 92029; (760) 471-4999; stonebrew.com; Brewery; $$. Stone Brewery is one of the largest of its kind in the area, and now sells its unique blends in nearly 40 states. Many of Stone's beers begin with a traditional recipe but take a quick shift into overdrive, with a number of brews reaching the low double-digit alcohol level. These beers aren't meant to be consumed in large quantities; rather, they should be savored for their complex flavors that excite the taste buds. A popular favorite is the Arrogant Bastard Ale. First released in 1997, this significantly hoppy, strong ale quickly became a favorite among craft beer aficionados. Considered one of the fastest-growing breweries in America in the past 15 years, they were named "All-time Top Brewery on Planet Earth" by *Beer Advocate Magazine* in 2008 and 2009. A visit wouldn't be complete without dining at the Stone Brewing World Bistro & Gardens, an 8,500-square-foot eatery serving beer-friendly cuisine since 2006. Stone is actually one of the largest restaurant purchasers of local, organic produce in San Diego County. Also be on the lookout for a hefty expansion into additional locations, and even a potential brew house in Europe. Open daily.

Stumble Foot Brewery, 1784 La Costa Meadows Dr., #103, San Marcos, CA 92078; stumblefoot.com; Brewery; $$. Opened for business this year, Stumble Foot has made the crucial transition from a nano to microbrewery. Owner Bill Randolph stated, "My biggest fear is that I will be over my head in success," as he was nearly sold out of an IPA during my visit. Popularity can grow rapidly for a small-production brewer that creates unique and flavorful styles, even in a city with a reputation for being a centerpiece for craft beer. Don't miss the smooth and spicy Chipotle American Stout, winner of multiple amateur awards, and a perfect example of human ingenuity. Plenty of additional unique blends are in production or under consideration.

Wet 'n Reckless Brewing, 10054 Mesa Ridge Ct., #132, San Diego, CA 92121; (619) 272-1756; wetnreckless.com; Brewery; $$. This small start-up is a perfect example of an up-and-coming nanobrewery. Relying on 20 years of experience creating unique beverages and striving for success in the tradition of many local crafters, Owner Dave Hyndman's hobby-turned-business offers *true* beer lovers a great place to drink amongst friends. The locals seem to resoundingly like the simplicity of the place with its bar/pub-like feel and local sense of camaraderie. Hyndman continues to take his science knowledge to new heights, creating unique flavors in every style he creates. Quite popular with the local crowd, be sure to try the Destroyer IPA and Super Ridiculous Stout.

Bars, Brewpubs & Gastropubs

Blind Lady Ale House (Uptown), 3416 Adams Ave., San Diego, CA 92116; (619) 255-2491; blindlady.blogspot.com; Brewpub; $$. A true beer bar in Normal Heights, Blind Lady Ale House doesn't serve spirits or beer cocktails, but takes pride in using a state-of-the-art, direct-draw draft system, ensuring a fresh and foamy pour from keg to pint. Master Brewer Lee Chase was one of the start-up members of Stone Brewing Company, and remained with the operation for 9 years. He brings this incredible knowledge and experience to new heights. With 26

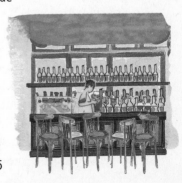

beers on tap, you might want to linger awhile, especially since the pizzas are made with organic ingredients from local farms. For 3 years in a row, *Draft Magazine* lists the Blind Lady as one of "America's 100 Best Beer Bars."

BUB'S @ The Ballpark (Downtown), 715 J St., San Diego, CA 92101; (619) 546-0815; bubssandiego.com; Bar; $$. A great sports bar, Bub's at the Ballpark is located in the East Village near Petco Park. It's a perfect spot to socialize before, during, and after a Padres game, but also has a loyal following in the off-season. Even during the crowded hours, you won't feel cramped, as the high ceilings, large garage door openings, and spacious tables and booths provide plenty of room. Plenty of plasma-screen TVs are streaming all types of sporting events. Sixteen beers are on tap, and pair well with the popular chipotle fish tacos, Russian Roulette chicken wings, or one of the gigantic "sammiches." Brunch is also served from 10 a.m. to 2 p.m. on weekends.

Downtown Johnny Brown's, 1220 3rd Ave., San Diego, CA 92101; (619) 232-8463; downtownjohnnybrowns.com; Bar; $$. Tucked away in the Civic Center Concourse, this Irish pub/sports bar has been open for 25 years. Claiming to be one of the first craft beer bars in San Diego, it was the location for Stone Brewery's first release party. It is a popular spot for the lunch crowd, as city workers and other businesses race to get a table in the expansive dining room. Nights are also busy with the theater crowd, sports fans, and beer lovers joining together for good conversation. Plenty of plasma TVs stream nonstop sporting events. They also have a pool table and shuffleboard, with a larger patio outdoors. Popular items include delicious burgers, bar food, or fresh fish of the day.

El Dorado Cocktail Lounge, 1030 Broadway, San Diego, CA 92101; (619) 237-0550; eldoradobar.com; Bar; $$. Knowledgeable and friendly bartenders are more than happy to educate you about your exclusive craft cocktail concoction at this laid-back lounge, reminiscent of an old-world Western saloon. Belly up to the bar and remember the "good ol' days" while sipping on an "Old-Fashioned" made with Angostura aromatic bitters, simple syrup, your favorite whiskey, and an orange peel garnish, or sip on "The Sidecar" composed of cognac, Cointreau, and lemon juice. A rustic interior boasts maroon-hued walls adorned by vintage cowboy scenes, wrought-iron chandeliers, and an enormous taxidermied white buffalo head (known by his Facebook friends as "Otis") perched high above the dance floor. Built floor to ceiling by an ownership team of three brothers and a close family friend, the modestly hip 2,000-square-foot venue has garnered international recognition for consistently showcasing up-and-coming DJ talent with near-nightly live sets.

Hamilton's Tavern, 1521 30th St., San Diego, CA 92102; (619) 238-5460; hamiltonstavern.com; Bar; $$. This traditional neighborhood alehouse is one of the oldest beer and wine licensed locations in San Diego. The bar is named after Herman Hamilton, a Marine veteran and South Park resident for over 35 years. Oftentimes, you will find him at the tavern telling stories and enjoying the conversation. The atmosphere is reminiscent of an old Irish pub, where many of the patrons are locals who visit frequently for the excellent beer selection and hearty pub food. Twenty-eight tap handles and 2 cask beer engines serve some of the best local beer craft beers, selected microbrews, and imports. They also offer over 200 bottled beers with an emphasis on traditional Belgian craft beers. On the food side, the specialty of the house is Hop Sausage, hand-ground meat and hop leaves that are cased, parboiled, and grilled in-house. Other favorites include several styles of chicken wings, sandwiches, burgers, and other traditional pub selections. Hamilton's was named in *Draft Magazine*'s Top 100 Best Beer Bars in 2012.

Knotty Barrel, 844 Market St., San Diego, CA 92106; (619) 269-7156; knottybarrel.com; Gastropub; $$. One of downtown's newest gastropubs, this cozy bar features a selection of over 60 local, domestic, and imported beers from around the world, including 16 craft beers on tap. You'll feel right at home when you enter, with barn board wood on the walls and a large hanging chalkboard depicting all of the beer selections available. Partnering with local farmers and vendors to source the freshest ingredients possible, the produce is exceptional and all of the meats served are hormone and pesticide free. Open for lunch and dinner, most menu items reflect traditional British pub grub. Big sellers include fried pickles, Italian truffle fries, and house-made mac and cheese. One of my favorites is the bison burger, with lettuce, tomatoes, red onion, and blue cheese on an egg bun, served with crispy french fries. Perfect with a locally crafted beer!

La Jolla Brewhouse, 7536 Fay Ave., La Jolla, CA 92037; (858) 456-6279; lajollabrewhouse.com; Brewpub; $$. Torn between visiting a beer pub or decent restaurant? At the La Jolla Brewhouse, you'll get the best of both worlds. A young but seasoned brewmaster is crafting a wide selection of beers on the premises. There is also a long list of craft beers on tap, as well as many bottle and can selections. The roomy interior is filled with live sporting events on nearly 30 flat-screen TVs, and there is also an outdoor patio and fire pit for enjoying the beautiful weather. The menu is extensive, and will cater to any mood, including sandwiches, burgers, pasta, traditional bar apps, salads, pizza, and more. A local favorite is Willys' Ring of Fire, a hand-tossed pizza that includes house-made marinara, mozzarella, parmesan, buffalo chicken tenders, spicy buffalo chili sauce, and chipotle cream. Beer-pairing dinners are scheduled regularly, so call in advance to get a seat.

Live Wire Bar, 2103 El Cajon Blvd., San Diego, CA 92104; (619) 291-7450; livewirebar.com; Bar; $$. Opened 20 years ago, this small bar is all about the beer and music blasting from a vintage juke box. Over 20 brews are available by tap or bottle, with a selection that features local and other popular labels. This is not a fancy or quiet place to sip a cocktail and carry on an intimate conversation. But if you're looking for a hip, happening nightclub with loud music and lots of energy, this is the place for you. No fancy food choices, plasma TVs, or patrons donned in clothes with expensive labels. Tattoos and piercings are the norm in this neighborhood hangout, a popular choice among locals.

Monkey Paw Pub & Brewery, 805 16th St., San Diego, CA 92101; (619) 358-9901; monkeypawbrewing.com; Brewpub; $$. With over 30 craft and local beers on tap, Monkey Paw also brews several styles in-house, including American Pale, IPA, Stout, Imperial Stout, and English Bitter. They also have a huge selection of domestic and international beers by the bottle, including many very unique or hard-to-find labels. Step into the open front and marvel at loads of dark wood with windows that highlight the view of downtown. The food menu is focused on traditional pub grub, including their popular Philly cheese steak sandwiches, hot wings, and crispy waffle fries. One of the best choices is the beefy cheese steak with Naughty Monkey Sauce, pepper jack cheese, and a spicy Serrano and onion slaw.

Neighborhood, 777 G St., San Diego, CA 92101; (619) 446-0002; neighborhoodsd.com; Bar; $$. This small but impactful downtown hot spot boasts 27 craft microbrews on tap, as well as a large selection of bottled beers, including some very rare labels. For a special occasion, order the 750 ml bottle of Deus Brut Belgian ale, or the special Samuel Adams Utopia, one of the strongest beers ever created (25 percent alcohol). For the latter, you'll pay $250 a bottle, and that's not a typo! When you get hungry, they offer finely crafted foods inspired from a traditional London pub, but made in a modern style. Small plates include classics like sweet potato fries, onion rings, and cheddar corn dogs. Two very popular main dishes are the stone smoked porter braised beef ribs, served with roasted jalapeño mac 'n' cheese, and the spicy Cajun-rubbed burger with pickled radish, onion, cucumber salad, and jalapeño mayo. Be sure to also scan the walls during your visit, as they are adorned with works from local artists, and they donate portions of the proceeds to local charities.

Noble Experiment, 777 G St., San Diego, CA 92101; (619) 888-4713; noble experimentsd.com; Bar; $$. There's something sexy and secretive about sneaking off with your significant other to a dark, converted loft located behind a secret wall of kegs. A cocktail bar only, the interior is small but feels spacious with its 20-foot ceilings and ivory leather booths. This place further defies expectations with Renaissance paintings and a striking crystal chandelier that illuminates light off a wall sheltered with thousands of gold-plated skulls. Head Bartender Anthony Schmidt says that the drinks on the suggestion list are the most popular, yet customers have different tastes. Some prefer stronger, more spirit-forward drinks, some prefer refreshing, citrus-driven drinks, and some will go for something creamy and decadent if they're looking for a dessert-style beverage. With over 100 spirits (alcohols used for drinks) on hand as well as the house-made syrups and fresh, local fruit, I guarantee you'll find something you like from the personal bartenders who are passionate about their specialty concoctions. You may also request cocktails that are not featured on the menu if you prefer. You can't afford a moment's hesitation, so be sure to secure your advance reservation via secretive text message.

O'Brien's, 4646 Convoy St., San Diego, CA 92111; (858) 715-1745; obrienspub.net; Brewpub; $$. Although it's on the smaller side and located in a strip mall, O'Brien's is a hidden gem. There's plenty of beer, wine, and a full lunch and dinner menu at this longest tenured craft beer bar, also named one of *Draft Magazine*'s Top 100 Best Beer Bars 2 years in a row. It has a standard pub interior with green walls, 4 big-screen plasma TVs, a huge front patio with heaters, comfortable chairs, and a dart board. This is a great place to watch soccer, as the walls are adorned with team pennants. There are 20 beers on tap and over 200 specialty domestics and international beers in the bottle, including Norway and Germany. Their menu is packed with a great variety of gourmet burgers, sandwiches, including corned beef and pastrami, grilled chicken, fabulous salads, fish specials, and delicious fish tacos.

Offshore Tavern & Grill (Mission Bay), 2253 Morena Blvd., San Diego, CA 92110; (619) 276-2253; offshoretavern.com; Bar; $$. This favorite Bay Park tavern and grill includes a vast wine selection, 16 draft beers, and a covered patio space. It's the perfect place to unwind after a hard day's work, or watching your favorite sports team on one of 20 plasma TVs. With a degree in culinary arts from Pennsylvania Culinary Institute's renowned Le Cordon Bleu, Executive Chef Adam Kettering likes to focus his expertise on seafood and gourmet California cuisine. He cooks up an array of specials, including bacon-wrapped meat loaf, lemon pepper grilled mahimahi, carne asada mac 'n' cheese, and an open-faced grilled rib eye sandwich.

Proper Gastropub, 795 J St., San Diego, CA 92101; (619) 255-7520; propergastropub.com; Gastropub; $$. Located right across the street from Petco Park, this traditional gastropub has a large upper-deck patio with expansive views. With a dozen rotating beers on tap and plenty more available in the bottle, you can choose from small microbrewery specialties or larger international favorites. Chef Sean Magee is doing his part to keep San Diego's food scene on the cutting edge by introducing patrons to food they've never eaten before, or changing up classical pub fare. A perfect example is the bangers 'n' mash: house-made banger corn dogs, celery root-parsnip mash, wild rocket greens, whole grain mustard vinaigrette, and mostarda. They also make their own sausage and grind burgers in the kitchen.

Ritual Tavern, 4095 30th St., San Diego, CA 92104; (619) 283-1720; ritualtavern.com; Bar; $$. Serving over 30 draughts on a rotating basis, there's something here for every distinctive taste. Ritual also has an extensive bottle list of every style, including pilsner, wheat, sour, IPA, ale, trippel, porter/stout, and more. Their food menu is diverse, ranging from traditional pub favorites to house specials. But unlike most rivals, Ritual focuses on serving food that is sourced locally, including produce from independent farms, seafood from Catalina Offshore Products, and artisan breads from Sadie Rose Baking Company. One of the more popular items is the shepherd's pie, made with natural lamb, beef, Suzie's organic seasonal vegetables, and topped with toasted mashed potatoes. Another favorite is the seafood bouillabaisse with mussels, scallops, locally caught fish, tomato sauce, and market vegetables.

Station Tavern, 2204 Fern St., San Diego, CA 92104; (619) 255-0657; stationtavern.com; Bar; $$. Located on a quiet corner in the neighborhood of South Park, it's the architecture that will create a positive first impression. The award-winning design utilizes reclaimed wood materials and themes reminiscent of the site where an old trolley station was located. There's plenty of indoor seating, but patrons flock to the large outdoor "backyard" area with picnic table seating and plenty of space to relax. Several local and international beers are available on draft and in the bottle. Although they offer a great selection of pub favorites, the most popular menu items are far from traditional. Be sure to try the house veggie burger made with chickpeas and spices, or the black bean burger, an all-vegetable patty blending black beans and bell peppers, topped with lettuce, onion, tomato, and lime cilantro spread.

Sublime Ale House, 1020 W. San Marcos Blvd., San Marcos, CA 92078; (760) 510-9220; sublimealehouse.com; Brewpub; $$. Located in a newer area of San Marcos, this North County gem serves 498 beers on tap, and plenty more by the bottle. Focusing on local, American, and international craft labels, you're bound to find an old favorite or something distinctively new. The offerings rotate frequently, and are selected to provide a huge array of flavors and styles. Even better, many of their food items include beer in the recipe. Feel free to ask the staff for a pairing recommendation, and you'll be pleasantly surprised. They are dedicated to using local produce in their dishes, and the fresh baked bread adds a wonderful aroma to the entire restaurant. Although the burgers are extremely popular, I am in love with the Mountain Summit Pizza with wild mushroom, artisanal sausage, caramelized onion, and an olive oil-garlic base.

Toronado, 4026 30th St., San Diego, CA 92104; (619) 282-0456; toronadosd.com; Brewpub; $$. This is an extremely popular uptown hangout, especially at night when the conversations and music reach higher decibel levels. Over 30 craft beers on tap and 2 available by traditional hand pump. My absolute favorite is North Coast Brewery's Old Rasputin Russian Imperial Stout, a selection that is sometimes difficult to find on draft. Also don't overlook the extensive bottle selection, where you can find labels from around the world, including the typical beer capitals like Germany and Belgium, but also lesser-known styles from Italy, France, and Japan. The most frequently ordered items on the menu include an array of sausage sandwiches and burgers. I suggest you first pick the food you're craving and then ask the staff for a beer that pairs well.

True North Tavern, 3815 30th St., San Diego, CA 92104; (619) 291-3815; truenorthtavern.com; Bar; $$. Just off University Avenue in North Park, the True North Tavern has all of the components of a great local hangout, including brick walls, large booths, plenty of seating inside and on two outdoor patios, pool tables, TVs, and two full-service bars, where a hearty selection of wine, spirits, and 20-ounce beers are offered. Over 20 taps pour mostly well-known labels of local crafts and larger domestics, with other choices available in the bottle. Sharing a kitchen with the popular **Urban Solace** (p. 203) restaurant next door, you'll find an array of delicious food choices. One of their signature menu items is the unique "Loaded Tater Tots," tossed in a house-made secret spice blend and buried under marinated carne asada, cheddar cheese, scallions, spicy crema and salsa fresco, and topped with a sprinkling of cilantro—perfect as a starter to your meal or to complement your beverage selection.

Urge Gastropub, 16761 Bernardo Center Dr., San Diego, CA 92128; (858) 673-8743; urgegastropub.com; Gastropub; $$. One of the more recent additions to this area, Urge Gastropub has the most extensive tap list in North County, featuring over 50 local and national American microbreweries. They also offer 100 labels by the bottle. Chef Marc Liautard incorporates beer and seasonally fresh produce into many of his recipes, including the popular Garbage Burger, a 50/50 mixed patty of Angus beef and ground smoked Wild Boar bacon, topped with sautéed button mushrooms, caramelized onion, Rogue Creamery Chocolate Stout cheddar, and horseradish aioli. For a lighter, vegan choice, try the organic ratatouille, a layered slab of squash, eggplant, tomato, and zucchini, sautéed and baked.

West Coast Tavern, 2895 University Ave., San Diego, CA 92104; (619) 295-1688; westcoasttavern.com; Bar; $$. West Coast Tavern, housed in the vintage lobby of University Avenue's historic Birch North Park Theater, is open until midnight every night for late dining. Enjoy trendy craft cocktails, imaginative appetizers, sliders, sandwiches, meats, and desserts in dimly lit surroundings. Enjoy one of the many craft beers on tap while sitting at the gigantic central bar. Executive Chef Eli Freebairn surprised diners with gourmet eats you wouldn't normally expect to find at a tavern, such as Maple Leaf duck confit with sweet potato puree and Vande Rose Farms all-natural pork ribs with bourbon glaze and Cajun-style barbecue sauce. I come here for the chicken 'n' waffle entree—simply divine!

The Yard House, 1023 4th Ave., San Diego, CA 92102; (619) 233-9273; yardhouse.com; Bar; $$. This large, open gathering place is a focal point in downtown. Business lunches, large gatherings, nighttime partygoers, and beer connoisseurs are seen here on a daily basis. A glass-enclosed keg room connects various beer styles directly to the large island bar, where more than 250 draft beers are available on a rotating basis. With one of the most extensive food menus available, it's a sure bet that you'll find one of the nearly 100 items to satisfy your taste. High-end selections are side by side with typical party favorites. Popular items include spicy jambalaya with blackened jumbo shrimp, spicy chicken–andouille sausage, red and pasilla peppers pan blackened with sweet crawfish, and Cajun tomato cream sauce with linguini pasta, jasmine, or brown rice; or the pepper-crusted filet, with parmesan mashed potatoes, asparagus, carrots, and brandy shallot cream sauce.

Food Trucks

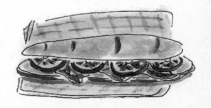

One of the hottest trends in larger cities is the increase in numbers and quality of street foods. Local restaurants and private companies have seen the value in taking their foods to the local communities via mobile kitchens. Although the typical street foods are always available, you can now find many interesting modifications to these simple recipes. You can find nearly any cuisine to satisfy your craving, and a number of vendors also utilize organic and locally grown products to support the community. Whether you're looking for a quick fix during a lunch break, a late-night snack after spending time with friends at the bar, or need a mobile caterer for an event, there's someone who can provide the solution.

Modern technology makes the search even easier, as many of the culinary coaches are tracked online via the web, including Twitter and Facebook. Although not nearly an exhaustive list (these businesses can be here today and gone tomorrow), below is a helpful guide to the many varieties of foods available. There are also a few online guides available that include updated locations/ times for many of the trucks in San Diego: sdfoodtrucks.com/, foodtrucksmap.com/sd/, and roaminghunger.com/sd.

Artistica Food, San Diego; (619) 500-MEXI (6394); Twitter: @ ArtisticaFood. Bringing the exquisite flavor and uniqueness of Mexican gourmet food to the San Diego streets.

Bitchin' Burgers, Carlsbad; (760) 458-7602; bitchinburgersfood truck.com. On the road in Carlsbad, Bitchin' Burgers serves up organic grass-fed beef topped with organic produce coming from local farms.

Casanova Fish Tacos, San Diego; (619) 822-8310; casanova fishtacos.com. Deep-fried Baja-style fish tacos, grilled chipotle fish tacos, shrimp ceviche, fish burritos, spicy shrimp tacos and burritos. Nominated Best San Diego fish tacos 2010 and 2011 by the *Union Tribune* and SignonSanDiego.

Chop Soo-ey, San Diego; (619) 929-0167; chopsooeytruck.com. Chop Soo-ey by Trucked-Up Productions is a creation of Chef Deborah Scott and the Cohn Restaurant Group. Asian-inspired barbecue.

Chubby's Food Truck, San Diego; (858) 752-3339; chubbys foodtruck.com. American classics with a Hispanic twist. From burgers to burritos, wraps, sandwiches, nachos, and fried Twinkies for dessert.

Corner Cupcakes, San Diego; (619) 800-CAKE (2253); corner-cup cakes.com. Corner Cupcakes is San Diego's mobile cupcake shop. Their cupcakes are baked daily from scratch. Lunch.

Crazy Wheel, San Diego; (858) 888-5592; joe@crazywheelsd.com; Twitter: @crazywheelSD. Nomadic coffee house with products from all parts of the world, also serving Asian-inspired food items, such as Filipino barbecue and Indonesian satay chicken.

CurioCity Catering, curiocitycatering.com; Twitter: @curiocitytruck. Offering a diverse menu focused on locally grown and produced ingredients, and dedicated to using seasonal, sustainable and organic whenever possible. The menu changes seasonally and spans different ethnicities.

Delicioso Food Truck, (619) 572-6463; deliciosofoodtruck .webs.com. Offers a variety of delicious Southwest food favorites, including California burritos with chipotle and cilantro tasting sauces, carne asada fries, barbecue fries, and more.

Devilicious, deviliciousfoodtruck.com. Serves "delicious madness for the mind" and was featured on season 2 of the Food Network's *The Great Food Truck Race.*

Dharma Dogs, facebook.com/DharmaDogs. Specializing in preparing hot dogs any way you like, or choosing from the daily menu for something truly unique.

The Dog Shack, facebook .com/TheDogShack. A mobile kitchen offering gourmet hot dogs to anyone and everyone in San

Diego. The menu also includes homemade curly fries with special house seasoning.

Eat at Recess, (760) 624-TOTS (8687); EatAtRecess.com. They make playtime mobile for breakfast, lunch, or private playtime (Recess Catering); they're here to make sure you have fun.

Espresso Urbano, (858) 349-5454; espressourbano .com. Provides gourmet beverage service from a mobile espresso bar and coffee truck. Menu items include hot drinks, iced drinks, and blended drinks to order, like lattes, mochas, cappuccinos, and more.

Flippin Pizza, flippinpizza.com. Serving the same delicious menu items available in their restaurant locations, the trucks are also available for birthdays, office parties, sporting events, and more.

Food Farm, foodfarmsd.com. All of Food Farm's sources are from local farms and ranches that practice organic and sustainable methods. They are proud to bring house-made food from the best sources to you on the streets of San Diego!

Food Junkies, (619) 339-4882; foodjunkiescatering.com. Specializing in catering special events, corporate and private parties with the best street food available.

The Gathering Spot, (619) 621-8722; tgsbistrotruck.com. Taking common and ordinary street foods we all know and love, and making them into extraordinary culinary creations.

Green Truck, (310) 204-0477; greentruckonthego.com. Not only do they serve fresh, organic, and locally grown foods, the Green Truck believes in a healthy environment. Their commissary kitchen is solar-powered, all of their packaging and utensils are either recyclable or compostable (compost is even sent back to local farms), even the vegetable oil used to cook foods is used to power food trucks the next day.

Groggy's, (619) 796-3124; followgroggys.com. Home of San Diego's original "Fat Sandwich," they also serve burgers, hot dogs, and other street items.

Jack in the Box, San Diego, CA; Facebook.com/MunchieMobile; Twitter.com/MunchieMobile. Jack in the Box restaurants' first ever mobile food truck! Dig into the Jumbo Jack and Spicy Chicken Sandwich to their famous tacos.

Joes on the Nose, (858) 373-8001; joesonthenose.com; Twitter: @joesonthenose. Serving organic coffee, tea, espresso drinks, and smoothies.

Linme's Gourmet Soul Food, (619) 631-2042; on facebook .com; Twitter: @lgsoulfoodtruck. Considered the only soul food mobile kitchen in San Diego, they cook everything from scratch.

Recipes come from over 110 years and 4 generations of family cooking. Specialties include fried chicken, meat loaf, and barbecue sandwiches.

Mad Maui, (760) 683-9BBQ; madmaui.com; Twitter: @MadMauiBBQ. Specializing in barbecue fusion, menu items include their famous Maui Wowee smoked pork sliders, Volcano Nachos, brisket sandwiches, and various tacos.

 **Mangia Mangia,** mangiamangiamobile.com; Twitter: @mangiatruck. Using the finest ingredients, they create spectacular Italian classics including paninis, lasagna, spaghetti, traditional desserts, and more.

MIHO Gastrotruck, San Diego; MIHOgastrotruck.com. Get tasty and affordable hand-crafted street food made from fresh, local, and thoughtfully sourced ingredients. Menu subject to change on a daily basis.

Mr. Pig's BBQ, San Diego; (760) 214-7336; thepigmobile.com. Real, honest barbecue for lunch and dinner. Serving pulled pork and brisket sliced sandwiches with all the popular sides.

Nana's Heavenly Dogs, Clairemont; (619) 663-6475; NanasHeavenlyDogs.com. This full-service cart specializes in hot dogs and sausage. Cash only, open late at night.

New York on Rye, Carlsbad; newyorkonrye.com. Jewish deli food truck with corned beef, pastrami, Reubens, knishes, and corned beef hash burritos for lunch and dinner.

Patty Melt, San Diego; (619) 929-0167; pattymelttruck.com. It's all about the patty melt at this food truck by Trucked Up Productions, a creation of Chef Deborah Scott and the Cohn Restaurant Group.

Pierogi Truck, North San Diego; (858) 205-3995; pierogitruck .com. Featuring 10 kinds of pierogi and plenty of other authentic Polish dishes.

Red Oven Artisan Pizza, Carlsbad; (760) 814-1688; RedOvenSD.com. Handcrafted pizza dough cooked in a completely mobile Mugnaini wood-fired oven is what makes this pizza so special. Breakfast, lunch, and dinner.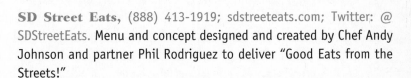

SD Street Eats, (888) 413-1919; sdstreeteats.com; Twitter: @ SDStreetEats. Menu and concept designed and created by Chef Andy Johnson and partner Phil Rodriguez to deliver "Good Eats from the Streets!"

Super Q Food Truck, (619) 995-4BBQ; superqfoodtruck.com/ bbq; Twitter: @SuperQFoodTruck. The best hickory-smoked barbecue this side of the Mississippi! All-American barbecue with elements of North Carolina, Texas, and St. Louis–style flavors and influence.

Sushi Ninjas, (213) 605-1089; sdsushininjas.com; Twitter: @ SDSushiNinjas. Serving the freshest sushi and handmade rolls in a mobile setting.

Sweets in Motion, (855) 7SWEETS; on facebook.com. Their gourmet sweets are made by hand. They specialize in all things sweet, including cupcakes, cheesecakes, brownies, cookies, cake balls, whoopie pies, and many more sweet treats.

Sweet Treats, (858) 603-8965; sweettreatstruck.com; Twitter: @ SDsweettreats. Their dessert truck features a full line of gourmet desserts all made fresh from great local vendors like Cupcake Love, Heaven Sent, and San Diego Desserts. Gourmet Ice Cream truck is also available.

Tabe BBQ, (858) 279-0040; tabebbq.com. Fusion of Mexican, Asian, and the tropical salsas inspired by Hawaii. Menu includes burritos, tacos, rice bowls, salads, and more.

Thai 1 On Eats, ohiii.com. Specializing in Thai cuisine, and home of their famous chicken satay, the menu also includes soups, salads, Thai entrees, and desserts.

Two for the Road, (619) 752-7104; twofortheroadsd.com. Specializing in American comfort food, including burgers, hot dogs, and regional specials like New England lobster rolls, Miami mojito chicken sandwiches or Seattle salmon burgers.

VineaGoGo, (877) 846-6246; vineagogo.com. The advanced sommelier and experienced staff are available for any level of service including personalized wine tastings, customizable wine parties, corporate events, and access to their wine club.

Where's the Fire Pizza, (760) 983-1414; wtfpza.com. Gourmet pizzas are 100 percent handmade Neapolitan style made with caputo flour using a wood-fired brick oven for a dangerously delicious experience.

Foodie
Day Trips

Whether you're just visiting our fair city or call San Diego home, be sure to broaden your horizons beyond our county lines. This chapter highlights several places to spend a day or weekend away from the routine. Each destination has its own unique charm and is within an hour's drive, which makes it easy to navigate. Most important, they all offer enough activities to keep you occupied, whether you're young or old, alone or with a large family. We would strongly recommend planning an overnight stay to maximize your adventure. Here you will find a Wild Western town situated among soaring mountain pine forests, a warm valley with endless rows of grapevines and citrus groves, a posh seaside resort frequented by the Hollywood elite, and an island retreat accessible only by boat or helicopter. Expand your horizons and enjoy the diversity!

Julian

For a historical day trip near San Diego, there's no better destination than Julian. Located approximately 1 hour east of San Diego in the pine and oak wooded mountains, Julian offers visitors a chance to step back into the Wild West. This small town was originally founded in the late 1800s as a centerpiece to the gold rush. One of the first mining claims in this area was filed in February 1870. Soon after, the town grew quickly to accommodate the many settlers looking for a better life. Today, it is considered the premier mountain retreat in San Diego County, and one of the rare local areas with distinct four seasons. In the spring you'll find meadows of blossoming flowers including daffodils. The summer is very warm and a perfect location for hiking, camping, picnicking, and star gazing. The cooler months of fall announce the beginning of apple harvest, one of the most recognizable attractions to this town. Winter days and nights are cool and crisp, with light snowfalls common between November and February. Where else could you snow sled in the morning and surf that same afternoon? The town center is only a few blocks long, and looks much like an old western settlement. Specialty shops feature handmade jewelry, antiques, artwork, and plenty of souvenirs. There are over 20 restaurants, a number of historic locations, and plenty of lodging choices, including bed & breakfast, lodges, cottages, and traditional hotels.

Visiting in the spring and fall months is especially nice when the foliage is just blooming or fruit is at the peak of harvest. Breakfast at the **Julian Cafe and Bakery** (2112 Main St.; 760-765-2712) is comfort food at its best. The chicken-fried steak and eggs, smothered in creamy gravy, with hash browns, homemade biscuits and jam, and coffee can last you all day. For lunch, a great stop is the **Miner's Diner** (2134 Main St.; 760-765-3753). Although they have a full menu for breakfast and lunch, the centerpiece is a sit-down bar with an old-fashioned soda fountain; a perfect place to rest your tired feet and enjoy a pick-me-up for the rest of the day. For dinner, try the **Bailey Woodpit Barbecue** (2307 Main St.; 760-765-3757; baileybbq.com). Featuring plenty of barbecue favorites and 16 craft beers on tap, there is also live music and dancing on the weekends.

There are three main bakeries in town, all located on Main Street. **Apple Alley Bakery** (2122 Main St.; 760-765-2532; facebook.com/AppleAlleyBakery) serves a variety of homemade apple pies, pastries, and cookies. They also have a great lunch menu. **Julian Pie Company** (2225 Main St.; 760-765-2449; julianpie.com) is a locally owned family business specializing in apple pies and cider doughnuts. They source their apples from nearly 17,000 local trees and serve delicious pies and pastries at both their Julian and Santa Ysabel locations. **Mom's Pies** (2119 Main St.; 760-765-2472;

momspiesjulian.com) has a large front window on Main Street where visitors can watch bakers prepare pies and baked goods throughout the day. Lunch is also available. If you plan to visit any of these proprietors, keep in mind that the lines for pies can get extremely long during Apple Harvest Season. Consider making the trip during the off-season or during the weekday.

Nearby you can visit a number of local wineries, as well as tour an inactive gold mine. Recreational gold panning continues to this day in a small area east of town called Banner Creek. There are also plenty of self-picking orchards available during the season. See the Julian Chamber of Commerce website for more information (julianca .com/index).

There are three major routes to access Julian. The northern access is via SR 76/SR 79, which links to northern San Diego and southwestern Riverside Counties, including routes to I-15. SR 78 comes to Julian from the west, providing access to Ramona and Escondido, and continues down the eastern slope of the mountains to SR 86 in Imperial County. The southern access is SR 79 through Cuyamaca Rancho State Park, which ultimately intersects with I-8.

If you choose to access Julian from the west on SR 78, be sure to make a pit stop at a landmark located in Santa Ysabel, at the intersection with SR 79. The now famous **Dudley's Bakery** (30218 CA 78, Santa Ysabel; 760-765-0488; dudleysbakery.com) was founded in 1963 and continues to have a loyal following. At the time it was established, many thought the expert baker Dudley Pratt was making a huge mistake, as Santa Ysabel was too far from San Diego and its neighboring communities. Nearly 50 years later, this small bakery continues to draw customers from all parts of the county. They serve over 40 different types of breads, fruit bars, and pastries (try the cinnamon raisin and Baja jalapeño breads). All of their items are also available online or at many grocery stores throughout San Diego.

Temecula

Located in the southwest portion of Riverside County, Temecula is approximately a 1-hour drive from many points near San Diego. Prior to the discovery of this area by Spanish missionaries in 1798, it is believed that the Pechanga Band of Luiseño Indians lived here for hundreds of years. After the Mexican-American War, many settlers began arriving in the area. This was the location for the second established post office in the entire state of California.

Primarily recognized for its burgeoning wine industry, Temecula is a major draw for visitors from both the southern San Diego areas, as well as many points north, Orange County, Riverside, Los Angeles, and Palm Springs. The most rapid growth was seen in the 1990s, when families were drawn by the affordable housing prices and warm climate. The major route into Temecula is using I-15, both north and south.

On the western end of the town, you will find Old Town Temecula, a collection of historic 1890s buildings within a walkable few blocks along Front Street. Here you will enjoy browsing through many antiques stores and dealers, specialty food stores, art galleries, boutiques, and gift shops. The Temecula Museum features exhibits about the local band of Native Americans, local natural history, and city development. A number of themed restaurants and bars are available for dining and nighttime entertainment. Hot air balloon rides and horseback riding are also very popular.

The first commercial wine grapes were planted in the 1960s, and the area now boasts over 35 wineries, with many more under construction. Spread over 35,000 acres of rolling hills and vineyards, you can easily spend a day tasting the many varietals available. The climate is perfect for growing Chardonnay, Merlot, and Sauvignon Blanc. In recent years, wineries have also begun producing Mediterranean varietals like Viognier, Syrah, and Pinot Gris. The hotter temperatures are also particularly well-suited to grapes such as the Rhône varietals, Cabernet Sauvignon, and Zinfandel.

Wine tasting is available at most of the wineries on a daily basis, as well as informative winery tours and large winery events, especially near harvest season. Along with remarkable wines, you'll also find excellent restaurants located in or near the wineries. **The Pinnacle Restaurant at Falkner Winery** (40620 Calle Contento; 951-676-8231; falknerwinery.com), includes sweeping views of the Temecula Valley and vineyards and specializes in daily Mediterranean-style cuisine. There's a BBQ picnic on Sundays. The **Creekside Grille at Wilson Creek Winery** (5960 Rancho California Rd.; 951-699-9463; wilsoncreekwinery.com) offers spacious dining both inside and outside, with a focus on

California Modern cuisine. Baily's Fine Dining is located in Old Town Temecula (28699 Front St.; 951-676-9567; baily.com) and offers dining at two distinct restaurants specializing in California Continental and American Modern cuisines.

If you choose to stay for more than 1 day, there are a number of intimate bed-and-breakfast inns and larger resorts to call home. The accommodations at the South Coast Winery Resort and Spa (34843 Rancho California Rd., Temecula; 951-587-9463; wineresort .com) are luxurious. Each villa room opens to a small patio and breathtaking views of the surrounding vineyards. Since there are no common walls between villas, it's like having your own private residence in paradise. The well-recognized spa is an oasis of relaxation. No visit would be complete without lunch or dinner at its award-winning Vineyard Rose Restaurant. The atmosphere during a warm summer night on the patio is beautiful. Candlelight and a great bottle of wine make this one of the more romantic getaways in Southern California.

Laguna Beach

Located halfway to Los Angeles, this seaside resort city is approximately a 1-hour drive from San Diego. From the south, you can reach Laguna Beach using Pacific Coast Highway 1, which intersects with

I-5 near Dana Point. PCH 1 also continues north to Newport Beach and the south Los Angeles area. From the east, you can utilize SR 133, which intersects with SR 73 (toll road) near Aliso Viejo. It is one of the premier destinations for visitors in southern California, with 20 sandy beaches and coves available for oceanfront recreation, including surfing, sunbathing, and swimming. Nearby you can catch a catamaran for whale and dolphin watching excursions.

What once started as a small community of artists looking for a home away from the busy Los Angeles city life is now home to more than 100 art galleries, studios, and boutiques. The city has more than 65 unique works of public art, designed and created specifically for Laguna Beach, including murals, statues, benches, and more. **The Laguna Art Museum** (lagunaartmuseum.org) is one of the oldest in the state and focuses on the cultural heritage of California and the unique history of the local area. Open Mon, Tues, and Fri to Sun 11 a.m. to 5 p.m.; Thurs 11 a.m. to 9 p.m. Closed Wed.

Two large art fairs run during the summer months, although there are many other art-related events throughout the year. Started in 1965, the **Sawdust Art Festival** features over 200 local artists showcasing paintings, jewelry, ceramics, photographs, sculptures, art glass, and textiles native to the area. You can also engage in demonstrations and workshops, with entertainment and lots to eat and drink throughout the day. Open 10 a.m. to 10 p.m. daily from late June to Labor Day. The **International Art Show** is also a main summer event, featuring over 125 international juried artists and master craftsmen. This event offers visitors a chance to browse through booths of original watercolors, oils, photography, sculpture, ceramics, glass, and more. You can also meet and talk with the artists. Open from 10 a.m. to 11:30 p.m. in July and August.

Over 70 restaurants are located in the area, ranging from casual street food to top-tier dining. **Las Brisas** (361 Cliff Dr.; 949-497-5434; lasbrisaslagunabeach.com), located in a landmark building first opened as the Victor Hugo Inn in 1938, is now a very popular destination for upscale Mexican cuisine. Another great upscale choice is the **Stone Hill Tavern** (1 Monarch Beach Resort; 949-234-3318; michaelmina.net/restaurants/locations/stoc .php), located within the magnificent St. Regis Monarch Beach Resort, featuring American cuisine inspired by award-winning chef Michael Mina. For authentic Italian dining, try **Ti Amo Ristorante** (31727 Coast Highway; 949-499-5350; tiamolagunabeach.com), with its romantic interior and fabulous pasta choices.

For a special occasion, or if you just want to feel pampered, the **Montage at Laguna Beach** is an experience like no other. Perched on an oceanfront bluff with expansive views of the Pacific Ocean, this luxury beach resort is situated on 30 lushly landscaped acres. There is also a 20,000-square-foot indoor/outdoor oceanfront spa. The crown jewel of this resort is the award winning **Studio** restaurant, a Craftsman-inspired building reminiscent of an elegant and charming beach cottage. Facing west over the Laguna bluffs, the doors and windows are often opened to panoramic views and pleasant ocean breezes. The California-influenced French cuisine and expansive wine list make this one of my preferred destinations. Located at 30801 Coast Hwy., Laguna Beach (949-715-6000; montagelagunabeach.com).

Catalina Island

Catalina Island is located about 22 miles south-southwest of Los Angeles across the Pacific Ocean. Two main ferries service the Island; *Catalina Express* (catalinaexpress.com) leaves from San Pedro, Long Beach, Newport Beach, and Dana Point, and the *Catalina Flyer* (catalinainfo.com) departs from Marina Del Rey. A one-way trip averages between 60 and 90 minutes, depending on the departure port. Some run more frequently than others, so it is important to plan ahead. The closest and most convenient option from San Diego is the *Catalina Express* in Dana Point, about a 1-hour drive north on I-5, exiting at Pacific Coast Highway 1 and following the signs to Dana Harbor. Helicopter service is also available at a steeper price, and only takes 15 minutes one-way.

The island itself is 22 miles long and 8 miles across at its greatest width. About a million tourists visit the island every year. The main destination is the town of Avalon, near the southeastern tip of the island. A vast majority of the tourist activities, lodging, and businesses are located in this area. Avalon was first developed as a resort destination in 1888 by George Shatto, who also built the first hotel and a pier to welcome guests. In 1919, chewing-gum mogul William Wrigley Jr. bought out controlling interest in the

Santa Catalina Island Company and invested millions in preserving and promoting the island. It wasn't until 1975 that the island's interests were deeded to the Catalina Island Conservancy, an organization that Wrigley helped create. A smaller resort village called Two Harbors is located on the northern isthmus. Only one restaurant, general store, and hotel are located here.

The use of motor vehicles on the island is restricted, so most residents use golf carts and bicycles for transportation. Tourists can hire a taxi from Catalina Transportation Services, but can also rent bicycles and golf carts in Avalon. A long list of activities are available to experience the Island and its many wonders. A number of small motor tours leave daily for a long loop through the backcountry, allowing visitors to view native bison and other wildlife, as well as experiencing stunning views of the island bluffs, beaches, and ocean. Other popular choices are helicopter tours, fishing expeditions, parasailing, snorkeling and scuba diving, hiking, and camping.

It's recommended you stay at least one night on the Island. For a special experience, consider the **Inn on Mt. Ada** (398 Wrigley Road, Avalon; 310-510-2030; innonmtada.com). This historic site was once owned by the Wrigley family and has since been restored to a stunning hotel with panoramic views of the island and Pacific Ocean. Another excellent choice is the **Hotel Metropole** (205 Crescent Avenue, 310-510-1884; hotel-metropole.com), an upscale oceanfront hideaway located next to the central marketplace. Avalon is also the center for shopping and dining. Strolling along the streets will transport you to a small Mediterranean village, and is perfectly designed to make window shopping enjoyable. You'll find clothing, jewelry, antiques, artwork, gift shops and boutiques, and plenty of souvenirs.

As you can imagine, there is a great mix of restaurants to choose from, including fine dining, casual, and fast food. There are also a number of excellent bakeries, ice cream shops, coffee houses, and even a few bars/nightclubs for entertainment. Several restaurants top the list based on quality of the food, as well as local popularity, reflected in their long-running establishment. **Antonio's Pizzeria & Cabaret** (230 Crescent Ave.; 310-510-0008; catalinahotspots .com) is located on the waterfront, and has a great selection of casual meals and excellent drinks. Seating is available both inside and on an open patio. The calzone pairs great with a cold beer. Surprisingly, they also have some of the best pancakes on the island. **Steve's Steakhouse** (417 Crescent Ave.; 310-510-0333; StevesSteakhouse.com) is a perfect destination for a more upscale dinner, with beautiful harbor views and a robust selection of quality meats and seafood. The rack of lamb is a local favorite. For a traditional Mexican breakfast, lunch, or dinner, be sure to stop by **Mi Casita Mexican Restaurant** (111 Claressa Ave.; 310-510-1772; catalinahotspots.com). The carne asada and margaritas are a great ending to a long day of shopping!